Splendiferous Speech

Splendiferous Speech

How Early Americans Pioneered Their Own Brand of English

ROSEMARIE OSTLER

First edition
Published by Chicago Review Press Incorporated
814 North Franklin Street
Chicago, Illinois 60610
ISBN 978-0-912777-05-4

Library of Congress Cataloging-in-Publication Data
Is available from the Library of Congress

Cover design: Jonathan Hahn
Cover illustration: Lindsey Cleworth Schauer
Typesetting: Nord Compo

Printed in the United States of America
5 4 3 2 1

Contents

Prologue

American Talk

WHAT DOES IT mean to talk like an American? To John Russell Bartlett, who wrote an 1848 dictionary celebrating colloquial American speech, it meant being partial to outlandish slang—*splendiferous*, *scrumptious*, *higgledy-piggledy*—and newly created verbs—*advocate*, *eventuate*, *demoralize*. It also meant borrowing new words as needed—*raccoon*, *tomahawk*, *tobacco*—and repurposing old ones—*fall* to refer to autumn, *mad* to mean angry, *corn* for a native grain.

Bartlett's *Dictionary of Americanisms: A Glossary of Words and Phrases Usually Regarded as Peculiar to the United States* also revealed some typical ways that Americans use language. For instance, they create vivid expressions out of everyday life. Real-world metaphors in Bartlett include *save someone's bacon*, *pull up stakes*, *fizzle out*, *cave in*, *sit on the fence*, *play possum*. Tall talk and hyperbole are also part of the mix. The picturesque boaster who claims to be "half horse, half alligator, and a touch of the airthquake" is a quintessentially American language user. So is the comic rural figure who confesses that he's been "knocked into a cocked hat" and "no two ways about it."

Bartlett (no relation to the quotations Bartlett) was not the first to record popular Americanisms, but most earlier writers only talked about them to criticize. John Pickering, who authored an 1816 collection of American words and phrases, apologized to his readers for publishing many questionable terms. He explains in his introduction that his main purpose is not to give these terms status but to show "those who would speak *correct English*" what they should avoid.[1]

Bartlett's purpose was the opposite. He wanted to showcase the linguistic traits that make American English unique, even if they don't exactly add up to proper speech. The *Dictionary of Americanisms* represents a turning point for the American language. For the first time, slang and popular expressions appeared in print without apology.

Bartlett was a businessman and independent scholar who became fascinated by the American way with words. An avid information gatherer and list maker, he decided to collect as much slang and folk speech as he could find. It turned out to be a lot. In ten years of combing novels, newspapers, speeches, and sermons, he found hundreds of examples reaching back to the earliest settlement days.

He discovered that certain aspects of American life were especially rich sources of vocabulary. The western frontier provided a continuous stream of new speech, starting with the 1803 expedition of Meriwether Lewis and William Clark. Like earlier colonists, Lewis and Clark helped themselves to Native American words—*calumet, sassafras*. They also combined existing English words in new ways—*turkey buzzard, sweat house, mule deer*. Later settlers continued the trend. The famous frontiersman Davy Crockett contributed more than a dozen memorable words and phrases, including *chip off the old block, a power of good, bark up the wrong tree, go the whole hog,* and *be stumped.*

The political world has always been a bubbling stew of slang and sensational rhetoric. Bartlett recorded words that entered the language or changed their meaning as Americans created a new government—*Congress, presidential, senatorial, legislate.* He also noted colorful terms like *gerrymander*—probably the first piece of American political slang—plus *caucus, lobby, stump speech, spoils,* and others. When Bartlett was writing his book, the intractable conflicts that led to the Civil War were just heating up. He captured the mood of the moment by including descriptive party nicknames like *Barnburners, Old Hunkers,* and *Locofocos.*

Newspapers were another excellent resource for slang. Besides introducing the latest political and sports terms, they crammed their articles with lively vocabulary that would amuse readers—*claptrap, fat in the fire, to gouge, to corner.* Newspaper writers also indulged in elevated language, such as saying *incarnadined* instead of *bloodied.* One critic of the florid style called them "big words for small thoughts,"[2] but Bartlett thought these words were "expressive," if not "remarkable for their elegance," so he swept them onto his list. He even added words that he himself considered "strange and barbarous," including words invented on the spur of the moment by popular preachers—*happify, to fellowship.*[3]

Although most of Bartlett's dictionary entries are familiar to modern Americans, not everything made it into the permanent vocabulary. Many one-of-a-kind words and expressions like *absquatulate* (leave in a hurry), *lickspittle* (a groveler), *blatherskite* (a noisy, blustering person), and *know b from a bull's foot* (know what's what) are now sadly obsolete. They nonetheless display the hallmarks of typically American slang—wordplay, homespun metaphors, unexpected compounds. Words come and go, but what makes English American hasn't changed all that much since Bartlett's day.

Besides its unabashed embrace of the country's low language, Bartlett's dictionary was remarkable for another reason. It was the first book of its kind that was favorably received by most critics. Although one or two reviewers complained about the preponderance of "mere slang words," most people were enthusiastic.[4] The *Christian Register* described it as "replete with amusement as well as instruction." *Littell's Living Age* predicted that it would provide a "fund of fun" for a winter's evening. When the fourth edition appeared in 1877, the *Providence Evening Press* called the book "a landmark in the literary history of the country."

This positive attitude was a sharp departure from earlier opinions on the value of American English. The British had been disapproving of the "American dialect" since the seventeenth century. Early British commenters joked uneasily about the infiltration of Indian words like *wampum* or disdainfully noted the use of *fall* to mean "fall of the leaf" rather than the biblical fall of Adam.[5] One British critic wailed, "Oh spare, we beseech you, our mother-tongue!" after reading a book by

Thomas Jefferson (*Notes on the State of Virginia*) that included the word *belittle.*

Many early Americans also worried about keeping the language pure. John Adams, among others, thought the government should establish an institution for "refining, correcting, improving, and ascertaining" the English language in America. Although Americans who wrote about the topic defended their speech against the most abusive British attacks, they still talked about purging the language of "vulgarities" and "improprieties." If innovations were accepted into American speech, warned one critic, the country would suffer the embarrassment of being "placed among those who use dialects" rather than standard English.

A likely reason why Bartlett's book escaped this sort of criticism is that it appeared at an auspicious moment. The year of its publication, 1848, found Americans in an unusually nationalistic mood. The Mexican-American War had recently ended with the Treaty of Guadalupe Hidalgo, which gave the United States over half a million square miles of new western territory, including California, where gold had just been discovered. That same year Zachary Taylor was elected president in the first national election to be held on the same day—the Tuesday after the first Monday in November—in all thirty states.

Americans were starting to see themselves as the political and cultural equals of the English speakers on the other side of the Atlantic. Along with that new self-confidence came a new appreciation of their own vernacular. Bartlett's dictionary made it clear that in the seventy-two years since the American Revolution, American English had decisively declared its own form of independence. Although built on a British foundation, it had developed a style and flair all its own. The story of Bartlett's *Dictionary of Americanisms* is the story of how Americans reshaped the English language to suit themselves. It's a progress report on a process that started in the seventeenth century and is still going on today.

1

One English Becomes Two

ENGLISH COLONISTS STARTED building the road to Bartlett's dictionary almost as soon as they landed on American shores. The first Americanisms were contributed by John Smith, a leading founder of the Jamestown, Virginia, colony. Smith sailed into Chesapeake Bay with 104 fellow settlers on April 26, 1607, and started recording new words right away.

In 1608 he sent home a letter describing his first meeting with the great Algonquian chief Wahunsonacock, also known as Powhatan. The story features an early version of one of the first naturalized American English words. Smith tells how two native guides ushered him into a large gathering around a fire, where he found the chief lying "uppon a Bedstead a foote high, upon tenne or twelve mattes, richly hung with manie Chaynes of great Pearles about his necke, and covered with a great Covering of *Rahaughcums*."[1]

It's doubtful that Smith intended to create a new English word. He was careful to underline *Rahaughcums* (italicized in the published version) to show that it was foreign. He simply wanted to describe the scene, and since no English word existed for the cloak of ring-tailed raccoon pelts that Powhatan wore, Smith borrowed the Algonquian one. Over time, he borrowed several more words from the same source. They made it into the permanent vocabulary because English needed them, and eventually they made it into Bartlett's dictionary.

Smith took several stabs at trying to represent the pronunciation of *Rahaughcum*. In the same letter, he writes, "The Empereur Powhatan, each weeke once or twice, sent me many presents of Deare, bread, *Raugroughcuns*." Several years later, describing Virginia wildlife, he says, "There is a beast they call *Aroughcun*, much like a badger, but useth to live on trees, as squirrels doe." By the time he wrote again about his first meeting with Powhatan in the 1624 *Generall Historie of Virginia, New-England, and the Summer Isles*, he had whittled the spelling down to the more English-looking *Rarowcun*. By 1672, others had standardized the word as *raccoon*.[2]

The earliest American words are all borrowed from Algonquian, a large language family that in the seventeenth century included dozens of member languages. It was spoken all along the East Coast as far north as Canada. Unfortunately, Algonquian languages aren't an easy fit for English. Meanings that English speakers express with several separate words come together in one word in Algonquian. *Powhatan*, for example, means "falls on a rapid stream," a reference to the James River falls, part of Powhatan's territory.[3]

To make matters more complicated, English spelling was pretty much do-it-yourself in the seventeenth century. No overall standard existed, and writers often spelled a word more than one way. That would have been even truer for words from other languages. The evolution of *raccoon* set the pattern for other adoptive Algonquian words. The English tried out several spellings, while also chopping off a syllable or two to get a word that looked more English.

These early linguistic innovations almost certainly passed unnoticed by the colonists. Their goals when they arrived in North America were economic, not cultural, and it would hardly have occurred to them that their actions would have a permanent impact on the English language. The British government's aim was to establish an outpost in North America. The French and Spanish had taken possession of American territories decades earlier, and James I thought it was time that England staked its own claim in the "new world."

The expedition's sponsor, the Virginia Company of London, was interested in the commercial possibilities of the new territory. The company instructed the men of Jamestown to travel as far as they could up any navigable rivers in search of the elusive Northwest Passage, the fabled quick route to the Pacific Ocean and the Orient. The colonists were also told to bring pickaxes to any likely-looking hilly areas and dig for gold. The Spanish were enriching themselves with gold and silver from Mexico and South America, and the English hoped for the same success on the East Coast. Rumors of "golden cities" had been circulating for years.

The Jamestown colonists would be frustrated in many of their aims. They traveled about sixty miles up the James River, only to discover a fall line that made the James and the area's other rivers impassable. That ended their hopes of finding a quick route to the Pacific. Then, after wasting many months mining iron pyrite ore—known as "fool's gold" to the initiated—they were forced to abandon their dream of quick riches. The London investors didn't see a return on their money until decades later, when the colony started growing tobacco for sale. Smith and his companions did, however, succeed in establishing England's first permanent North American colony.

Although the Virginia Territory stretched from what is now New England to the Carolinas, the colonists chose to settle in the tidewater area of the Chesapeake because earlier explorers recommended it. The weather was mild for much of the year and the soil was fertile. Several large rivers emptied into the bay. Smith would later declare that "heaven and earth never agreed better to frame a place for man's habitation."[4]

Still, it was alien territory. Unlike the heavily cultivated countryside of England, the land here looked wild and overgrown. Dense hardwood forest grew almost down to the beach. The bay, which was thirty miles across at its widest point, was dotted with large and small islands, some wooded, others covered with grass. Unfamiliar animals populated the woods. The land surrounding the river mouths was marshy. Even though the men had just spent four months crowded onto three small ships, they must have felt some trepidation at their first sight of their new home.

Their misgivings could only have increased when the next day's scouting party was greeted with a volley of arrows. Seventeenth-century North America might have looked wild to English eyes, but it wasn't untenanted. At least two dozen Native American tribes, probably between fifteen thousand and twenty thousand people, lived in a scattering of small villages around the Chesapeake area. These included Powhatan's people, called the Powhatan. They lived by harvesting the bay's plentiful fish and shellfish, as well as hunting and gathering wild plants. They also grew corn, beans, pumpkins, tobacco, and a few other crops.

The Jamestown colonists needed to get on good terms with the Powhatan. They were ill equipped to survive on their own. About half were upper-class gentlemen who had never done manual labor and considered themselves above it. Some of the rest were workers with practical skills, such as carpenters and bricklayers, but even they weren't prepared to build a self-sustaining community from scratch.

Luckily for the English, tribal leaders saw advantages in trading corn and venison for copper, hatchets, knives, and other English products. Although violence continued to break out at intervals, and worsened once the Indians realized that the English were planning to stay permanently, there were many periods of truce over the next several years. As a leader of the colony, Captain Smith made frequent trips to Indian villages to negotiate for corn and other food and to try to establish friendly relations.

A former soldier, the twenty-seven-year-old Smith had adventured all across Europe before joining the Jamestown expedition. Although he stayed in the colony for only two years before returning to England, he was an interested and alert observer of the land and native cultures. He was also eager to share his exploits with those back home. He wrote about everything he saw and did.

He described the region's flora and fauna, borrowing an Algonquian word whenever he couldn't find an English one. "The *Opassom*," he writes, "hath a head like a Swine, and a taile like a Rat, and is of the bignesse of a Cat." The word *opassom*, like *raccoon*, went through a

A portrait of Captain John Smith on a tobacco card, with the story of his rescue by Powhatan's daughter, Pocahontas, depicted in the background. The card was produced in 1888 by W. Duke, Sons & Co. tobacco manufacturers as part of the "Great Americans" tobacco card series. *Prints and Photographs Division: Library of Congress, LC-DIG-ppmsca-39614*

few iterations, sometimes being spelled *apossoun*, with *possum* finally emerging in 1670. He also notes an exotic fruit tree: "The *Putchamin* is first green, then yellow, and red. . . . When it is ripe it is as delicious as an Apricock." Other writers called this fruit a *Pishamin* or a *Pessemmin*, before finally settling on *persimmon*.[5]

Besides slipping Algonquian words into his narratives, Smith collected them in lists. Most of these words didn't make it into the English vocabulary. Two that did are *tomahawk* and *moccasin*. Smith was also the first to note certain northeastern Algonquian words. His 1614 visit to New England yielded *hominy*, *muskrat*, and *moose* ("a beast bigger than a Stagge").[6]

Smith also recorded many details of native life. One of these is the probable origin of an early political term. The Chickahominy people, Smith says, "are governed by the Priests and their Assistants, or their Elders, called *Caw-cawwassoughes*."[7]

Years later, an Americanized version of the word with simplified spelling appeared in the May 5, 1760, *Boston Gazette*. Noting a new political trend, the newspaper describes a dozen or so men who have "been known to combine together, and are called by the Name of the New and Grand Corcas." By this time, the meaning had evolved from a tribal elder to a group of like-minded individuals (like party elders) who met to discuss policy. By the 1780s, the word was being spelled *caucus* and had acquired its modern political meaning. Like so many American nouns, it had also spawned a verb—*to caucus*.

Caucus was one of the first of several native words that the English appropriated for political purposes. Eighteenth-century men's clubs had a habit of borrowing Native American terminology to name their organizations or officers. New York's notorious political organization Tammany Hall owed its name to Chief Tamanend, a seventeenth-century Delaware chief in what is now Pennsylvania.

An intriguing aspect of Smith's narratives is the amount of conversation he records between the English and the Algonquians. Describing his first meeting with Powhatan, he recounts how the chief welcomed him with "good wordes" and assurances of friendship. Before negotiations started, they exchanged stories. Powhatan asked why the English had landed at the Chesapeake, and Smith told him a tale of being forced into the bay by extreme weather. The chief in turn related what he knew of the land and people on the other side of the James River's fall line.

With these preliminaries out of the way, they struck a deal: "Hee promised to give me Corne, Venison, or what I wanted to feede us; Hatchets and Copper wee should make him, and none should disturbe us." This initial trade negotiation was only the first of many extended discussions that the two men shared during Smith's time in Virginia. Smith's retelling of these meetings often includes Powhatan speaking improbably fluent seventeenth-century English. "Your kind visitation doth much content me," Smith quotes him as saying on one occasion.[8]

Was the chief really speaking English? Was the captain speaking Algonquian and translating Powhatan's remarks? Or, in reality, were they both frantically gesticulating? It could have been a little of all three. Smith no doubt embellished the dialogues to some extent. He also must have spoken some Algonquian. By the time he met Powhatan, he had been bartering with various tribes for several months and had plenty of opportunity to pick up a few words.

At some point, he learned enough to interpret for the others. One of the men who accompanied Smith on a February 1608 visit to Powhatan describes "the great kinge and our captain" renewing their acquaintance with "many pretty discourses." He then quotes a Powhatan speech in ordinary English and follows it with the remark, "Captain Smith being our interpreter . . . told us his [Powhatan's] intent was but to cheat us."[9] The way this incident is presented suggests that Powhatan's "English" speeches were either translations or paraphrases.

It's likely that the chief also knew a little English. The Jamestown settlers weren't the first Englishmen he'd ever met. English speakers had been making landfall along the North American coast for nearly a century before Smith and his companions arrived. These earlier visitors also traded with the Indians. Some language exchange would have been all but inevitable.

Or maybe Powhatan learned English from an Algonquian speaker who had been in England. For decades, English explorers routinely captured two or three Indians and brought them back to London. After the Indians learned English, they would be taken back to America to act as interpreters for later expeditions.

Several Powhatan made the voyage east, including three men who caused a sensation in 1603 by paddling their canoe up the Thames River. No one knows what happened to these three—no Algonquians were on the ships that sailed for Jamestown. However, one or more of them could have returned to Virginia on an unrecorded sailing.[10]

Many early encounters between the English and the Algonquians obviously relied on gestures. In a 1607 report, Gabriel Archer, a member of Smith's exploring party, tells of flagging down some natives who were passing in a canoe. The Indians realized that the English were asking for directions, and one obliged by drawing a map of the river, first in the dirt with his foot, then with a pen and paper provided by Archer. This incident was probably more typical of interactions between the two groups than the long conversations detailed by Smith. It seems clear, though, that words were being traded along with goods.

The second permanent English colony benefited even more from English-speaking natives. In most ways, the men and women who founded the Plymouth Colony in 1620 were the antithesis of the Jamestown men. They were not adventurers in search of quick riches but religious dissenters who came to America for a chance to practice their faith without interference from the English government. They were industrious people, many with families, better organized and more focused than their Jamestown compatriots. The settlers that we know as the Pilgrims were like the Jamestown settlers in one important way though—they were poorly prepared for survival in America.

Although the colonists who set sail on the *Mayflower* in September 1620 have come down in history as the Pilgrims, they never called themselves that. The word appears only once in *Of Plimoth Plantation*, governor William Bradford's record of the colony. Describing the group's departure from the Netherlands, where they had settled a decade earlier, he alludes to a passage in the New Testament Epistle of Paul to the Hebrews. He writes, "So they lefte that goodly and pleasant citie, which had been ther resting place near 12 years; but they knew they were pilgrimes, and looked not much on those things, but lift up their eyes to the heavens."[11] (Like all seventeenth-century writers, Bradford had his own individual spelling style.)

The word *pilgrim* had, of course, been around for centuries. It could mean someone who traveled to a sacred place as an act of religious devotion or, as Bradford meant it, a person for whom the world was merely a temporary stopping place on the way to heaven. Except for quotations or paraphrases of Bradford's original sentence, the word wouldn't be used as a reference to the Plymouth colonists until about two hundred years later.[12]

The term *Pilgrim Fathers* is first recorded in a speech given by the New England statesman Daniel Webster. Speaking at a celebration of the two hundredth anniversary of the *Mayflower* landing on December 22, 1820, he talked of coming together to pay homage to "our Pilgrim Fathers." Webster must have liked the phrase because he used it again in later speeches.[13]

By the mid-nineteenth century, *Pilgrim* with a capital *P* was the common name for the Plymouth settlers. Around the same time, the word without an initial capital picked up a new meaning. It started being applied to greenhorns on the western frontier. John Wayne later made this usage famous in *The Man Who Shot Liberty Valance* and other movies, but it was probably not that common when Bartlett wrote his book. He doesn't include it in any edition, although a few entries mention capital-*P* Pilgrims.

The *Mayflower* colonists' initial destination was the mouth of the Hudson, but violent November storms off Cape Cod forced them to anchor in what is now Provincetown Harbor. They founded their new colony on Cape Cod instead. The *Mayflower* anchored in Plymouth Harbor on December 16, three months after the start of the trip.

"The Landing of the Pilgrims at Plymouth, Mass., Dec. 22nd, 1620," an 1876 print by Currier & Ives. As the Pilgrims struggle ashore, a snowshoe-clad Native American greets them. *Prints and Photographs Division: Library of Congress, LC-DIG-pga-09270*

Cape Cod looked less like wilderness than the Chesapeake. Many areas near the shore had been cleared for planting. The first scouting party almost immediately came across a cornfield, as well as buried baskets full of multicolored ears of harvested corn. (To the English it was *Indian corn*—the word *corn* alone covered any type of grain.) The men also saw houses and other indications of village life. However, the inhabitants themselves were scarce. Except for one or two abortive attacks that were easily repelled, the natives avoided the Englishmen. When the colonists approached them, they fled.

Several years before the Pilgrims landed, two calamitous events occurred that would have a big impact on their relations with the Native Americans in the region. The most recent was an epidemic that had swept through New England only a year or two earlier, wiping out as much as three-quarters of the population. The exact nature of the disease is unknown. It might have been smallpox or some other European disease carried by the fishermen and fur traders who landed frequently along the New England coast. By the time it ran its course, only a few thousand people were left alive.

The second event had occurred six years before, but the repercussions still lingered in 1620. A ship's captain named Thomas Hunt, on his way to Spain, stopped near Plymouth and tricked twenty-seven Indians into boarding his ship. When he reached his destination, he sold his captives into slavery. This outrageous act, which got Hunt banned from future commercial voyages, naturally infuriated the Cape Cod tribes, who cut off trade dealings with the Europeans. It also vastly complicated England's immediate settlement plans. However, it resulted in an unexpected benefit for the Pilgrims.

As some of the men were holding an outdoor meeting in March 1621, they were startled to see a lone Indian approaching the settlement. He walked up to the gathering and, to the colonists' astonishment, welcomed them to America in broken but understandable English. His name was Samoset, and he was not a local but an Abenaki from Maine. He had learned English from the sailors who came to fish off the Maine coast. He now lived in Patuxet, a once-thriving village close to the Plymouth settlement that the epidemic had turned into a ghost town.

Samoset was the first native the Pilgrims had a chance to talk to, and they eagerly questioned him about the region and the neighboring tribes. He told them about Massasoit's people, the Wampanoag, who were their nearest neighbors. They had been hard hit by the epidemic, and the tribe's warriors were now down to sixty. He also told them of the Hunt incident and the resulting anger against the English.

Samoset identified himself as a sagamore, or chief, of his people. *Sagamore*, and the related word *sachem*, also meaning chief, were two of the earliest Algonquian terms that the Pilgrims learned. They appear in Bradford's writings and other accounts of early colonial days. John Smith reported in his description of New England that the Massachusetts tribes "call . . . their Kings there abouts *Sachems*," while the Penobscot used the term "*Sagamos*."[14]

Like *caucus*, these words eventually made the move from Native American culture to American politics. By the nineteenth century, both were being used to refer to big men in the party. High officials in the Tammany organization were called Sachems and the leader the Grand Sachem. *Sagamore* even crossed the Atlantic. An 1882 article in the London periodical *Academy* includes the line, "Readers on this side of the Atlantic cannot be supposed to owe allegiance to every local sagamore of learning." Although neither word is heard much anymore, as late as July 18, 1977, *Time* magazine referred to "party sachems."

Samoset continued to visit the colony. On one occasion, he brought a friend who spoke even better English than he did. The friend's name was Tisquantum, which the Pilgrims simplified to Squanto. Squanto was one of the few remaining members of the Patuxet. He was one of the men that Hunt had kidnapped seven years earlier. After rescue from the Málaga slave market by local monks, he left Spain and made his way to London, probably by ship. There he was taken in by an officer of the Newfoundland Company. He learned English, became an interpreter for the company, and eventually returned to North America on a trading vessel.

Squanto immediately proved his value to the colonists. He announced that Massasoit was waiting nearby and wanted to meet with them. This meeting, and the brokering of a mutually beneficial trading arrangement, was the beginning of a long period of generally peaceful relations between the colonists and the Wampanoag. Squanto stayed on at the Plymouth Colony until he died of an illness in 1622. Besides teaching the colonists survival skills, such as how to grow corn, he continued to act as an interpreter and negotiator in their dealings with the surrounding tribes.

Squanto's language skills were crucial for the Plymouth colonists. While John Smith collected Algonquian words and recorded many details of native culture, Bradford had no apparent interest in the language or culture of the neighboring tribes. *Of Plimoth Plantation* is almost entirely about the doings of the colonists. He only records native words when they're needed to tell his story. Even so, he did make contributions to the permanent vocabulary.

Besides *sachem* and *sagamore*, Bradford was probably the first to record a version of the word *powwow*. Relating an incident that happened before the Puritans arrived, he writes, "Before they came to the English to make freindship [*sic*], they got all the Powachs of the cuntry for 3 days togeather."[15] In this passage, Bradford is referring to the priests or shamans of the tribe. During the seventeenth century, *powwow* referred to people, not events. The translation of the word is "he who dreams."

By the early eighteenth century, the English meaning was starting to shift to refer to a ceremony conducted by shamans. One 1708 observer describing such an occasion writes, "The Indians . . . had a *Powwow*, or sort of conjuring." The same writer also uses the word as a verb: "They *Powwow* often."[16] In common with most other Algonquian borrowings, *powwow* went through several spelling changes, sometimes being spelled *Powaw*, *Pawaw*, *Powah*, or *Pauwau*. The word's shortness and relative ease of pronunciation suggests that the problem was more with the lack of clear English spelling rules than with the original Algonquian. The spelling stabilized at *powwow* sometime during the nineteenth century.

As early as 1812, *powwow* had already joined *caucus* in the American political lexicon. The June 5 *Salem Gazette* for that year told its readers, "The Warriors of the Democratic Tribe will hold a powow [*sic*] at Agawam on Tuesday next." Native Americans have recently taken the word back from English. Tribes around the country now use *powwow* as a name for gatherings that feature traditional dancing.

Later New Englanders collected several other words from Algonquian languages, including *squash* (originally *asquutasquash*), *hickory* (*pohickory*), *pecan*, *skunk*, *chipmunk*, and *wigwam*. They also modified certain terms with the adjective *Indian*. This name for American natives had been in use for a while. As every schoolchild knows, it originated with Christopher Columbus, who mistook the Bahamas for the coast of India. Within a short time, Europeans realized Columbus's mistake, but the misnomer stuck anyway.

Both Bradford and Smith use the term *Indian corn*, and Smith talks about *Indian pumpkin*, *Indian beans*, and *Indian cakes* (presumably cornbread). *Indian pudding* and *Indian bread*, both made out of cornmeal, were added to the language later in the seventeenth century. The word also became a popular identifier for American plants that looked vaguely similar to something familiar, as in *Indian plume*, *Indian bell*, *Indian paint brush*, *Indian basket grass*, *Indian ginger*, and *Indian rice*.

More significant than plant names are the cultural terms, which usually have more to do with how the colonists viewed the Indians than with genuine Native American activities. *Indian file* (single file) and the pejorative *Indian giver* (someone who gives a present but expects an equivalent in return or asks for it back) were in use by the mid-eighteenth century. Sitting *Indian style* (cross-legged) came in about a century later. Bartlett also lists the now obsolete *Indian bed*, a bed of clams on the ground that are roasted by having a fire kindled on top of them.

Indian summer, an autumnal spell of unusually fine weather, was a common expression by the late eighteenth century. Its origins are uncertain. An English term for the phenomenon already existed—*St. Martin's summer*—but the colonists apparently associated the same type of weather in North America with the Indians. One possibility is that it refers to the habit that some tribes had of burning grass and underbrush in the fall. Some early definitions of *Indian summer* include mentions of smokiness.

When John Smith says that a possum "hath a head like a Swine" we understand what he means, but no one today, either American or British, would say it that way. The language that the first settlers brought to America was just beginning to evolve into modern speech. It's easier to read than the English of the Middle Ages—like Chaucer's *Canterbury Tales*, for instance, which opens, "Whan that Aprille with his shoures soote"—but it's also different from modern English in some noticeable ways.

Doth and *hath* for *does* and *has* were common, and *-eth* was used more often than *-s* on verbs that followed third-person nouns and pronouns. Describing the female possum, Smith says, "Shee hath a bagge, wherein she lodgeth, carrieth and suckleth her young." Bradford comments, "Man may purpose [propose], but God doth dispose."[17]

Seventeenth-century English speakers also used *be* in many places where we use *is*, *was*, or another form of that verb. Some examples include *for those that be aged*; *although it be now too late*; *if the difference be not great*. The word *not* typically comes after the verb. Instead of saying *we do not know the Indians' loss*, Smith says, "the Indians losse wee know not."[18] So-called double negatives like *not never* and *not neither* were common.

Many verb forms were different from modern forms, especially in the past tense. Seventeenth-century English speakers used *holp* for *helped*, *bare* for *bore*, *riss* for *rose*, *holden* for *held*, *durst* for *dared*, and *brake* for *broke*. We read in Bradford, "their freinds [*sic*] of the Company, which still clave [cleaved] to them." Smith writes, "This he spake [spoke] only to win time."[19]

They also sometimes used different verb tenses than we do now—"they would have eate it up" or "this being the first New-England water they drunke of."[20] If we saw those sentences in a modern book, we'd assume the author was uneducated, but to Bradford's readers, they seemed just fine. He and other people also used double comparatives, such as *more sadder*, *more better*, and *most fearfullest*, which are now banned from standard English. They put *-est* on words where it would be wrong now, such *chiefest* and *miserablest*.

The written English of the first colonists might be challenging for modern readers, but their spoken speech, if we could hear it, would be even trickier. The English of that time was still in the end stages of a series of changes that started centuries earlier, when vowels began to shift from the archaic English pronunciation to the modern English version. Evolving vowel sounds are one reason why spellings of the era were so haphazard. Free-form spellings have an advantage though—they give us a clue about how words sounded. When in doubt, writers spell a word the way they pronounce it.

In Smith and Bradford's day, the *er* of certain words—*persons, search, merchant, concern*—was pronounced like *ar*—*parsons, sarch, marchant, consarn*. The sounds of short *i* and *e* were often interchangeable—*assest* for *assist* and *sperit* for *spirit*, but *chist* for *chest* and *divil* for *devil*. The *oi* sound was pronounced like long *i*—*biling pint*. *Ure* was pronounced like *er*—*critter* for *creature*, *paster* for *pasture*, *figger* for *figure*. *See* was more like *seh* and *name* was more like *nem*.

Consonants were different too. Words like *daughter*, *thought*, and *brought* were pronounced closer to *dafter*, *thoft*, *broft*. For certain words borrowed from Latin, an *l* had recently been added to the spelling to reflect their origin, but it was not yet widely pronounced. Examples include *fault*, *falcon*, and *vault*, which were pronounced something like *fawt*, *fawcon*, and *vawt*. The initial *h* was dropped from short words, so *his* and *hit* sounded like *is* and *it*. The ending *-tion* was pronounced *-syon*, as in *proclamassyon*.

By 1600, the notion of a standard was emerging, with the speech of London and the royal court considered the "best" sort of English, although pronunciations and grammar were still in a state of flux. Most of the earliest colonists came from London and the surrounding areas, so the London way of talking would have been dominant in Jamestown and Plymouth. However, the dialect of the first settlers didn't stick. Later immigrants had a greater impact, with each stream of new settlers bringing their own regionalisms from home.

One place where the English of the first colonists left lasting traces was in the American vocabulary. Besides borrowing words from the natives, they occasionally took the easier path of borrowing from their own language. Features of the landscape were assigned English labels, even if the things named weren't exactly the same as the English variety. For instance, American rabbits are really hares, and American orioles and swallows are different birds from their English counterparts. Walnut, beech, and hemlock trees also refer to different species in the two places.

In England creeks are inlets of the sea, but by the early seventeenth century in America, they could be tributaries of a river or simply small streams.

The English term *hole* means a deep place in a river, but the colonists used it to mean a small bay or a grassy valley. A *fork* in America can be the junction or branching of two rivers, as well as its traditional British meaning of a dividing place in a road. *Rock*, which refers to a land mass such as a cliff in England, can refer to a large stone in America. *Bluff*, an adjective that in the old country describes a rounded, almost perpendicular shoreline (*bluff banks*), is a noun meaning a steep cliff in America. In the eighteenth century, repurposed *bluff* would gain the distinction of becoming the first Americanism to be attacked in print.

To the English, *buffalo* traditionally meant the kind of oxen found in India. In America, the English applied the word to bison, a different species. We usually imagine buffalo roaming the Great Plains, but in the seventeenth century, they ranged as far east as colonial Maryland, where one observer listed them among other wild animals of the territory. "In the upper countrey," he writes, "there are Bufeloes, Elkes, Lions, Beares, Wolves, and Deare."[21]

Certain seventeenth-century words or meanings gradually dropped out of favor in England but lived on in America, such as *fall* for *autumn*, *mad* to mean angry as well as crazy, *clod* for a lump of dirt, *quit* for *stop*, *stock* for *cattle*, *bug* to mean any insect (not just a bedbug, as in England), *notify* for *inform*, *wilt* for *wither*, and *sidewalk* for *pavement*. All these words are labeled Americanisms now but were good British English in the seventeenth century. Smith uses "fall of leafe" in his *Historie of Virginia.*

British critics of later centuries stigmatized the expression *I guess* as an American barbarism, but when the first settlers arrived in America, the phrase was British English. Luminaries like William Shakespeare and the philosopher John Locke used it in their writing. Nonetheless, by the early nineteenth century, *I guess* had become entirely an American expression. Bartlett lists it as an Americanism used to mean *believe, suppose, think, imagine,* or *fancy.*

The changed use of *corn* from England to America reflects how central this native crop was to the first colonists' existence. *Corn,* a general term for any type of cereal crop, was interpreted differently depending on what was grown in the area. In Ireland it normally referred to oats, but in England to wheat.

When Columbus arrived in the Caribbean he noted an unfamiliar grain that the natives called *mahiz.* He brought the word back to Europe, where it entered Spanish, French, and several other languages. The English naturalized it as *maize.* Europeans still use some version of *mahiz* to refer to American corn; but, for unknown reasons, when the colonists encountered the grain in North America, they called it *Indian corn.* Over time, the *Indian* part was dropped in favor of plain *corn.*

One reason why the colonists might have referred to maize as corn is that it was the major cereal crop in the places where they settled. Corn, not wheat or oats, was the staff of life for the early settlers. The Jamestown men would have starved before their first winter was out if the Algonquian people in the area had not been willing to provide copious supplies of corn in exchange for English knives and copper. The Pilgrims, too, relied on native corn harvests. The English grains they planted didn't sprout. When wheat was finally grown successfully in America, it was at first called *English corn.*

Algonquian also gave us the words *pone,* which meant a roasted or baked food; *hominy,* meaning ground or beaten corn; and *succotash,* a word for boiled corn kernels. American breads made from corn include *ash cake*, *ash pone* (both cooked in the ashes of the fire), *corn flipper*, *corn fritter*, *corn dodger*, *hoecake*, *batter cake*, *spoon bread*, *hush puppies*, *johnnycake*, and *slapjack*. Later, *corn syrup*, *cornflakes*, and *popcorn* were added to the American food lexicon. The American spirit bourbon was first known as *corn whiskey*, and from the eighteenth to the early twentieth centuries, *corned* or *corned up* meant drunk.

In other American slang, *corny* and *cornball* have meant old-fashioned or sentimental since the nineteenth century. Country bumpkins are *corncrackers*, *corn pone*, or *cornhuskers*. An easy-to-catch high fly ball in baseball is called a *can of corn*. From the early nineteenth century until well into the twentieth, *corn* was slang for money, a testament to the crop's economic importance. The seventeenth-century colonists would have had no trouble seeing the connection.

Once it was clear that the first two settlements had managed to survive, the English government flung open the gates for the next rush of colonists. In 1624 the Crown took over the management of Jamestown from its private investors. However, the king, unlike the Virginia Company, wasn't interested in managing Jamestown himself. Left to their own devices, the local leaders quietly began expanding their tobacco cultivation.

Although James I published a pamphlet titled "A Counterblaste to Tobacco" in 1604, in which he warned his subjects that smoking was a habit "loathsome to the eye, hatefull to the Nose, harmfulle to the braine," and "daungerous to the Lungs," its popularity continued to grow. Tobacco sales were booming, not only in England but elsewhere in Europe. By 1664, fifteen million pounds a year were being produced. An enormously wealthy landowning class sprang up because of tobacco.[22]

Optimistic younger sons of aristocrats flocked to Virginia, taking advantage of their political connections to acquire property and start their own tobacco plantation. By 1675, at least forty thousand gentry and their servants had settled in the Chesapeake Bay area.[23] Nearly all of them came from the southern and western counties of England, an area with a distinctive way of talking. These speech patterns took root in Virginia and formed the basis for southern American speech.

The soft, low-pitched intonation of western England evolved into the characteristic southern drawl. Many words that are now considered countrified or archaic first appeared in Virginia with the late seventeenth-century planters. These include *bide* for *stay*, *passel* for a collection of things, *skillet* for a frying pan, *disremember* for *forget*, *poorly* for *ill*, and *favor* for *resemble*. Putting an *a-* before certain verbs, such as *a-hunting*, *a-crying*, *a-going*, also originated in western England.

The early Virginians were also responsible for an explosion of tobacco terms. The word *tobacco* came from the Spanish, who got it from the natives of Haiti. By the 1580s, both the word and the plant were familiar in England, and smoking pipes full of tobacco was on the way to becoming a popular fad. *Tobacco smoke* first appeared in print in 1598, and *tobacco breath* and *tobacco fumes* in 1609.

Tobacco shops for buying the substance, and *tobacco houses* where like-minded men gathered for a smoke, were both common at the beginning of the seventeenth century. The day's supply was carried in a *tobacco bag*. Contemplating the beginnings of the tobacco trade in his *Historie of Virginia*, John Smith comments that "there are so many sofisticating Tobaco-mungers in England."[24]

Virginians created terms to talk about growing, harvesting, and selling the plant. By the end of the seventeenth century, these included *tobacco trade*, *tobacco planter*, *tobacco warehouse*, and *tobacco worm*. Tobacco was cured in buildings called *hangers*.

Tobacco was responsible for bringing the first women to the colony. Between 1620 and 1623, dozens of women arrived to enter into arranged marriages. They were called *tobacco brides* or *tobacco wives* because the future husband paid for his spouse's passage with tobacco—120 pounds of it, according to most sources.

The hallucinogen *Datura stramonium* also grew in Jamestown and was common enough to be named *Jamestown weed* or *jimsonweed.* It's first mentioned in a 1687 letter from Rev. John Clayton, who toured Virginia and sent reports back to the Royal Society in London. Clayton recounts how several soldiers went to gather wild greens for a salad and collected large handfuls of "an Herb called James-town-weed." After eating it, the soldiers were "rendered apish and foolish, as if they had been drunk, or were become idiots." Early settlers also applied jimsonweed as a poultice to burns or inflammations.[25]

While would-be planters and their wives were swelling the population of Jamestown, Puritans were arriving in Massachusetts. In 1629 five ships of settlers founded the Massachusetts Bay Colony north of Plymouth. Their chosen governor was John Winthrop, a Cambridge-educated lawyer from a well-to-do family. While on the ship en route to the colony, Winthrop delivered a sermon titled "A Model of Christian Charity." In it he reminded the new colonists that the world would be watching their success or failure. Taking a phrase from Jesus's Sermon on the Mount, he said, "For we must consider that we shall be as a city upon a hill."[26]

Politicians of later centuries adopted *city upon a hill* as a metaphor for American uniqueness and positive ideals. The phrase also appears in the form *shining city on a hill.* In recent times, presidents John Kennedy, Ronald Reagan, and Barack Obama have all alluded to America's status as a city upon a hill.

The first five Puritan ships were only the beginning. From 1629 until 1641, hundreds more ships arrived in Massachusetts Bay, depositing more than twenty thousand settlers. They came mainly from East Anglia, an area in the east of England encompassing Norfolk, Suffolk, Essex, and Cambridgeshire. As with the Chesapeake Bay settlers, the Puritans of Massachusetts had a distinctive dialect. They spoke in a high-pitched, nasal voice that has sometimes been called the "Norfolk whine."[27]

In New England it established itself as the "Yankee twang." Later English visitors to the region often commented on the nasality of American speech. Dictionary maker Noah Webster, writing more than a century after the colony's founding, complains about "the drawling, whining cant" of New Englanders, whose lazy pronunciations found "a passage thro the nose."[28]

New Englanders owned other distinctive pronunciations that lingered over time, especially in country districts. They pronounced a long *i* to rhyme with *alive* in words such as *motive* and *ensign*. They slipped in an *e* before *ow*, so *cow* became *keow*. They said *hev* for *have*, *gineral* for *general*, *ar* for *air*, and *yestidy* for *yesterday*. They also inserted *r*'s in some places where they weren't normally found, such as in *foller* (*follow*) and *arst* (*ask*). The Puritans' way of talking was the beginning of the "down-east" accent that nineteenth-century humor writers would caricature as typical American yokel speech and that modern writers still use to mark rural New England folks.

Colonial New Englanders lived close to the land. Fishing and timber harvests formed a large part of the economy, and most people also grew their own food. When they first arrived, they had to clear a piece of property before they could farm it or build on it. Their engagement with local landscape, plants, and animals called for a host of new descriptive terms.

One popular way to get them was by combining two English words. Early words for landscape features that mattered to settlers include *bottomland* and *backcountry*. Colonists also invented the terms *cold snap* and *landslide*. Other original terms for the terrain are *canebrake*, *pine barren*, *salt lick*, and *foothill*, as well as the new nouns *clearing* and *rapids*. Animals named for what they seemed like to the colonists include *catfish*, *blackbirds*, *bullfrogs*, *groundhogs*, *flying squirrels*, *rattlesnakes*, *copperheads*, and *bald eagles*. Several novel berries were named—*cowberry*, *bilberry*, *huckleberry*, *thimbleberry*, and *cranberry*.

The first known use of the word *swamp* appears in John Smith's *Historie of Virginia*. Describing the area around Jamestown for the

London investors, he says, "Some small Marshes and Swamps there are, but more profitable than hurtfull." He doesn't say how the swamps could be profitable, but swamps to early Americans were not necessarily bad. The word referred to a rich tract of low-lying land, too watery for cultivation but full of trees and other wild vegetation. Smith might have been thinking of logging the swamps or harvesting other plants. A later writer notes that the swamps yield "course [coarse] Hay" for winter use.[29]

Although the first recorded use of *swamp* refers to the American landscape, it was probably already a local English word. Smith clearly expected his correspondents to know what sort of land he was talking about. There's some evidence that the colonists did try to benefit from the swamps—the terms *swampland*, *swamp lots*, and *swamp meadows* came in soon after. Not until the nineteenth century was *swamp* used figuratively to mean a miserable, hard-to-escape place.

Americans have been footloose from the first. *Pull up stakes*, one of the earliest American expressions, entered the language in the seventeenth century. Settlers' property boundaries were marked by driving sharp wooden stakes into the ground (*setting stakes*). When owners or tenants moved, they pulled the stakes out of the ground. Besides describing a literal activity, *pull up stakes* was being used figuratively by 1640. Bartlett quotes an English visitor to Boston who wrote to a friend that year to say that he would soon be returning home: "I am loath to hear of a stay, but am plucking up stakes as soon as I may."[30]

The last major seventeenth-century English migration was the wave of Quakers who poured into the Delaware Valley beginning around 1675. Most settled in Pennsylvania, founded by William Penn in 1681. Penn, the son of Admiral Sir William Penn, joined the Society of Friends, usually known as Quakers, at a young age. When Penn's father died, he left the young man a fortune, including a land grant from Charles II that Penn turned into a Quaker refuge.

Penn was politically active in England and didn't spend much time in his newly acquired American territory. Yet he showed a flair for American-style word creation, including what may be the first use of the word *Americanize*. He wrote in a 1686 letter, "I aime at Americanizeing my famely [family]."[31] Other words that first appear in his writings are *boatable*, *cancellable*, *nullable*, *revealable*, and *sayable*. He also created *unconcern*, *unman*, and *unbottom*, meaning to unsettle someone. He added *black perch* and *swamp oak* to the list of American natural features. Penn also inspired the expression *avoid like the plague*, writing that "an able bad Man is an ill instrument, and to be shunn'd as the plague."[32]

Penn made the first in-print mention of the food called *hotcakes* while writing about a festival of the Delaware Indians. Penn says, "Their entertainment was a green Seat by a Spring, under some shady Trees, with hot Cakes of new Corn, both Wheat and Beans, which they make up in a square form, in the leaves of the Stem, and bake them in the Ashes."[33] The expression *sell like hotcakes* has been current since the early nineteenth century.

The settlers who colonized Pennsylvania and the Delaware Valley were more linguistically mixed than those of Virginia and Massachusetts. Most of the English Quakers originated in the North Midlands, an area that covers Cheshire, Lancashire, Yorkshire, Nottinghamshire, and Derbyshire, but they came from other parts of England and other European countries as well.

Not much remains of the purely North Midlands way of talking in what's usually called American midland speech, but a number of vocabulary words are still found in both places. These include *abide* meaning tolerate, *apple-pie order*, *bamboozle*, *brat*, *chock-full*, *crib* for a child's bed, *egg on*, *elbow grease*, *gab*, *gallivant*, *guzzle*, *nailed* for caught doing something wrong, *nap* in the sleeping sense, *rumpus*, *slam*, and *tiff*.

The Quakers also influenced the language through their use of *thee* and *thou*. Both words had been part of the vocabulary since the days of Old English. Originally, *thou* was the second-person subject pronoun (*thou art*) and *thee* was used as an object (*I love thee*).

You signified the plural but was also used to politely address a social superior. Quakers addressed everyone as *thee* and *thou* because they didn't believe in recognizing social hierarchies. In America Quakers started using *thee* in both positions (for example, *thee is*), an instance of English moving in a different direction from the mother tongue shortly after leaving home.

By the eighteenth century, non-Quakers had pretty much replaced both *thou* and *thee* with *you*, which now stood for singular as well as plural second person. However, *thou* and its corresponding verb forms (*thou art, thou hast, thou wast*) continued to appear in American grammar books as "correct" speech until well into the nineteenth century. Quaker usage may have helped keep the words in the written vocabulary long after they disappeared from everyday English.

Changes in the language didn't go unnoticed back home. Purists were soon complaining about the influx of American barbarisms into the King's English. The earliest known complaint comes from the English traveler Francis Moore, who wrote about his voyage to Georgia in 1735. Describing the location of Savannah, he says, "It stands upon the flat of a Hill; the Bank of the River (which they in barbarous *English* call a *Bluff*) is steep, and about 45 foot perpendicular."[34]

The English dictionary maker Samuel Johnson was also hostile to American words and usages. Commenting on a collection of American-written essays, he says, "This treatise [is] written with such elegance as the subject admits, tho' not without some mixture of the *American* dialect, a tract [trace] of corruption to which every language widely diffused must always be exposed."[35]

A more lighthearted commentator suggests that someone should write a glossary of "the words, figures, and forms of speech" of the American colonies. He says that such a guide would have greatly helped him when trying to interpret a recent letter, which he then quotes: "At a meeting of Sachems it was determined to *take up the hatchet*, and *make the war-kettle boil.*" The letter also includes the word *scalp* and an early version of *smoke the peace pipe*—"smoak the calumet of peace."[36]

This trickle of commentary and complaint became a flood as time went on. The growth of American English was about to shift into high gear, and what started as the almost accidental adoption of a handful of necessary words evolved into a full-fledged alternative idiom.

Dozens of new words and changed meanings entered the language in the decades before the Revolution. Pronunciations in America and England began to diverge. More noticeably, speech styles diverged as Americans started to develop their own characteristic ways of talking. And countering the outrage of the linguistic traditionalists were the colonial patriots, ready to argue ferociously for the superior virtues of the American tongue.

2

The Two Englishes Part Ways

By the eve of the American Revolution, candidates for entry into Bartlett's dictionary had grown from a brief list of Algonquian terms, courtesy of John Smith, to a substantial collection of words and phrases from a variety of places. Some were borrowed from other languages. Many were retooled or newly constructed out of English parts. The English language in America was gradually but inevitably drifting away from its parent. While Captain Smith and his Jamestown companions clearly spoke the same English as their British sponsors, even if it included a few novelties like *raccoon*, George Washington and his fellow citizens spoke something recognizably different.

This state of affairs wasn't at all remarkable. Languages change over time, slowly but continuously. Sounds shift, words enter or leave the vocabulary, new grammatical patterns emerge, and old ones fall out of use. Dialects form when speakers of a language split into geographically distant or culturally distinct groups. Both branches of the language will continue growing and changing, but almost always in different directions, especially if physical or political barriers (like an ocean) make it hard for the two groups to interact. After centuries of limited contact or none at all, dialects may grow so far apart that they're no longer mutually understandable. What started as a single language—say, Algonquian or Germanic—will morph into multiple languages—for instance, Ojibwe, Cheyenne, and Cree, or English, Dutch, and Swedish.

Matters hadn't progressed that far in the century and a half since the first colonists left England. British and American English speakers were in regular contact, and besides, a relatively short amount of time had passed. Cracks were nonetheless starting to appear in what was once a solid linguistic edifice. Some words and usages that were still current in America had gone out of style in England, while new trends in the home country often didn't make it to the colonies. Americans went their own way, collecting new vocabulary and developing fresh ways of talking. As a result, American speech in the late eighteenth century was archaic in some ways but innovative in others.

George Washington's diaries show evidence of both traits. He still attached the prefix *a-* to certain verbs, an old-fashioned grammatical structure that had come to Virginia with the first planters. He writes, "Went a ducking between breakfast and dinner and killed 2 mallards and 5 bald-faces," using the American word for a wigeon. He also uses the southern regionalism *righted up*, a Scottish term that was in the process of turning into an Americanism: "The old fence round Field No. 2 was righted up to keep creatures out of it." Other archaic verbs likely to be part of his vocabulary include *cotched* (*caught*), *fotch* (*fetched*), *holp* (*helped*), and *mought* (*might*). All were still fairly common.[1]

Washington also embraced new word creations, such as *back shed*, meaning a shed attached to the back of a house; *branch*, the American word for a small stream; and verbs that were heard only or mainly in America. Some examples that appear in his writings are *to obligate*, *to council* (meet in a council), *to populate* (increase in population), and *to predicate* (to affirm on the basis of some fact).

Although Washington's spelling is much more recognizable to modern readers than that of John Smith or William Bradford, his pronunciation would still sound strange. The word *creatures*, for example, would have sounded more like *creetyur*, maybe even verging on *critter*. Washington and his fellow colonials would have pronounced many words differently from both modern British speakers and modern Americans—words like *cowcumber* (*cucumber*), *obleege* (*oblige*), *chaw* (*chew*), and *froncheer* (*frontier*). They would have pronounced *Constitution* as *konsteetushun* and *American* as *Amereekan*. Today we might stigmatize these words as countrified, but in the late eighteenth century, they were the ordinary pronunciations of an educated future president. The same is true for two common grammatical usages, *ain't* and *you was*. These wouldn't be deemed marginal until well into the next century.

American English speakers weren't as easily distinguishable from British speakers as they are today, but certain pronunciation differences that signal an American or English accent were becoming noticeable. In two high-profile cases, Americans stayed with the older sound while the British went with something new.

When the first settlers arrived in Jamestown and the Plymouth Colony, all English speakers pronounced the letter *a* like the vowel in *hat* rather than the first vowel in *bother*. During the eighteenth century, the English who were still in England started to say *a* more like *ah* before consonant combinations such as *lf*, *nc*, and *th*—*cahf* for *calf*, *dahnce* for *dance*, *bahth* for *bath*. Aside from some areas of New England, most Americans never made that switch. They adopted that *ah* sound before two consonants only in a few words, for example *calm* and *father*, and before most *r*'s, as in *car* and *large*. In George Washington's day, the few changes to *a* that Americans did make were only starting to filter through. Washington probably pronounced *father* to rhyme with *rather*.

An even more distinctive change was affecting the *r* sound. For the most part, the first colonists always pronounced their *r*'s, as did their relatives back home. (One exception was in words like *burst*, *curse*, and *horse*. Lower-class speakers said *bust*, *cuss*, and *hoss*, a pronunciation that lingered in America and can still be heard in casual or regional speech.) As with *a*, the situation started changing during the eighteenth century.

The English upper classes adopted a trend of dropping or minimizing the *r* at the end of a word or between a vowel and a consonant. By the end of the century, the new pronunciation was widespread. An English grammarian writing in 1791 says, "In England, and particularly in London, the *r* in *lard, bard, card, regard,* etc. is pronounced so much in the throat as to be little more than the middle or Italian *a,* lengthened into *laad, baad, caad, regaad.*"[2]

In America, *r*-less speech took root only in a few places. It caught on in port cities like Boston and Charleston, where British fashions arrived first and British visitors were more common than elsewhere. It also spread through much of the South, where plantation owners identified with the English aristocracy. As a Virginian, George Washington might well have adopted this new British speech style. The majority of Americans, however, continued to say their *r*'s. The *r*-pronouncing dialect expanded across the continent, while *r*-lessness never spread beyond its original strongholds. Saying your *r*'s is now an identifying feature of American speech.

Washington's language patterns—lagging behind those of the old country in some ways but surging ahead in others—were typical of American speech. Language reflected the larger push-and-pull relationship between Great Britain and its American possessions. The colonists were still tied to England in various ways. Trade laws largely prevented them from doing business directly with countries outside the British Empire, so they relied on British imports for luxuries such as tea, rum, and sugar, as well as practical goods like cotton and silk fabric. Americans also counted on England for books, including schoolbooks. Colonial children of the time learned to read and write from textbooks written in England.

England was nevertheless a foreign place to most Americans. Few colonists had ever heard British speech. Long-distance travel was expensive and onerous, so people who emigrated from England seldom returned. Native-born Americans were even less likely than immigrants to visit the mother country unless they were very well off. Communication between the two places was largely in writing, and written language is slow to reflect changes in the vernacular. Often it doesn't reveal pronunciation changes at all. This lack of feedback made it even easier for the two countries to follow separate verbal paths.

At the same time as the colonies grew more politically and culturally estranged from England, they were connecting more with each other. By the 1770s, the Crown laid claim to an unbroken stretch of the East Coast from Georgia to what is now Maine, encompassing a population of well over two million people.[3] Travel between regions was getting easier all the time. Only the rich owned carriages, but a primitive stagecoach service ran between major towns. Water travel was comfortable and cheap on the small, single-masted sloops that ran along the rivers and the coast. Colonists not only traveled more in neighboring regions but also frequently upped stakes and relocated permanently.

These restless habits had an impact on the American language. Colonies that were originally settled by English speakers from a specific place—for instance, Yorkshire or Essex—became home to people with a variety of cultural and linguistic histories. Their speech patterns mingled to such an extent that it's now difficult to draw a straight line between any regional American dialect and a single ancestral region of England. Traces remain—archaic words like *disremember* in southern speech, the "down-east" accent of New England—but the overlap is only partial. The regional speech styles that were already developing before the Revolution were a mix of old and new.

The need for new words to capture the experience of living in North America kept inventive new terminology flowing into colonial English. Combining two familiar words—for example, *underbrush*, *watershed*, *pitch pine*—was still a popular form of word creation. Sometimes one compound led to a proliferation of similar terms. For instance, by the late eighteenth century, American English included not only *backcountry* but also *backlands*, *backwoods*, *back road*, and *back settlement*. Benjamin Franklin used *back settlements* in 1759 when writing about the hinterlands of Pennsylvania and Virginia.

A characteristic of many new terms was that they started out with literal meanings but added figurative ones over time, enriching the language in two ways. For example, *back track* first meant a track leading backward or toward a starting point. "We lay still and kept scouts upon our back tracks to see if there would any pursue," writes a Massachusetts colonist in a 1724 journal entry.[4] By the early nineteenth century, *take the back track* meant to retreat from a position taken or "walk it back," as we would say now. The *Congressional Globe* for March 19, 1838, records a congressman complaining about the twists and turns involved in passing a revenue bill: "We were suddenly ordered to wheel about . . . and take a back track." Later, *backtrack* became a verb in its own right.

Turning nouns into verbs was a favorite method for creating new words. Although English speakers had been verbing nouns for centuries, Americans seemed to have a special knack for it. Some verbs made the transition just by adding *to*, as *to deed*, *to dump*, *to blow*, *to cord*, *to scalp*, *to progress*. The endings *-ate* and *-ize* were also popular ways to transform a word into a verb. *Locate*, *eventuate*, *advocate*, and *appreciate* (with the meaning of rising in value) were all early American creations. The *-ize* ending gave us *jeopardize*, *deputize*, *energize*, and many other words, including some now arcane terms like *citizenize*. Bartlett defines *citizenize* as "to admit to the rank and privileges of a citizen," noting that it's "rarely used."

George Washington was not the only founding father to indulge in Americanisms. John Quincy Adams coined *antagonize*, and Alexander Hamilton used the now defunct verb *to retrospect*. Noah Webster took credit for *demoralize*, another example of a word that started with a literal meaning and then expanded into metaphor. For Webster, it meant corrupting someone's morals. The modern meaning of undermining someone's morale or self-confidence appeared in the early nineteenth century.

Thomas Jefferson wholeheartedly embraced new words, even in formal writing. His view of English in America, as he wrote to a friend, was that "so great growing a population . . . must enlarge their language, to make it answer its purpose of expressing all ideas. . . . The new circumstances under which we are placed call for new words, new phrases, and for the transfer of old words to new objects." He predicted that an American dialect would establish itself in time, although he conceded that it might take a while. Until then, he tells his correspondent, "necessity obliges us to neologize."[5]

Neologisms that Jefferson invented or popularized include *democratize*, *ambition* used as a verb ("This is what I ambition for my own country"), and *avail* meaning to give the benefit of ("avail Mr. Barclay of that fund"). One of Jefferson's coinages, *belittle*, drew a firestorm of British criticism when it appeared in his 1785 *Notes on the State of Virginia*. Describing the ideas of the Count de Buffon, a French naturalist who claimed that animals of the same species tend to be smaller in America than in Europe, Jefferson writes of "the tendency of nature to belittle her productions on this side of the Atlantic."[6] By *belittle*, Jefferson meant literally to make smaller.

This usage deeply offended a reviewer for the *European Magazine and London Review*. "*Belittle!*" he gasps, "What an expression! . . . Why, after trampling upon the honour [*sic*] of our country, . . . perpetually trample also upon the very grammar of our language? . . . Freely, good sir, will we forgive all your attacks . . . upon our *national character*; but for the future spare—O spare, we beseech you, our mother-tongue!"[7] The reviewer's plea was in vain. Only a few years later, *belittle* took on the figurative meaning of disparaging a person or thing or dismissing its importance.

Bartlett gives only the literal definition of *belittle* in the 1848 edition of his dictionary, saying the word is rarely used. By the time of the 1877 edition, however, the metaphorical meaning was well-enough established for him to add the definition, "To speak of a thing in a depreciatory, or contemptuous way." Like many other Americanisms excoriated by British critics, figurative *belittle* was, after a time, accepted in the old country. The novelist Anthony Trollope used it in his 1862 book *North America*, saying, "Washington was a great man, and I believe a good man. I, at any rate, will not belittle him."[8]

The eighteenth century saw one more burst of immigration from the British Isles. Beginning around 1700 and continuing for most of the century, a steady stream of new arrivals—more than two hundred thousand by most counts—made their way to North America, mostly from Ulster (Northern Ireland) but also from Scotland and the north of England. They were collectively known by the Americanism *Scotch Irish*. (This term isn't heard in the British Isles, where *Scotch* is supposed to refer only to whisky, not people. There the group is more typically known as Ulster Scots. These are Scots who migrated to Northern Ireland in the early seventeenth century as part of James I's plan to establish a Protestant, English-speaking presence there.)

Scotch Irish immigrants were unlike earlier colonists. Although they were mainly Presbyterians, a disenfranchised religion in England, religious freedom wasn't their primary motive for leaving. Nor were they sponsored by investors. They came to escape poverty and the political unrest of Ulster and the Scottish border regions and to build a more prosperous life than they could have hoped for at home.

Established colonists viewed the newcomers as competition for increasingly scarce land and pressured them to move on from their arrival ports of Boston or Philadelphia. Most were pushed into the backcountry of western Pennsylvania, then into the southern Appalachian Mountains. Eventually they spilled into the frontier territories of Kentucky and Tennessee. In these isolated regions, the Scotch Irish clustered in tight-knit communities, creating a culture of strong extended families and keeping their music and folklore, Presbyterian religion, and other traditions alive. For a while, they also kept their distinctive way of talking. It would form the basis of an iconic American dialect.

A number of words that can be heard today in regions of Scotch Irish settlement started life in Scotland (and in some cases are still there). These include *airish*, meaning chilly or breezy weather; *biddable*, meaning obedient; *chancy* to mean doubtful or risky; *ill* for *bad tempered*; and *mind* for *remember.* In Pennsylvania *redd up* is used for *tidy up* and *anymore* can mean something like nowadays, as in *all the good jobs are in the cities anymore.*

The Appalachian backcountry preserved some old-fashioned verb forms. Bartlett's dictionary lists as examples *seen* for *saw*, as in *I seen it*, and *done* for *have*, as in *they done gone* and *he done did it.* The region was also home to what Bartlett calls "intensive and extravagant" modifiers, such as *all-fired, splendiferous*, and *powerful.* Words like these were later put into the mouths of southern and western stereotypes—the mountain men and cracker-barrel philosophers of nineteenth-century comic novels.

During the height of immigration from Ulster and the north of Britain, Americans distinguished a Scotch Irish–like accent from other types of English, although exactly how it sounded is unclear. Recent arrivals were often described as speaking "broad Scottish" or having "an Irish brogue." Many of these descriptions appeared in newspapers, where the masters of runaway indentured servants posted advertisements to track them down. For instance, the *Boston Gazette* for the week of January 2–9, 1738, features the ad, "Ran-away . . . an indented Servant called Archibald Kier . . . talks pretty broad Scotch."

One runaway, "a native Irish servant named Edward Coalman," is identified in the *Pennsylvania Chronicle* for November 11, 1767, by what was apparently a known Irish trait: "very seldom answers yes or no, but I will or I did, or I will not or I did not."[9] Using *will* instead of *shall* after *I* was also an Irishism. American and British language critics of the mid-nineteenth century complained that the Irish were responsible for the virtual disappearance of *shall* in the United States.

Andrew Jackson, the first president to hail from Scotch Irish territory, "occasionally betrayed his lineage by the slightest possible twang of Scotch-Irish pronunciation," according to biographer James Parton. Jackson's parents had been part of the exodus from Northern Ireland. Writing in the mid-nineteenth century, Parton claims that there is "still a smack of the North-Irish brogue" to be heard in the Jackson family. Parton gives examples of their talk—"He went *till* Charleston," meaning *to* Charleston, and "there never was seen the *like* of him for mischief."[10]

After a while, the newcomers lost their foreign accents and developed a regional way of talking. One of the first to comment on the backcountry accent was the writer Anne Royall. Royall was a widow, a resident of Washington, DC, who supported herself by traveling around the United States and writing about the people she met, including their speech habits. She had a good ear but seldom liked what she heard.

Writing in the 1820s about the rural residents of what is now West Virginia, she complains that they have "so mangled" the English language that "it is hardly known to be such." As examples she gives *blaze* pronounced *bleez, handkerchief* pronounced *hancorchy, waun* for *one*, and *cheers* for *chairs*. Twenty years later, Bartlett comments in the introduction to his dictionary on a similar trait of western and southern people: "the giving of a broader sound than is proper to certain vowels; as *whar* for *where, thar* for *there, bar* for *bear*." This way of saying vowels later became an identifying trait for Davy Crockett and other rugged frontier types.[11]

Royall also remarked on the region's nonstandard word use. Her West Virginia acquaintances always used *road* for *way*, as in *Put them cheers out of the road*. She records the nonstandard past tense *comed* and notes an unusual way of using *let on*. "When they would say *pretence*," she writes, "they say *lettinon* [*letting on*]. . . . It signifies a jest, and is used to express disapprobation and disguise; . . . 'Polly is not mad, she is only lettinon.'"[12]

When *let on* was brought from Scotland and northern England, it originally meant to divulge something, and that's still the standard meaning. Bartlett defines *to let on* as "to mention, to disclose." He says that it is "often heard among the illiterate" in all parts of the United

States. The word continued to evolve in the mountains, however, until it gained the new meaning that Royall noted.

Because of the geographic isolation and homogeneity of Appalachian settlers, a myth sprang up sometime during the nineteenth century that mountain people spoke "the language of Shakespeare" or "Elizabethan English." Language observers noticed that obsolete verb forms like *holp* for *helped* and *drug* for *dragged*, double negatives (*never no more*), double comparatives (*worser, more crazier*), and other antiquated usages were still common in the mountain areas of the South. Some of these same words and phrases are also found in the works of Shakespeare, who wrote many of his plays during the late sixteenth century, when Elizabeth I sat on the throne. Based on this evidence, those observers concluded that the descendants of the Scotch Irish settlers had preserved a "pure" form of Elizabethan speech.[13]

Sadly for romantics, the truth is that language never stays frozen in time, even in secluded mountain settlements. The changed meaning of *letting on* that Royall records shows that backcountry English was evolving. When the first Scotch Irish began immigrating, the Elizabethan age was already a century in the past, and there's no evidence that residents of Ulster and the Scottish border territories preserved any more of that period's language than other English speakers.

Some of the old words and uses later attributed to the Scotch Irish were actually more widespread. The settlers of Jamestown and Plymouth (already post-Elizabethan—the queen died in 1603) also used *holp*, *drug*, and other now obsolete verbs, some of which didn't die out in America until well into the nineteenth century. Grammar books published as late as the 1840s list these and other unfamiliar verb forms like *spake*, *wrought*, and *hast*.

More important for American English than the speech patterns that arrived with the Scotch Irish were the striking expressions that sprang up in their new home. Many reflect settlement activities or aspects of the natural world—for instance, *blaze a trail*, *cave in*, *sit on the fence*, *cotton to*, *play possum*. Others express parts of the culture such as challenging your enemies—*get even, settle someone's hash*—or making a break for new horizons—*clear out, make tracks, be among the missing*. This colorful mode of self-expression eventually traveled beyond its backcountry birthplace to become a defining feature of the American language.

Another way that America was changing English was in the adoption of words from other colonial languages. Spain and France had sunk colonial roots into the Americas long before the arrival of the first permanent English settlers. Both impinged on British territory by the late 1700s. New Spain included Florida and the areas that are now Texas, New Mexico, and California. France claimed most of present-day Canada, as well as the Louisiana Territory, which stretched south to New Orleans and west to the Rockies.

Although the territories were vast, they were thinly settled by Europeans. Neither country was committed to building permanent communities of the sort that the English founded. Spain concentrated on extracting treasure from the gold and silver mines of Peru and Mexico and shipping it back home, while the French presence in North America consisted mainly of itinerant traders, trappers, and cod fishermen. Their linguistic influence reflected those limitations.

The first colonial Spanish loan words entered the English language shortly after Christopher Columbus's return from the Bahamas. Like all the early borrowings, they came from Native American languages and named an unfamiliar plant, animal, or cultural practice. Unlike later Native American loan words, they filtered directly into England from Spain. Because of that, they didn't trouble British language purists as much as the new terminology that later came from Jamestown and Massachusetts.

Cannibal, introduced by Columbus, was one of the earliest. It's a form of the tribal name for the Carib people of the West Indies, who were thought to consume human flesh. By the eighteenth century, it had generalized to a word for anyone who eats human flesh or any animal that eats its own species. Another Carib word, *hurricane*, was used to describe Atlantic "tempests" as early as 1555. Other early borrowings were *canoe*, adopted from a Central American language around the same time as *hurricane*, and *coyote*, a Mexican word first written down in 1628.

Food words that we now think of as American rather than Spanish include *chocolate*, first mentioned in 1604, from Nahuatl *chocolatl* and Spanish *chocolate*; *tomato*, from Mexican *tomatl* and Spanish *tomate*, which appeared around the same time; and *potato*, used as early as 1565. The original Spanish word, *patata* or *batata*, referred to sweet potatoes. White potatoes at first were known as *Virginia potatoes*.

Barbecue, from Haitian *barbacoa* and the same word in Spanish, came into colonial English at the end of the seventeenth century, and Americans quickly made it their own. Originally it named an iron frame used for grilling meat. Later the meaning extended to the meat itself. By 1730 *barbecue* was being used to designate a social event that centered on grilling meat. George Washington mentions attending barbecues more than once in his diaries.

French colonial borrowings didn't begin entering English until late in the seventeenth century. Most result from the experiences of the trappers and explorers who roamed French territory. *Caribou*, which was being used as early as 1672, came originally from Algonquian. New Englanders borrowed *chowder* from Newfoundland in the mid-eighteenth century, a version of the French *chaudière*, a cooking pot. The name expanded to cover the food cooked in the pot as well.

The French word *prairie* entered English around 1682 and was used first in England, but its meaning changed in America to describe a different landscape. In France and England, *prairie* referred to a meadowland. In America, the word meant rolling grasslands in most of the country, or marshlands in the South. Westward expansion would bring a proliferation of compounds, including *prairie dog*, *prairie hen*, *prairie fire*, *prairie wolf* (coyote), and many names for plants, such as *prairie flower*. The large covered wagons that carried settlers across the continent were known as *prairie schooners*. (The origin of *schooner*, which normally refers to a sailing vessel, is unclear. Dutch and Scottish are two possibilities for the original language. Wherever it came from, the American version of the word was almost certainly coined in Massachusetts, where it was in use by 1716.)

Place names were the major linguistic contribution of the Spanish and French before the Revolution. As Americans pushed west during the nineteenth century, they found ready-made territorial names, such as Nevada, Colorado, and California, from Europeans who had come before. Hundreds of towns are named for Spanish saints—California alone boasts San Bernardino, San Jose, Santa Rosa, San Francisco, and dozens more. French explorers, besides naming Louisiana for their king, gave descriptive names to many locations, including Eau Claire ("clear water"), Des Moines ("of the monks"), Pend Oreille ("hang from the ear," for the large earrings of the Kalispel Indians), and Deschutes ("of the falls").

Native American languages also influenced American English through place names. Most of the original colonies were named after their founders or royalty, but *Massachusetts* comes from the Massachusett tribe who lived near Massachusetts Bay, and *Connecticut* from the Mohegan name for the area around the Connecticut River. *Adirondack*, *Allegheny*, *Potomac*, and *Niagara* were also early borrowings from the local tribes. As Americans moved farther west, more Native American loan words entered English, including names for the Kentucky, Tennessee, Illinois, Mississippi, and Ohio Territories.

The colonial language that made the strongest impact on English is Dutch. By the time of the Revolution, the Dutch empire in America had long been absorbed into the British colonies, but their linguistic influence still reverberated.

The Dutch adventure in America started in 1609, when an Englishman named Henry Hudson, an employee of the Dutch East India Company, sailed into New York Harbor. His arrival there was incidental—like other navigators of the time, he was looking for an easy route to Asia. Since he was there, however, he claimed the territory for his employers, who named it New Netherland. Shortly afterward, Dutch traders established an outpost near what is now Albany. Settlement started in earnest in 1626, when Dutch colonists famously purchased Manhattan (which they named New Amsterdam) from the Munsee Indians for goods worth about twenty-four dollars.

Around nine thousand Europeans were living in New Netherland when it changed hands thirty-eight years later.[14] During one of the periodic wars between the English and the Dutch over control of world trade routes, Charles II decided to confiscate New Netherland and hand it over to his brother James, who was then Duke of York. In August 1664, he sent four warships into the harbor, and Governor Peter Stuyvesant, realizing that he was massively outgunned, surrendered without a fight. Overnight, New Netherland turned into New York.

Dutch residents didn't abandon their culture as easily as they gave up their colony. The Dutch language continued to be heard in both New York and New Jersey until well into the nineteenth century. An early historian of New York, writing in 1757, records that "the Dutch dialect . . . is still so much used in some Counties, that the Sheriffs find it difficult to obtain Persons sufficiently acquainted with the *English* tongue, to serve as Jurors in the Courts of Law." Services in the Dutch Reformed Church continued to be held in Dutch, as noted by a young Noah Webster in 1786. After attending an Albany, New York, church service, he wrote in his diary, "Hear the Dutch parson Westils—understand not a word." He adds that "the Dutch have no taste for the English language."[15]

At the same time, a number of Dutch words were Americanizing. These included several food terms, such as *coleslaw*, *cruller*, *waffle*, and *cookie*. (Food terms loom large as word borrowings because they're so culture specific. If the English didn't eat waffles until introduced to them by the Dutch, they wouldn't have a ready-made word for them.) *Snoop*, from Dutch *snoep*, originally had the food-related meaning of a person who sneaked delicacies. Bartlett describes the word this way: "Applied to children, servants, and others, who clandestinely eat dainties or other victuals which have been put aside, not for their use." He adds that "the term is peculiar to New York." The broader definition of spying or poking into other people's business replaced this specialized meaning by the later nineteenth century.

Dope, from the Dutch *doop*, originally meant a dipping sauce. The word first labeled any sort of thick, semi-liquid concoction, but by the late nineteenth century, it was slang for opium, which was mixed into a molasses-like goo for smoking. From there, it naturally expanded to encompass any kind of drug. *Dope* can still apply broadly to anything that comes under the general heading of "a mixture of stuff," from gossip ("What's the dope on *x*?") to preparations for waxing skis.

Boss, one of the first Dutch English words, first appears in writing in John Winthrop's 1635 history of New England. Describing recent newcomers to the colony, he writes, "Here arrived . . . one Gardner, an expert enginer or work base."[16] *Work base* was Winthrop's way of spelling the Dutch *werk-baas*, or "work master," the title given to a supervisor or business manager.

Bartlett defines *boss* as "a master, an employer of mechanics or laborers." In his 1877 edition, he tells readers that the *o* in *boss* is pronounced like the *a* in *all*, suggesting that the word was not yet common. However, it was beginning to replace the traditional English term *master*: "We hear of a *boss*-carpenter, a *boss*-bricklayer, *boss*-shoemaker, &c., instead of master-carpenter, &c." Bartlett also includes the verb *to boss*, "to rule over, to direct."

Dutch place names are thickly scattered around New York. Any name that incorporates *hook* ("point of land"), *dorp* ("village"), or *kill* ("channel") originated with the Dutch—New Dorp, Schuylkill, Peekskill, Red Hook, Kinderhook. Other Dutch names are not as obvious, such as Brooklyn (for the Dutch town of Breuckelen) and Coney Island (Conyne Eylandt, or Rabbit Island). The Bowery was originally a *bouwerij*, or farmstead.

At first glance, Flatbush doesn't look especially Dutch, but *bush* in the sense of backcountry comes from the Dutch *bos* or *bosch*, woodland or uncleared countryside. When the Dutch settled the Flatbush area of Brooklyn, it was a flat, wooded plain. *Bushwhacker*, now associated with life on the frontier, first appears in Washington Irving's 1809 comic history of New Netherland, *A History of New York, from the Beginning of the World to the End of the Dutch Dynasty*, published under the ultra-Dutch pseudonym Diedrich Knickerbocker. Describing a great (fictional) gathering of Dutch warriors at the south end of Manhattan, Irving lists among them the Van Bunschotens of Nyack and Kakiat, who were "gallant bushwhackers and hunters of raccoons by moonlight."[17]

Irving's book also gave New Yorkers their title of *knickerbocker*. Knickerbockers started out as descendants of the original Dutch settlers, but by the 1850s, the nickname covered all New Yorkers. At around the same time, *knickerbockers* or *knickers* became a name for loose-fitting knee breeches, apparently a reference to the outfits shown in an early illustrated version of the book.

In later editions of the book, Irving, who was born in New York in 1783 to Scottish immigrants, offered his "Author's Apology" for having made fun of the early Dutch residents. He believed that Dutch New Yorkers had forgiven him, however. They now prided themselves on being "genuine Knickerbockers," he said, and used the label "to give the home stamp to everything recommended for popular acceptation, such as Knickerbocker societies; Knickerbocker insurance companies; Knickerbocker steamboats;" and many other product names.[18]

"The Knickerbockers at Practice," a pen-and-ink drawing by Homer Davenport. One of the first-ever baseball teams, the New York Knickerbockers wore knickers as part of their uniform. *Courtesy of the Miriam and Ira D. Wallach Collection of Arts, Prints, and Photographs, New York Public Library*

Whether purposely or not, Irving provided one of the earliest American stereotypes: the would-be intrepid, but unsophisticated, colonial Dutchman. Several American expressions that incorporate *Dutch* tell us something about the negative English view of the people whose colony they had taken over. A *Dutch treat* is a social occasion when each person pays his or her own way, or in other words, no one treats. *Dutch courage* is the kind of bravery that comes from swigging alcohol.

Dutch comfort, telling someone to be glad things aren't worse, is not very comforting. To be *in Dutch* is to be in trouble and run the risk of having someone scold you, or *talk to you like a Dutch uncle. That beats the Dutch,* the only halfway positive expression, was a common way to describe a surprising event. It was said that the Dutch, with their powerful navy, could beat the devil, so beating the Dutch was quite a feat.

The Dutch opinion of the English was no more flattering. *Yankee,* that most American of words, likely grew out of a derisive Dutch nickname for the English in America. Several explanations have been floated for the word's origins (for example, that it's based on a Native American word for an Englishman), but the most plausible is that it comes from the Dutch *Janke* (pronounced *yan-kuh*), a diminutive of *Jan* (John), which means something like "little John." At the time, *John Bull* was a nickname for a typical Englishman. The Dutch in New York would surely have gotten some satisfaction from referring to their new overlords as little John Bulls.

Originally, *Yankee* meant a New Englander, but the British picked up the term and generalized it to refer to any American. It was current by 1758, the time of the Seven Years' War, fought on North American soil between the British and the French. British general James Wolfe wrote to one of his commanders, "My posts are now so fortified that I can afford you two companies of Yankees," adding dismissively, "the more as they are better for ranging and scouting than either work or vigilance."[19]

The song "Yankee Doodle" was the brainchild of a British army surgeon named Richard Shuckburgh, who set the words to an old English folk tune. No one is sure of the lyrics of the original verses, but they apparently ridiculed the scruffiness and lack of discipline of American troops. Most Americans couldn't afford uniforms, so they came to the war in their work clothes.

The word *dandy* in the chorus was contemporary slang for a well-dressed young man devoted to fashion. *Macaroni* meant more or less the same thing, probably a reference to London's Macaroni Club, a collection of aristocratic dandies who had traveled in Italy (and presumably developed an appreciation of *maccheroni* pasta). Both were slaps at Americans' supposedly primitive notions of what constituted elegance—they were so unsophisticated, they would stick a feather in their caps and "call it macaroni."

At the start of the war for independence, British troops composed aggressive verses like this one sung at the Battles of Lexington and

"The Macaroni. A Real Character at the Late Masquerade." In this mezzotint by Philip Dawe, the Macaroni is not wearing a feather in his cap but is otherwise dressed in the height of fashion. *Courtesy of the Lewis Walpole Library, Yale University*

Concord: "Yankee Doodle came to town / For to buy a firelock [musket] / We will tar and feather him, / And so we will John Hancock." Later, as the tide began to turn in favor of the Americans, Yankees took the word back. They made it a term of pride in expressions like *Yankee ingenuity* and *Yankee grit*, and American Revolutionary soldiers adopted "Yankee Doodle" as their anthem. They wrote new verses that praised General Washington and warned of English defeats to come. By the end of the war, the song was a national folk tune. The American army band chose to play it on October 19, 1781, at Yorktown, Virginia, as General Cornwallis's troops surrendered their arms.[20]

Other languages in pre-Revolutionary America contributed a scattering of words to the developing vocabulary. Tens of thousands of Germans, mostly Amish or Mennonites, poured into western New York and Pennsylvania around the same time as the Scotch Irish. They didn't interact much with English speakers though. They continued to speak their home dialect, a variety of German that became known as Pennsylvania Dutch (from *Deutsch*, the German word for *German*). Word borrowings from the time are limited to *noodle*, *pretzel*, and *sauerkraut*. Pennsylvania Dutch, which is still spoken, also gave rise to local expressions that are literal translations of German terms, such as *all* for *all gone* (*the potatoes are all*) and *leave* for *let* (*church leaves out at noon*). The main German influence on American English, however, came with the later German migrations of the nineteenth century.

Millions of speakers of West African languages also lived in early America. The first Africans came to the colonies in 1619, when a Dutch sea captain brought twenty captive Angolans to Virginia. A regular slave trade developed during the eighteenth century, and Africans continued to be brought into the country until 1808, when the trade was banned. Although their numbers were relatively large, their language use was restricted in ways that limited their contributions to early American English.

Captives were taken from all over West Africa, which is home to over one thousand languages, including thousands of local dialects. No single language predominated. To thwart attempts at mutiny, slave traders made deliberate efforts to keep people who spoke the same language apart. After arrival, the enslaved people were dispersed to different plantations, ensuring that the linguistic mix stayed random.

To communicate with each other and, more imperatively, to understand the speech of their masters, enslaved Africans needed to learn English as quickly as they could. Most apparently acquired passable English within a fairly short time. Like the ads for runaway Scotch Irish servants, notices for runaway slaves often include their level of English skills. Recent arrivals were described as speaking "but few words of English" or "little to no English," but those who had been in the country even a year or two typically spoke "pretty good" or "very good" English. Those who were born in America were of course native speakers.

In spite of the repression of Africans' native speech, early American English did absorb several loan words from different African languages. They follow the usual pattern of naming food and customs not found in Europe. One of the earliest, *banana*, was first noted in a 1597 book about recent European explorations. It comes from Guinea by way of Spain or Portugal. (The word is identical in those two languages.) *Okra*, originally from the Ibo language of Nigeria, appears in a 1679 account of colonial Jamaica. The Bantu word *gumbo* also means okra. Bartlett lists it with the spelling *gombo* and defines it as "the Southern name" for what Northerners call okra. Over time the meaning shifted to refer to a soup or stew made with okra.

Yam, another early word adoption, appears in several exotic travelogues. One from 1589 describes yams as "a kind of roots" much eaten in Benin. "They call it Inamia," the author says, and "it is pleasant in eating."[21] *Yam* likely comes from the Fulani word *nyami*, meaning to eat. Like *banana*, it detoured through Spanish or Portuguese, undergoing a couple of radical spelling changes before taking its current form in English. In America, sweet potatoes are sometimes also called yams from their resemblance to the latter, but the two plants are different species.

Voodoo and its variant *hoodoo* originated in the Fon language of Benin. They were brought to America by enslaved workers who came from the West Indies. Early examples of *voodoo* are often spelled *voudou*, and the word could refer to the practitioner as well as the religion. The fantastically shaped pillars of rock found in several western states have been called hoodoos since the late nineteenth century, apparently because some people found them eerie.[22] *Gris-gris*, the word for magic charms, is another West Indian borrowing, but probably came to English through French.

Other small linguistic enclaves existed around the time of the Revolution, such as the Swedes of the Delaware Valley and the Welsh Quakers of Pennsylvania and New York. These communities didn't have any lasting effect on American speech, but they did add regional color until at least the mid-nineteenth century. Bartlett claimed in 1848 that in New York's Oneida County, "one may travel for miles and hear nothing but the Welsh language."[23] Gradually these islands of foreign speech disappeared, engulfed by a rising tide of English.

By the time the colonists were ready to part ways with the old country, the notion that Americans had a different way of talking was already widespread. Just how distinctive American English was—and whether or not that was a problem—were matters of perspective.

Eighteenth-century travelers from England often remarked approvingly on the uniformity of American speech across regions and classes. Lord Adam Gordon, a Scottish nobleman visiting the colonies in 1764, was pleased by "the propriety of Language" displayed by Philadelphians. He was also impressed with Bostonians, whose language and manner, he thought, "very much resemble the old Country." William Eddis, a visitor to Maryland until the Revolution sent him home to England, wrote to a friend, "In England, almost every county is distinguished by a peculiar dialect; . . . but in Maryland, and throughout adjacent provinces . . . a striking similarity of speech universally prevails." He thought the speech of nearly everyone he met showed "accuracy and elegance."[24]

Another Englishman, Nicholas Cresswell, spent three years in the colonies before he too was driven out by the war. Cresswell explored most of British America, including the backcountry, and concluded that Americans "in general speak better English than the English do. No County or Colonial dialect is to be distinguished here." The exception, according to Cresswell, was New England speech, which had "a sort of whining cadence that I cannot describe."[25] He was referring to the so-called Norfolk whine (mentioned in chapter 1). Others also noticed this legacy of the Massachusetts Bay settlers. More than one observer of the time mentioned the twang peculiar to New Englanders.

Americans themselves were more likely to spot the linguistic differences from place to place—usually with disapproval. Anne Royall's view of Philadelphia speech contrasts sharply with that of Lord Gordon. She writes, "The dialect of the citizens, particularly of the children, . . . is very defective." She prefers the dialect of her home territory of Washington, DC, praising it as "the most correct and pure of any part of the United States."[26] People then as now tended to think of their own speech as the most correct and accentless.

Another American who collected regional variations was Noah Webster. Writing shortly after independence, he cataloged dozens of pronunciations that he considered problematic. Some had been around for a long time, such as the archaic *marcy* for *mercy*, *keeow* for *cow*, and *motive* to rhyme with *drive*, still in vogue among the yeomanry of New England.

Southerners "almost omit the sound of *r*" in words like *ware* and *there*, Webster says. Many residents of the middle states, even "some well bred people," flatten out the vowel in *off* and *soft* so it sounds more like *aff* or *saft*. "The words *either*, *neither*, *deceit*, *conceit*, *receipt*, are generally pronounced, by the eastern people, *ither*, *nither*, *desate*, *consate*, *resate*. These are errors," he states flatly. Although Webster championed American speech, he condemned "local peculiarities," believing that uniform pronunciation and word use would encourage political unity throughout the country.[27]

How could so many problematic pronunciations be apparent to Royall and Webster but not to English visitors? The English travelers quoted above were writing about a slightly earlier time, but regional speech differences had existed since the seventeenth century. The language wouldn't have changed that much between the 1770s and the early 1800s. One possible explanation is that aristocratic visitors from England spent most of their time with "well-bred people," so they may not have heard the full range of distinctive accents.

Another reason why American English might have sounded so uniform to British visitors is that they were comparing it with the language of England. By the eighteenth century, English dialects had had a much longer time than American ones to divide into ever smaller bubbles of local speech. As William Eddis remarked, almost every county could be said to have its own dialect. That was true for upper-class as well as lower-class residents. The standard form of speech known as Received Pronunciation, which would later make educated people sound very similar all over England, was just starting to spread out of London.

Another mitigating factor is that Americans moved away from their birthplaces more often than the English did, so they were exposed—and exposed other people—to different kinds of accents, which may have had a flattening-out effect. They were also more literate. Most men and many women could read, which meant that they were more inclined to pronounce words the way they were spelled.

The British were more struck by American word choices than pronunciations. Nicholas Cresswell notes the use of *a-hunting*, the verb *jerk* to mean curing meat, and, after a clash with three American patriots, a new meaning for *torified.* Normally the word means to be converted to the conservative political views of the Tory Party. In this instance, it meant to punish someone for being pro-English. "Taylor threatened to tar and feather me," records Cresswell. "Find I shall be torified if I hold any further confab with these red-hot liberty men."[28]

Other commenters noticed the use of words that were defunct in England, such as *fall*; unfamiliar terms like *slops* for the leavings fed to pigs; and word expansions, such as the wholesale use of *fix*. According to the popular British author Frederick Marryat, traveling in postwar America, "The verb 'to fix' is universal. It means to do anything." Bartlett's definition seems to agree with that assessment. He says it means "to put in order; to prepare; to adjust; to set or place in the manner desired or most suitable." Marryat was on the alert for outlandish word creations during his travels. He reports on several, including a discussion of investments with a man who claimed he could "not only have *doubled* and *trebled*, but . . . *fourbled* and *fivebled* my money."[29]

Sometimes, as in Cresswell's case, novel usages were noted without judgment, but more often they were attacked as barbarities or corruptions. Marryat deplored the many provincialisms he heard. "It is remarkable how very debased the language has become in a short period," he mourns. The large tolerance of, even admiration for, American pronunciation didn't extend to the American penchant for casual word invention.

After the war, new words accumulated even faster, much to the disgust of the English, who were now smarting from their military defeat and loss of territory. Hostility toward American language innovations grew, and howls of outrage like the one heard over Jefferson's use of *belittle* became more common. At the same time, some Americans wanted to distance themselves even more from their former compatriots by establishing a national form of American English.

3

An American Tongue

When New York City held a Grand Procession on July 23, 1788, to celebrate the adoption of the Constitution by ten states, the Philological Society of New York proudly joined in. The young men of the society—formed a few months earlier for the purpose of "ascertaining and improving the American Tongue"—were strongly pro-Constitution, but supporting the federal government was only part of their aim. They were also there to boost their plan for a national brand of English. (*Philology* comes from the Greek for love of words.) Aside from occasional half-joking suggestions that the United States adopt Hebrew, Greek, French, or some other language as the national speech, Americans accepted that they would have to continue using English, the language of the enemy. Nonetheless, many linguistic patriots wanted to make it as distinct from the British variety as possible—and not only different but also better.[1]

After the war, Americans were eager to emphasize their separateness from the old country. The main point of the Grand Procession was to spur New York's warring constitutional convention to vote for ratification, which it did on July 26. However, the parade was also a showcase for American abilities and self-reliance. The whole city participated. One eyewitness estimated that the procession included at least five thousand marchers and extended farther than a mile and a half. Thousands more thronged the streets or hung out of windows and doors to cheer the marchers on.

First came the workers' guilds. Tailors, bricklayers, shipbuilders, and many other craftsmen marched together, carrying the implements of their trade and flying a pro-Constitution banner or other device.

Scholars and professionals marched too. The president of Columbia College strode along in his cap and gown, accompanied by professors and students. Judges and lawyers marched in their robes. Clergymen, physicians, and independent scholars walked together, carrying a blue flag with the motto UNITED WE STAND, DIVIDED WE FALL.

The Philological Society brought up the rear of the procession, dressed all in black to show their intellectual seriousness. Members carried implements that advertised their commitment to American English. The standard bearer flew a flag crowded with linguistic symbols, including three tongues representing language, a key signifying "language, the key of knowledge," and Gothic letters alluding to the Germanic origin of English. The group's secretary carried a scroll listing "the principles of a Federal language."[2]

"Parade in Honor of the Adoption of the Federal Constitution, 1788." This drawing by David McNeely Stauffer shows a parade float carrying the "Federal ship *Hamilton*." The figures atop the fort are the president and members of Congress. When the float pulled even with the fort, it stopped and fired a thirteen-gun salute. *Courtesy of the Miriam and Ira D. Wallach Collection of Arts, Prints, and Photographs, New York Public Library*

The scroll is now lost, so no one knows exactly what those principles were, but we can get some idea from Noah Webster's writings of the time. Webster was the moving force behind the Philological Society. He founded the organization shortly after coming to New York in November 1787 to edit the *American Magazine.* When the magazine collapsed in 1789 and he returned to his native Hartford, the society disbanded without achieving its goal.

Webster himself remained committed to Federal English. Although his first dictionary was still years in the future, he was already the author of a three-volume set of language textbooks and well known as a writer and lecturer on language. In his 1789 *Dissertations on the English Language*, he advocates for an American language, writing, "As an independent nation, our honor requires us to have a system of our own in language as well as government. Great Britain . . . should no longer be our standard."[3]

Webster's guiding principle was uniformity. As an ardent Federalist, he believed in a strong Union and thought that local dialects create "a dissocial spirit between the inhabitants of the different states," leading to political discord. Differences in pronunciation or word use, he claimed, "excite ridicule" and cause people in different parts of the country to feel mutual contempt. To make the language and the country stronger, Americans needed to smooth out the regional wrinkles in their speech.

Where should they look for guidance in deciding which usage was correct? The British relied on their upper classes to determine acceptable speech, but Americans didn't have an aristocracy. Besides, Webster noted, fashions change. Basing the linguistic standard on the whims of a single class of people would be like "fixing a light house on a floating island." He thought the answer to this conundrum was to base standard American speech on "the rules of the language itself, and the general practice of the nation."

Most of the time, Webster explained, Americans everywhere use the same words the same way and pronounce them similarly. When they don't, "principles of analogy"—the form of a word that conforms most closely to the general pattern—should be the deciding factor. Webster disapproved of pronouncing words like *motive* with a long *i* because it was contrary to what the majority of speakers did. Most people outside of New England pronounced *motive* with a long *o* and a short *i*, so that should be the practice all over the country.

Webster recognized that language inevitably changes, but he thought that permanent standards for deciding acceptability could be established. Furthermore, he believed that Americans had an unprecedented chance to "ascertain and improve" English until it outshone the British original. "We have . . . the fairest opportunity of establishing a national language, and of giving it uniformity and perspicuity, in North America, that ever presented itself to mankind," he writes in *Dissertations*. "Now is the time to begin the plan."

The idea that English (and other languages) could be strengthened and perfected was current on both sides of the Atlantic, part of the larger eighteenth-century belief that societies can make progress toward ever-higher stages of development. Many Americans were convinced that only in the United States did such a project have a hope of reaching fruition. At the heart of Americans' linguistic boosterism was the belief that England was on the wane, while America was set to achieve great things.

Webster believed "the general practice of the nation" should guide language use, but most people who thought about the issue were in favor of appointing an authority. As early as 1774, a writer who styled himself "An American" sent a letter on the subject to the *Royal American Magazine*. Addressed to "The Literati of America," the letter suggests organizing an academy dedicated to analyzing American English. Members would convene annually to suggest how to "correct, enrich and refine it, until perfection stops their progress." In the letter writer's patriotic view, "The English language has been greatly improved in Britain within a century, but its highest perfection, with every other branch of human knowledge, is perhaps reserved for this Land of light and freedom."[4]

Academies for exploring certain branches of knowledge, such as the natural sciences, were a popular concept in Europe. Proponents of an American language academy envisioned an organization similar to the French Academy, which acted as an arbiter for the French language (and still does—the academy routinely bans Americanisms like *le week-end*, typically with little effect). An American academy never became a reality, but proposals for it continued to circulate until the 1830s.

Founding father John Adams was one of the leading supporters of such an authority. In a letter to the president of the Congress, he urged Congress to form a "public institution" for "correcting, improving, and ascertaining the English language." Adams was more inclined to use British English as a basic model but agreed with Webster that the United States would be more unified if Americans could establish their own linguistic standards. Besides making pronouncements on language use, he hoped officers of the academy would collect a library of language books that citizens could consult to resolve usage quandaries.

Describing his idea a few weeks later in a letter to a friend, Adams imagines the English taking advantage of this piece of American ingenuity. "After Congress shall have done it," he writes, "perhaps the British king and parliament may have the honor of copying the example." He adds jokingly, "England will never more have any honor, excepting now and then that of imitating the Americans." It wasn't entirely a joke though. Both Webster and Adams predicted that the country's growing population would one day make American English one of the world's most significant languages.[5]

Naturally the English didn't see things from the same perspective as their former colonies. Bitterness over Americans' evident belief that they were the cultural equals of the British reached a height during and after the War of 1812. Often called the Second War of Independence, it was militarily a draw but decisively ended British political control over the United States. Britain's cultural influence was also lessening as Americans started writing and publishing their own books, including schoolbooks. The English expressed their resentment of what they saw as American arrogance by sneering at nearly all the American writing that made it overseas.

Literary critics scoffed at the idea that the United States had enough intellectual heft to create an independent literature. "Nothing can obstruct American improvement more than the absurd persuasion . . . that she has acquired an extent of knowledge that renders her as independent in her literature as she is in her government," remarks one reviewer. Opines another, "The Americans are too young to rival in literature, the old nations of Europe." An article on education in the United States claims, "In all that relates to classic learning, they are totally deficient."[6]

British critiques of American English often exaggerated the linguistic distance between the old and new countries, always with the assumption that British English was unquestionably the superior version. An article in the *New Monthly Magazine* of December 1820 titled "On Americanisms" argues, "The Americans have been gradually making a decided progress towards the formation of a separate language." The author predicts that the British will eventually require a translation to read American writings, and concludes, "It is not necessary to say who would be the losers in such an event."[7]

The Scottish writer Thomas Hamilton, who visited the United States in 1831, also thought the speech of the two countries would soon become mutually unintelligible. He complains in his book *Men and Manners in America* that "the language of Shakespeare and Milton" is being gratuitously degraded. He says, "The privilege of barbarizing the king's English is assumed by all ranks and conditions of men." Unless Americans developed better taste and judgment, they would be speaking a different tongue from Englishmen within a century, or in his words, "a jargon as novel and peculiar as the most patriotic

American linguist can desire."[8] He sees this result as a clear disaster for Americans.

Washington Irving's *Sketch Book* was one of the few early books by an American that was positively received. Many British literary critics considered Irving the exception that proved the rule. He probably helped his own cause by living and writing in England. Irving's family had business interests in London that had been seriously neglected during the War of 1812. He traveled to England in 1815 to see what he could salvage and ended up staying for the next seventeen years.

The Sketch Book, a collection of essays and short stories that includes "Rip Van Winkle" and "The Legend of Sleepy Hollow," was published in installments, beginning in 1819. It appeared simultaneously in England and the United States and was a hit in both places. Even so, some British reviewers took a patronizing tone. A writer for the *Quarterly Review* praised the book but couldn't resist wrapping up his discussion with a few sententious remarks: "We wish well, and have always wished well to America. We sincerely hope she may become wiser as she grows older; but, as a first step toward improvement . . . she should learn to divest herself of that over-weening self-conceit, which has filled her with such exaggerated ideas of her own importance." A prime example of American conceit, according to the reviewer, was Americans' insistence on the validity of their own speech.

One of the reasons the reviewer likes Irving is that he doesn't use too many Americanisms. The reviewer reports that he looked up a few suspect phrases in the dictionary and found that they could be "defended by authority," although the stories do contain "outlandish" words like *deviltry* (an American variation on *devilry*) and *umbratile* (a rare word describing a recluse). He ends with the usual warning that "without continued care," the writings of England's great men will soon be unintelligible to American readers.[9]

Americans' free and easy way with vocabulary was almost always the main source of outrage for the British. (Remember the flap over *belittle*.) To be fair, some of the words that reached their shores were unquestionably strange. American poet Joel Barlow's patriotic epic *The Columbiad* almost seems designed to enrage linguistically sensitive English readers. The poem tells the story of Hesper, the "guardian Genius" of North America, who visits the elderly Christopher Columbus in a Spanish prison. Hesper shows Columbus a vision of America's future glories, beginning with Jamestown and reaching a peak with the founding of the United States.

The Columbiad, which is more than eighty-three hundred lines long, introduced dozens of new coinages and rare words. A few, such as *millennial*, later entered the mainstream vocabulary. Many more—for instance, *multifluvian*, *ludibrious*, *reseek*, *homocidious*, and *transbord*—were arcane, obsolete, or invented for the poem.

A scathing essay in the *Edinburgh Review* comments, "We have often heard it reported, that our transatlantic brethren were beginning to take it amiss that their language should still be called English; and truly we must say, that Mr. Barlow has gone far to take away that ground of reproach." Many of the words, says the reviewer, are as "utterly foreign as if they had been adopted from the Hebrew or Chinese."[10]

Barlow provided a rich target for reviewers, but most of the usages that offended British ears seem to have been singled out arbitrarily. Just as pet peeve lists today often include the same handful of supposedly misused words (*decimate*, for example), certain stock Americanisms were repeatedly held up for scorn. Their problematic status was taken for granted, just as that of *decimate* is now, without the peevers feeling the need to look into the words' origins or take into account the processes of language change. Sometimes the so-called Americanisms were originally British English or were used in both countries. Other terms were genuine Americanisms but had been created following normal rules of English word formation.

Thomas Hamilton points out several usages that were common sources of annoyance for language sticklers, such as the use of *expect*, *reckon*, *guess*, and *calculate* to mean *think*. To English critics, these usages illustrated the American tendency to degrade the meanings of established words, even though *expect* and *reckon* could also mean *think* in England, and *I guess* had come over with the first settlers. They also deplored the American way of turning nouns into verbs. In fact, the practice had been going on for several centuries—English features hundreds of noun/verb pairs, some going back to Early Modern English.

The English also disapproved of Americans' wholesale use of one word to mean myriad things. *Fix* to "do anything" is one example. Another that Hamilton gives is *clever*. In England, he says, it means smart, but in the United States it means "pleasant or amiable. Thus a good-natured blockhead . . . is a clever man."[11] To his astonishment, he also hears of a clever house, a clever sum of money, and a clever ship with a clever cargo. Like *expect*, *reckon*, and *progress*, this word might have been less of an Americanism than Hamilton supposed. One American writer of the time claims, "A native of England may be distinguished as readily by the frequent use of the adjective *clever* as the native of New-England by that of the verb *guess*."[12]

The provenance of the words and expressions that Americans used really didn't matter as much as the critics' perception that they deviated from the current literary norm. The English had as much of a problem with outdated British words as they did with American creations. They saw the use of old expressions like *I guess* or provincialisms like *reckon* as proof of Americans' cultural primitiveness. New words and definitions caused a different problem. They cluttered the language with unnecessary terminology that competed with established British words. The only universally accepted Americanisms were words for items that didn't exist in England, like raccoons and powwows.

This paragraph from the May 1808 *Monthly Review* parodies several supposed Americanisms: "In America, authors are to be found who make use of new or obsolete words, which no good writer in this country would employ; and if it were not for my *destitution* of leisure, which obliges me to hasten to the *occlusion* of these pages, as I *progress*, I should *bottom* my assertion on instances from authors of the first grade; but were I to render my sketch *lengthy*, I should *illy* answer the purpose which I have in view."[13]

Most of the italicized "Americanisms" in this paragraph started life in England. *Destitution* meaning lacking in something and *bottom* meaning to support a position had both entered the language centuries earlier and could still be found in British writing. *Occlusion* came into English from Latin in the seventeenth century. *Illy* had been used to mean *badly* in both countries since the sixteenth century, although it was considered substandard (and has since disappeared). *Grade* to mean *degree* is probably an Americanism, but British writers were using it by the nineteenth century.

Lengthy to describe a speech or piece of writing that is long and tedious is also an Americanism. It's a good example of a coinage that was singled out for attack simply because it was new. An early instance comes from John Adams's diary entry for January 3, 1759: "I grow too minute and lengthy." Although the word was created in the traditional English way of forming an adjective by adding *-y* to a noun (*dusty, hairy, needy, rainy*), commentators treated it as a verbal abomination. Reviewing a report on American manufacturing, the *British Critic* huffs, "We shall at all times, with pleasure, receive from our transatlantic brethren real improvements of our common mother tongue: but we shall hardly be induced to admit such phrases as . . . *more lengthy*."

Another verbal critic, an Irishman teaching school in Charleston, deplored Thomas Jefferson's regular use of the word. He says, "Mr. Jefferson . . . uses words unintelligible to an *Englishman*. Where the devil did he get the word *lengthy*? *Breadthy* and *depthy* would be equally admissible." (That's true—they would be. Their absence from the vocabulary is what linguists call an "accidental gap.")

Even many American writers rejected the word. An essay in the 1801 edition of the *New-England Palladium* makes the argument—still popular when criticizing a recent word invention—that *lengthy* is illegitimate because "it can be found in no English dictionary." Five years later, it would appear in a dictionary, but not an English one. *Lengthy* would have to wait for Noah Webster's 1806 *Compendious Dictionary of the English Language* to gain official status as a "real" word.[14]

Lengthy did have its defenders. "Lemuel Lengthy" (thought to be the playwright and satirist J. K. Paulding) wrote a six-page letter to the editor of the *Analectic Magazine*, stoutly defending American "words of our own invention." He insists that Americans have the right to do as they wish with the language: "It is ours by right of conquest, for when we wrested these states from England, we subdued the language with them." Therefore, he claims, if "we should think it proper to make a new grammar, alter the pronunciation and spelling, and invent a dozen more letters . . . I don't see that anybody would have a right to complain."[15] Paulding was writing tongue in cheek, but he also genuinely appreciated American English. His writings include such sterling Americanisms as *horse sense*, *muddle-pated*, *by hookey*, and *teetotaciously*.

In spite of its illegitimacy, *lengthy* was too useful to pass up. Like *belittle*, it eventually infiltrated the British vocabulary. By the time Bartlett wrote his dictionary, he was able to report that, although the word had almost disappeared from written English for a time, it was making a comeback in both countries. He then lists a number of British publications where the word recently appeared, including the *British Critic*, the *Quarterly Review*, and others that frequently attack Americanisms. Bartlett also notes that the English have "made some improvements" on the word. He has seen both *lengthiness* and *lengthily* in books by British authors.

The word *Americanism* was coined by John Witherspoon, president of Princeton University from 1768 until his death in 1794. Witherspoon was not a native-born American. He was born near Edinburgh and lived in Scotland until moving to Princeton, New Jersey, at age forty-five. Being a speaker of another deprecated regional dialect might have heightened his awareness of the differences between American and British language use.

Witherspoon introduced *Americanism* in a series of articles about American words and expressions written in 1781 for the *Pennsylvania Journal.* He defines Americanisms as "phrases or terms, or a construction of sentences . . . different from the use of the same . . . in Great-Britain," explaining that he means the term to be parallel to *Scotticism* (an English word found only in Scotland).[16] The definition later expanded to encompass any word or phrase that originated in America, even if the British or others later adopted it.

Although Witherspoon defined the term neutrally, he clearly viewed Americanisms with concern. His opening commentary in the first essay displays the mixed feelings that were shared by many American writers and critics of the time. He starts from the premise that the English of England is the benchmark for proper speech. He predicts that Americans will one day develop their own standards for language use, but until then, deviations from British English must be considered "improprieties."

Witherspoon was one of the first to collect American words and phrases with the idea of telling people what not to say. He sorts the words under discussion into terms heard only in America, regional words, "vulgarisms" (unrefined speech) heard in both countries, slang, and simple blunders in language use. The lists are short and random. Under the heading of genuine Americanisms, he includes some standard examples—*clever*, *notify*, *mad* to mean *angry*, *spell* for a period of time. He also notes one or two instances of grammar that strike him as odd, such as omitting *to be* in a sentence like "These things were ordered delivered to the Army." Regional words include *tote* for *carry*, a Southernism, and *chunks* for half-burned pieces of wood, heard in the middle states. As a slang word, he offers *bilk.*

His vulgarities mostly consist of nonstandard verbs—*know'd*, *see'd*, *drownded.* He also decries the trend of reducing *not* to *n't*, as in *can't*, *won't, don't,* and the like. Although these usages are found in England as well as the United States, he lists them because he believes that "persons are at less pains to avoid them here than in Britain." One source of frustration for critics was that the general American population not only deviated from approved British speech standards but also was very comfortable doing so.

Witherspoon's essays inspired readers to send in their own lists of pet peeves. These include *slack-baked* to mean "deficient in understanding," *grand* for *excellent, tarnal* for *eternal, sarten* for *certain,* and substitutes for swear words, such as *darn.* Some of the items are standard today—*once in a while* to mean *sometimes, occasion* to mean *opportunity.* The lists are not so much organized attempts to collect American vocabulary as catalogs of the words and uses that the compilers would like to see stamped out. That would be true of most collections of Americanisms until Bartlett's.

Meanwhile, hundreds of words and phrases continued to teem into the language unabated and largely unnoticed. A random selection of words that appeared in the years after independence includes new verbs like *Americanize, electioneer, obligate, opine, swap, stump* meaning to campaign, and *kick* meaning to object. Words for new objects like *lightning rod, snowplow,* and *grain elevator* were also created. Ironmongery became hardware in the United States and shops became stores. Slang and colorful expressions were also part of the mix—*all-fired, work like a beaver, give someone a black eye* (in the shame or defeat sense). Nearly all were quickly absorbed into the language unchallenged, even by language purists, while selected words like *notify* kept reappearing on complaint lists.

Not all Americans were ready for linguistic independence. When Noah Webster published *A Compendious Dictionary of the English Language* in 1806, the hostility that greeted it shows how far many people still had to go in respecting their own homegrown speech. The general populace easily adopted novel verbs and colorful turns of phrase, but critics didn't, and their readers remained scandalized. Webster's dictionary, the first serious attempt at a complete record of American English, was ahead of its time.

The blowback started in 1800, when Webster first announced his intention of writing a dictionary. Skeptics scorned the idea that the language even needed such a thing. In 1755 the British writer Samuel Johnson (nicknamed "Dictionary Johnson") had published the first comprehensive dictionary of English words and definitions. Johnson spent eight years writing it, and it was widely considered the final statement on the English language. Purely American words that Johnson hadn't vetted were not thought to be worth preserving. One typical editorial calls Webster's project "folly" because English has "arrived at its zenith . . . and . . . requires no introduction of new words." The writer goes so far as to describe Webster's plan as a "projected volume of foul and unclean things." Another editor accuses Webster of venal motives: "The plain truth is that he means to make money."[17]

A sarcastic commentary on Webster's "dictionary plan" speculates that "as Mr. Webster's dictionary is intended to be a complete asylum for fugitive words," such "idiotisms" as *hern* and *yourn* and *fotch* and *cotch* will no doubt be included. "We will no longer use the word *carry*," the writer predicts, "but substitute the more expressive phrase *to tote*." *Right*, as in *right good*, will replace *very*. The reviewer touches on all the usual suspect words—*guess*, *lengthy*, *occlude*—before ending with the suggestion that Webster comb the writings of Thomas Jefferson if he needs more material.[18]

When the dictionary came out, critics found more reasons for censure. Some had to do with the contents of the dictionary, others with Webster's contentious style. The preface alone was enough to inflame the majority of reviewers. Webster devotes a large part of it to attacking the revered Samuel Johnson, criticizing his scholarship and pointing out numerous definitions and word histories that he thinks are inaccurate.

Reviewers jumped to Johnson's defense. One regrets that Webster "has commenced . . . with . . . indiscriminate and malignant abuse of Johnson's Dictionary." Another expresses grave concern that Webster is encouraging a departure from standards by undermining Johnson. The same reviewer picks apart several of Webster's own definitions that he considers equally weak and sums up by saying, "We hope his own ill success will teach him not to exult over the miscarriages of others."[19] (Lexicography was an infant science in the early nineteenth century. Both Johnson and Webster included definitions and word histories that haven't stood the test of time.)

Reviewers were also unhappy with another major feature of the dictionary: Webster's extensive spelling innovations. Along with Benjamin Franklin and a few others, Webster had long been eager to establish a more rational spelling system. He announces in the preface that he made a few "trifling changes" to the traditional spelling of words.

Several of his simplifications were already becoming common in the United States. These include omitting the *u* in words like *honour* and *colour*, switching *re* to *er* in words like *sceptre* and *theatre*, dropping the *k* from words like *publick* and *musick*, and changing *qu* to *k* in words like *musquet* and *pacquet*. Webster went a bit further than that with his "trifling changes" though. The dictionary included several drastic respellings—*aker* for *acre*, *tung* for *tongue*, *wimmen* for *women*. Webster also dropped the silent final letter from many words—*fugitiv*, *imagin*, *thum*—as well as "extra" letters from the middle of some words, such as *lether* and *det*.[20]

One commenter called the system "injudicious and impracticable," asking, "What advantage would a new orthography procure equivalent to the confusion and perplexity of such an alteration?"[21] Most Americans agreed. People who already know how to spell are deeply resistant to learning a new system, even one that's more logical. Webster's dictionaries did change American spelling, but only by popularizing the simplifications that were already making their way into the written language—*honor*, *scepter*, and the rest. His more radical changes never caught on.

Webster's most significant achievement—his addition of over five thousand words never before recorded in a dictionary—also aroused the most ire. Webster says in the preface that he believes it to be "by far the most complete" list of words extant. He considers a dictionary of American terms essential for those living in the United States, writing, "English, like every living language, is in a state of progression. . . . The descendants of the settlers . . . will continue to speak the English language, but with numerous variations." Americans will "originate new words, or give to old words new signification, which will never be generally received or known in Great Britain."[22]

Webster notes in the preface that many of the new terms come from chemistry, botany, and other sciences—*pyrometer*, *telegraph*, *vaccination*. He also added words that were either invented in the United States or used with different meanings. New terms include *dutiable* and *irredeemable*. Words with new meanings include the verbs *girdle* (choke off trees to kill them) and *gin* (process cotton). He has also included new government terms, such as *constitutionality*, and updated the definitions for business and legal terms like *speculation*, *default*, *bankrupt*, *authority*, and others.

Reviewers were appalled at this attempt to legitimize words that hadn't received official literary sanction. "The fault of most alarming enormity in this work is the approbation given to the vulgarisms of some of our illiterate writers, and the unauthorized idioms of conversation," exclaims one writer. The predictable list of outrages follows—*advocate*, *obligate*, *appreciate* to mean rise in value, *test* as a verb, the new adjectives *presidential* and *governmental* ("barbarisms"), and of course *lengthy*. ("We might as well make *strengthy* to mean strong.")[23]

Webster defended his choices in a letter to his brother-in-law Thomas Dawes. He downplayed the extent of his spelling innovations, arguing that he was only offering sensible suggestions. He also defended himself against charges that he was adulterating the language.

He admits that he has introduced a handful of local terms and one or two "cant" (slang) words but argues that such terms exist, "and will exist, in spite of lexicographers or critics. . . . Must they be left unexplained, because they are local? This very circumstance renders their insertion in a dictionary the more necessary." For good measure, he points out that the great Johnson himself recorded such oddities as *jiggumbob*.[24]

Although Americans would remain unconvinced about Webster's spelling reforms, he was on firmer ground with the vocabulary. Some of his additions (*customable*, *imprescriptible*) later disappeared, but most were accepted into the permanent lexicon. Bartlett later looked to Webster's dictionaries for definitions and examples of dozens of words, from *advocate* to *woodchuck*.

John Quincy Adams gave the dictionary his qualified approval, saying, "Where we have invented new words or adopted new senses to old words, it appears but reasonable that our dictionaries should contain them." A reviewer for the *Panoplist* also approved of recording words "peculiar to America." He was even willing to give the spelling a pass, relieved that the more extreme ideas of Benjamin Franklin hadn't been enacted. On the whole, he was pleased to see "a literary work which bears such strong marks of deep research . . . produced by one of our fellow-citizens."

The physician Samuel Latham Mitchill, then a senator from New York, went even further. He wrote to ask Webster why Native American words such as *papoose* and *terrapin* were excluded. He also suggested adding *journey cake*, *canvasback*, *yellow fever*, and several other terms to the next edition. Enthusiasts like Mitchill, however, remained in the minority for some time to come.[25]

The next glossary of Americanisms appeared in 1815 in an unexpected place. The list of 273 terms was appended to a play—a little-known work titled *The Yankey in England*, by David Humphreys. Humphreys was a native of Connecticut who enlisted in the Continental Army in 1774 and acted as an aide-de-camp to Washington. After the war, he followed a career as a diplomat, with postings to London, Portugal, and Spain. Humphreys wrote throughout his life. He was best known as a poet but also produced biographies and essays, as well as two plays.

Billed as "a drama in five acts," *The Yankey in England* features a complicated plot involving shipwrecks, mistaken identity, star-crossed lovers, and other twists. The main character, a man named Doolittle, is the first example of the so-called stage Yankee, the larger-than-life city folks' version of the New England rustic. When the play opens, Doolittle has just escaped death by shipwreck. His first speech jams together countrified pronunciations, dialect words, euphemisms, and homespun expressions: "Had that darned old vessel . . . been a stun's throw furder off from land, I shood never have swimmed to shore, dead or alive, to all atarnity, I swamp it; Oh Doolittle! Doolittle! You've brought your pigs to a fine market."[26]

Doolittle displays all the hallmarks of an American yokel. He uses *I guess* constantly, as well as *argufy*, *ain't I*, *mad* to mean *angry*, and other classic Americanisms. He threatens his enemies in extravagant language: "I'll be even with you if it rains pitchforks—tines downward." He boasts of his courage by saying, "We wan't brought up in the woods, to be scart by an owl in an ivy bush."[27]

Humphreys added the glossary to his play either to underline his point or because he genuinely believed that his readers might have problems following Doolittle's conversation. Many of the words are common words respelled to approximate a rural New England accent—*afeerd*, *hansum*, *keow*. Others are typical examples of Americanisms—*clever*, *lengthy*, *calculate*. The list also includes a number of words that were nonstandard but found in England as well as the United States—*hoss*, *pester*, *twistical*.

The play's performance history is obscure. Only one performance is on record—a January 1815 amateur presentation in the author's hometown of Humphreysville, Connecticut.[28] However, later writers of "Yankee" plays borrowed freely from the glossary. When writing the *Dictionary of Americanisms*, Bartlett took several examples of New Englandisms from the play—*Sabbaday* for *Sabbath Day*; *spark it*, meaning to court; *how fare you*, pronounced *how fa' ye*, according to Bartlett (Doolittle's answer to this query: "Cleverly."); and *farziner*, a pronunciation of *as far as I know* that is "extensively used through New England and New York."

Only a year later, Humphreys's glossary was overshadowed by the first dictionary devoted to "unauthorized" American words and phrases, John Pickering's *A Vocabulary, or Collection of Words and Phrases Which Have Been Supposed to Be Peculiar to the United States of America*. Pickering was born in Salem, Massachusetts, the son of Timothy Pickering, secretary of state from 1795 to 1800. The younger Pickering graduated from Harvard in 1796 and spent four years as a diplomat, first in London, then in Lisbon. Later he returned to Salem and became a lawyer.

While Pickering was in England, he started to note down Americanisms "*for which there is no authority*," as he wrote to his father in 1800.[29] At that point, he had collected only three obvious culprits: *lengthy*, *to progress*, and *to advocate*. After he returned home, he continued to collect words and phrases. Pickering was a talented linguist and language scholar who spoke or read several European languages and was familiar with Turkish, Arabic, Persian, and Chinese. It's not surprising that the workings of American English drew his attention.

Pickering eventually compiled over five hundred words. While Noah Webster was concerned with giving accurate definitions and word histories, Pickering's main purpose was to tell Americans which words and expressions they should avoid. His *Vocabulary*, which appeared in 1816, was prefaced with an obsequious essay calculated to warm the hearts of British critics. He begins by emphasizing the importance of preserving the purity of the English language. If Americans want to communicate effectively with British readers, he says, "they must write in a language that Englishmen can read with pleasure."[30]

It can't be denied that Americans have strayed from the true linguistic path. They have formed new words, added new meanings to old words, and stubbornly continued to use obsolete words after the English have dropped them. Pickering quotes a number of British critics on the subject and advises his American readers to take these criticisms in a humble spirit, as they are the "general opinion of the literary men of Great Britain." Americans have a right to propose new words, but they shouldn't use any that "English authors of reputation" reject. Correct English is what the British say it is.

Pickering takes a swipe at Webster, although he doesn't mention him by name. "We have thirsty reformers," he writes, "who would unsettle the whole of our admirable language for the purpose of making it conform to their whimsical notions of propriety." One of Pickering's friends, after reading an early draft of the book, gloats in a letter, "I cannot help indulging a malignant pleasure in considering that our American Philologist Webster will be stopped in the ridiculous career he has engaged in, of murdering the English language."[31]

At least three-quarters of the deprecated words in Pickering's dictionary are in general use today. The book includes not only words that are labeled vulgarisms, such as *gumption*, *swap*, and *clever*, but also words that are used differently in England, such as *creek* to mean a stream instead of an inlet. Pickering includes political words like *gubernatorial* and a number of New England regionalisms, including *awful*, *crow-bar*, *freshet*, *gawky*, *spry*, and *tidy*.

He lists verbs that are either newly created—many with an *-ize* or *-ate* ending—or archaic. These include frequently stigmatized words like *locate*, *infuriate*, *immigrate*, *jeopardize*, *organize* (in the political sense), and *systematize*. Of *to test*, he says, "a *verb* only in writers of inferior rank." He quotes the British critics on the wrongness of *to progress*. He admits that *I guess* is occasionally heard in England but dismisses it as a provincialism, not an expression that educated people would want to adopt.

Pickering often condemns an Americanism with the statement "not in English dictionaries." Webster's *Compendious Dictionary* doesn't count as an authoritative source. On the contrary, Pickering uses it to prove that words are unauthorized. He says of the new use of *to girdle*, for instance, that Webster includes it but "apprises his readers that it is peculiar to *America*." Of *lengthy*, he says, "Mr. *Webster* has admitted it to his dictionary; but (as need hardly be remarked) it is not in any of the *English* ones." Even being in an English dictionary doesn't always count. Noting that the critics have pronounced *obligate* a "low colloquial inaccuracy," Pickering says, "It is in the dictionaries, and is sometimes used by English writers; but it is not considered as an authorized word."

The critical reception of Pickering's *Vocabulary* was vastly different from that of the *Compendious Dictionary*. "With great pleasure we acknowledge the . . . labours of Mr. Pickering," gushes a writer in the *North American Review*. "We are fully aware that the publick stands in need of literary guardians."[32] (This reviewer's verbal conservatism is evident from his refusal to adopt the new spellings of *labor* and *public*.)

The only dissenting voice was, predictably, Noah Webster's. He wrote a forty-page "letter" to Pickering on the subject of his vocabulary, which was published in 1817. He opens uncompromisingly by saying that he has examined the vocabulary, and "I found in it many things which appeared to deserve animadversion, and thought it incumbent on me, whose Dictionary you have often cited, . . . to correct what I apprehend to be erroneous opinions on the subject."[33]

Webster takes issue with Pickering's assumptions about language change and the creation of new words. He argues that everyone has the right to form new words using standard affixes (like *-ize* and *-ate*), and if others find the resulting words useful, then those words should be given a place in the language. Making verbs out of nouns is an old and respected linguistic process. In Webster's view, there's no reason why Americans shouldn't create new words this way. Webster has also noticed Pickering's frequent comment that a word may be found in Webster but is not in English dictionaries. He explains that he wrote his dictionary for that very reason.

The same *North American Review* reviewer who praised Pickering's *Vocabulary* when it first appeared felt moved to respond to Webster's letter. Besides taking issue with Webster's tone, he disagrees with nearly all of Webster's points, especially his contention that anyone has the right to turn a noun into a verb or make other contributions to the language. Instead, he supports Pickering's view that the vocabulary of the best British authors should be enough words for anybody. Many of those who read his comments no doubt nodded in agreement.

While the critics and the reformers were arguing about how different American English could or should be, the language continued to grow and reshape itself regardless. A prime source of new speech was the country's continuously westward-moving frontier. As Americans settled farther afield from the original colonies, the language that flowed from west to east began to have a profound impact on the American vocabulary.

4

Words from the West

THE FIRST RUSH of new western words came from Meriwether Lewis and William Clark. When Lewis and Clark set off to trek across the continent in 1804, President Thomas Jefferson charged them with collecting detailed information about every aspect of the country they passed through—plants and animals, landscape features, climate, and societies. In their effort to describe these things accurately, they created nearly two thousand words and phrases. They invented compounds, used old words with new meanings, and borrowed words and phrases from the people they encountered during their trip.

Lewis and Clark didn't plan to invent new language, any more than John Smith had. It grew out of the task at hand. The main purpose of the Corps of Discovery, as the Lewis and Clark expedition was called, was to explore and map the vast Louisiana Territory, which Napoleon had just sold to the United States for the bargain-basement price of $15 million. This vast swath of land was largely unknown to Americans. Now that the United States held title to it, President Jefferson wanted a clearer picture of what was out there.

Organized as an army unit, the corps had twenty-nine permanent members. The leaders were Lewis and Clark, both former army officers who hailed from Virginia. Lewis was Jefferson's secretary when he received the assignment. Other members included fourteen soldiers from the regular army, two French boatmen, a hunter who also acted as an interpreter, Clark's slave York, and nine civilians recruited by Clark, known as "the nine young men from Kentucky."

Later a French fur trader named Toussaint Charbonneau joined the expedition, along with a Shoshone woman named Sacagawea, whom

Charbonneau had purchased from her Hidatsa captors. Sacagawea's translating skills would be valuable when they reached her home territory. Interpreters were crucial for the expedition. The corps would cross paths with several Native American tribes—Lakota, Arikara, Mandan, Blackfeet, Shoshone, Nez Percé, Chinook, and other smaller groups—all speaking different languages.[1]

The corps began their travels in May 1804 after several months of training and preparation. They left from St. Charles, Missouri, journeying up the Missouri River in a fifty-five-foot keelboat and two pirogues laden with supplies. On May 25 they passed the last European settlement, "a small French village of seven houses and as many families," according to Clark.[2] Villagers sent eggs and milk out to the boats, the last the corps would enjoy for a while. From there, they would follow the Missouri into the northwestern interior. Their ultimate goal was the Pacific coast. The grueling trip out and back took more than two years.

Jefferson had several aims for the expedition. The dream of the Northwest Passage—the coast-to-coast water route that had eluded explorers since John Smith's day—was still alive, and Jefferson hoped the expedition would discover a river linking the Missouri with the Pacific. The president also wanted to open trade negotiations with the various tribes in the region. Lewis and Clark were charged with making friendly overtures toward any Indians they met, while noting as many details as possible about their lives. The long list of things that Jefferson wanted to know ran from concrete facts such as population numbers and types of possessions to more abstract knowledge, including morals and religious beliefs.

The leaders' communication skills would be taxed to the limit, but the linguistic challenges didn't end there. Jefferson also wanted copious information about the natural world. Besides mapping the route "with great pains and accuracy," Lewis and Clark were to take note of its significant landscape features. Things they were supposed to pay attention to included "the soil and face of the country"; any unusual plants; animals, "especially those not known in the U.S."; minerals, especially limestone and pit coal; and climate, including high and low temperatures, numbers of cloudy and clear days, first and last frost dates, and prevailing winds. On the way home, they were charged with "making such observations . . . as may serve to supply, correct or confirm those made on your outward journey."[3]

The Corps of Discovery's cross-continental journey finally demonstrated beyond a doubt that there was no water passage between the Atlantic and the Pacific. However, Lewis and Clark amply fulfilled Jefferson's other requirements. The journals they brought back were packed with careful descriptions. In spite of the sheer physical exhaustion entailed in crossing the northern plains, portaging around waterfalls, struggling through the mountains, and canoeing down western rivers, both men wrote in their journals nearly every day, meticulously recording every notable feature of the passing scene. When necessary, they created the language needed to do it justice. Many of the terms they repurposed or invented have since entered the permanent American vocabulary.

An easy way to create new terms was to combine a familiar noun with a new adjective, according to what the thing in question looked like or how it behaved or was used. They made up hundreds of terms of this type. A good example of the process comes from their naming of unfamiliar deer.

Crossing the plains of what is now South Dakota on September 17, 1804, Clark records in his journal that one of the men had killed "a curious kind of deer (*Mule Deer*)." His description makes it clear why the deer has been given that name—"the ears large & long." The tail featured "a tuft of black hair" at the tip, so Clark sometimes referred to the animal as "black-tailed deer," the French term for it. However, he gradually concluded that the black tail hair was "by no means characteristic of the Animal." He decided that the long ears of the creature made the name *mule deer* much more appropriate.

Lewis also talks about black-tailed deer in his journal, but he means a different animal. Writing on February 19, 1806, while at Fort Clatsop, Oregon, he describes a Pacific Northwest variety of deer that he doesn't recognize. "The Black-tailed fallow deer are peculiar to this coast," he writes. Like mule deer, the ears are "rather larger than the common deer." The tail is white, but the hair of the sides and top "quite black." In his opinion, the animal is similar to but not exactly the same as the mule deer. He concludes—correctly, as it turned out—that the black-tailed deer of Oregon was a different subspecies.

It's a tribute to Lewis's powers of observation that zoologists later agreed with his assessment. They gave the mule deer the scientific name *Odocoileus hemionus* and named the black-tailed deer *Odocoileus hemionus columbianus.* Their common names are still *mule deer* and *black-tailed deer*, the labels settled on by Lewis and Clark.

Often the two men named plants or animals for salient features. A sample of the word combinations that make their earliest written appearance in the journals includes *bighorn sheep* (a translation of the French name), *tumblebug* (a kind of dung beetle), *black woodpecker*, *tiger cat* (a lynx), *red-tailed hawk*, *red elm*, and *snowberry*.[4] Sometimes they named animals for their behavior, as with the *burrowing squirrel* (a ground squirrel) and the *whistling swan* (a small swan that Lewis discovered along the coast and named for its "peculiar whistling note.") They identified plants and animals according to their habitat—*prairie lark*, *Osage apple*, *mountain trout*, *sandhill crane*—or their uses—*buffalo grass* (where buffalo grazed) and *gig pole* (for spearing fish).

They occasionally had some difficulty deciding the best name for a plant or animal. Lewis named a "little animal found in the plains of the Missouri" a *barking squirrel* because of its warning cry. However, Clark called the creature by its now-common name of *prairie dog*. Both men described the same features, but its squirrel-like qualities were more important to Lewis, while its doglike bark was the most distinctive feature for Clark. The name may have been inspired by the French. Clark notes in his diary for September 7, 1804, that the French call the animal "Petite Chien" (little dog).

Naming the grizzly bear took several tries. The men of the corps referred to the unfamiliar animal variously as a white bear, a white-ish bear, or a yellow bear. A member of the corps named Ordway, who kept his own journal, noted that "Capt. Lewis . . . had killed a Whiteish bair . . . but is not white but light collour." In a later entry, he says that "the natives and the french traders" call the animal white but it is really light brown.[5]

After the party shot several of these bears and got a chance to examine the skins up close, they noticed that the tips of the fur were often silver. They started to call the bears *grizzly*, which can mean gray-haired. On June 13, 1805, Lewis wrote, "I am induced to believe that the Brown, the white, and the Grizly bear of this country are the same species only differing in colour from age." In a diary entry for May 31, 1806, he describes consulting with a band of Idaho Nez Percé, who confirmed that grizzlies came in a range of colors. Later he humorously suggested that it might be best to call the animal "the variegated bear."

The explorers preferred using English words when naming their finds, even if it meant extending common terms to a new species or subspecies (*blue jay*, *dogwood*, and *tree frog*, just to name a few). However, they occasionally borrowed terms from the French traders and boatmen. Aside from *bighorn*, few of the names stuck. (For instance, Lewis and Clark sometimes referred to the antelope by its French name of *cabrie*, but that word never became part of the vocabulary.) One translation that did make the cut was *Yellowstone*.

They also borrowed words from the native languages they heard, although they found them difficult to fit into English, and most were never adopted by anyone else. The Nez Percé *camas* (a plant with an edible bulb), Ojibwe *kinnikinnick* (a Native American tobacco substitute), and Cree *pemmican* (a cake of dried meat and fat) are three that succeeded. They also attached *Indian* to various items, as earlier

English speakers had done. They note a small bird (a bittern) that they call *Indian hen* and a type of lobelia that was smoked, which they call *Indian tobacco*.

They were among the first to use the terms *council house*, *sweathouse*, and *sweat lodge*. They also introduced a number of terms that incorporate *medicine*, probably a translation of an Ojibwe word—*medicine bag*, *medicine dance*, *medicine man*, and *medicine song*. They interpreted *medicine* to mean, in Lewis's words, "whatever is mysterious or unintelligible." They also wrote about the *Great Spirit*, again probably from Ojibwe, although they were not the first to use the term. In the May 2, 1805, journal entry that explains *medicine*, Lewis connected "big medicine" with "the presnts [presence] of the great Sperit."

"Captains Lewis and Clark holding a council with the Indians." This etching appeared in the published journals of Patrick Gass, a member of the Corps of Discovery. The event took place in present-day Nebraska. According to Gass, the Indians were Oto and Missouri, so they would have spoken Chiwere, a Siouan language. *Prints and Photographs Division: Library of Congress, LC-USZ62-17372*

The journals of Lewis and Clark are linguistically fascinating not only for their new word inventions but also for the picture they present of early nineteenth-century American speech. The men used many words that had evolved in meaning in America, such as *baggage* for *luggage* (a nearly obsolete meaning in England) and *biscuit* to refer to a small cake rather than the English cracker-like bread. They used *bug* for all kinds of insects, not just bedbugs as in England, *sick* for *ill*, and *mad* for *angry*.

Words for aspects of the terrain like *knob*, *fork*, *rapids*, *bottom*, and *prairie* were all used with their American meanings. They called bison by their American designation of *buffalo* and created several terms from the word—*buffalo berry* (found on the upper Missouri), *buffalo clover* (found on the prairie), *buffalo road* (a trail formed by the migrating herd), and *buffalo beef* (bison meat).

Some of the American meaning changes they adopted were fairly recent. Predictably, most were terms that came in handy for describing their daily activities. They said *hunting shirt* to refer to a shirt made of deerskin and *overall* for a sturdy pair of trousers worn while traveling, both current only since the late eighteenth century. *Keelboat* had only recently begun to refer to the large, flat-bottomed boats seen on American rivers. Other recent combinations in the journals include *buckshot*, *saddlebag*, and *backtrack*.

Clark was one of the first people to use *raft* to mean a mass of floating material ("a raft of Drift"), and also to use the word as a verb ("They were obliged to raft or Swim many Creeks"). Lewis and Clark use the Americanism *jerk* both as a noun referring to dried strips of meat and as a verb referring to the drying process. On June 5, 1804, Clark writes, "After Jurking the meat killed yesterday . . . we set out at 6 oClock."

The journals are full of new verbs and verb combinations. Both men had adopted *blaze* for marking a trail—"Blaze-notch a tree" from Clark and "blaize the trees with a tomahawk" from Lewis. They also used *hobble* to mean tying together the legs of a horse so it couldn't stray, *head* for what streams do when they rise from their source, *cache* for *hide*, *clear out* for *leave*, *quarter* to mean walk or climb up slantways, and *make along* or *make down* to mean extend in a certain direction ("the gullies which make down from the hills"). They wrote of chinking a wall, running a river, and raising a house. They also used the new American word *tote* for *carry*.

Both men had the American habit of using *fix* with a variety of meanings—adjust, put in order, arrange. The expedition carried *fixed ammunition*, that is, a charge of powder and shot wrapped together. Writing to his brother-in-law before the start of the expedition, Clark says he is waiting for Lewis, "who has been at St. Louis to fix off the Osage chiefs," meaning to come to an agreement with them.[6]

Both Lewis and Clark also made frequent use of another recently Americanized meaning that came in for criticism—*balance* to mean the remainder of anything, not just a sum of money due or left over. The ever-vigilant British reviewers began to notice the problem in the early nineteenth century. Complaining that Americans had perverted the word, a writer for the *New Monthly Magazine* writes, "They say, 'I spent a part of the evening at a friend's house and the balance at home,'" or even more deplorably, "'Half the enemy were killed and the *balance* taken prisoner.'" He cries, "What a specimen is this last sentence of the attachment of Americans to commerce!"[7]

Lewis mentions the balance of the day several times. On May 16, 1805, he writes about damaged supplies, mostly medicine, but "the ballance . . . some gardin seed, a small quantity of gunpowder, and a few culinary articles." In the same journal entry, he also describes the remains of a half-eaten deer that had been killed by a panther as "the ballance" of the animal. On July 26, 1804, Clark writes about a piece of bottomland with "one-half the distance wood & the bals. [balance] plain high & Dry."

Both Pickering and Bartlett call this usage a Southernism, so Virginians Lewis and Clark might have been aware of the new meaning early in its evolution. Pickering describes it as "a mercantile word . . .

signifying *the remainder of any thing.*" He notes that it is frequently used in congressional debates, but only by Southern members. By 1848, when Bartlett was writing, he could say that, although originally Southern, the word was now common throughout the United States.

The journals include various nonstandard words and usages. Ordway wrote *attacted* for *attacked*, a verb form first noticed by John Witherspoon in his articles about Americanisms. Clark used *learn* to mean *teach*, and Lewis wrote *drowneded* for *drowned*. They also use typical Americanisms such as *clever* for a good-natured person, *considerable of* to mean *many*, *tolerable* for *very*, and *illy* for *badly*.

Clark had more of a tendency than Lewis to use casual expressions like "He did not hurt me any" and to make up words like *increditable* (not credible). He also spelled many words phonetically, preserving the pronunciations of that time. Some examples are *deturmined*, *obstickle*, *extrodanary*, *sperit* (*spirit*), *squar* (*squaw*), and *bisquit* (*biscuit*). Clark usually wrote the name of the French trader as *Charbono* and the interpreter as *Sarcargahwea*.

The Lewis and Clark expedition revealed the continent to Americans. They discovered that it was much wider than they believed but crossable, even though an easy water route didn't exist. The expedition provided an accurate mapping of the rivers, plains, and mountains on the way. The corps introduced Americans to many unfamiliar plant and animal species. They also made connections with Native American tribes with very different languages and cultures from those in the East.

Lewis and Clark's word inventions didn't filter into the language for a while. One of the party, Sergeant Patrick Gass, published his journal in 1807, but it wasn't until 1814 that a version of the leaders' journals appeared. When they did, much of the scientific material had been edited out, which meant many of the words for plants and animals were missing. Lewis and Clark's impact on the American vocabulary was thus not as noticeable as it might have been.

More than thirty years later, as Bartlett was beginning to collect words for his dictionary, the territory that Lewis and Clark explored was still mostly empty of American settlers, although the first move across the Appalachian Mountains came in 1775. That year Daniel Boone, a hunter and trapper born in western Pennsylvania, led a party of about thirty men through the Cumberland Gap into the Kentucky Territory. They blazed what became known as the Wilderness Road. By 1800, more than two hundred thousand settlers had followed these pathfinders over the trail.[8]

Western colonization accelerated after the Revolutionary War, when England ceded all the territory running west to the Mississippi River. Between 1790 and 1840, around 4.5 million settlers swarmed into the western regions.[9] Typically, people went directly west—southerners into what is now Tennessee, Kentucky, Mississippi, and Alabama, and those from farther north into Indiana, Illinois, and Ohio. Many of the migrants were late-arriving Scotch Irish immigrants, looking for uncultivated land where they could stake a claim, either legally or not.

As Americans constantly pushed westward, what "the frontier" referred to changed. For the first half of the nineteenth century, few people went much beyond the Mississippi, where land was still plentiful. The frontier in those days lay just on the other side of the Appalachians. Migration across the plains didn't begin in earnest until 1843, when around one thousand settlers followed the Oregon Trail from Independence, Missouri, to what is now the Willamette Valley of Oregon. As more Americans began populating the continent's interior, the frontier kept shifting farther west. The connotations of *frontier* also evolved.

The word is as old as modern English (originally from a French word meaning forehead), but until the English started arriving in North America, its most common meaning was the part of a country that faced another country. The phrase *cross the frontier* still means to travel across the border between one country and the next.

When English colonists arrived in America, they needed a word to describe a kind of territorial boundary that didn't exist in England—the dividing line between their settlements and what they saw as untamed wilderness. In other words, the frontier was the border between where they lived and where Native Americans lived. George Washington used the word that way in 1756 when writing to the commander of Fort Dinwiddie during the Seven Years' War: "The intent of sending men hither was to protect the frontier inhabitants."[10] Washington refers to the frontier numerous times in his letters and reports during the war, and he usually means the area where settlers and natives clash. Its specific location could vary.

Early compounds from the word include *frontiersman*, first used in the early nineteenth century, and *frontierswoman*, which appeared around the middle of the nineteenth century. Other early combinations were *frontier post*, *frontier customs*, *frontier inhabitants*, and *frontier law*. *Frontier* gradually took on other meanings. Later in the century, when most Native Americans had been confined on reservations, the frontier became less about skirmishes and more about development. A new definition of the word was based on the presence or absence of a substantial settler population.

In 1874 census officials defined the frontier as a dividing line between areas with a population density of two or more settlers to the square mile and areas with fewer or no settlers. In 1890 they declared that no clear line separated settled from unsettled areas and therefore the frontier was closed. By that time, the word *frontier* had a mythic significance. It conjured up the post–Civil War Wild West, a place of wide open spaces, where the inhabitants were tough and self-reliant, and civilized behavior was a luxury.[11]

As settlers moved into new territory, they necessarily added words to the vocabulary, beginning with the vehicle that got them there: the Conestoga wagon. Conestoga wagons are named for the Conestoga River valley of Pennsylvania. (*Conestoga* is the name of an Iroquoian tribe whose homeland covered parts of Pennsylvania and Maryland.)

The first Conestogas are thought to have been built by Mennonites in the early eighteenth century. Designed for hauling freight, they were sixteen to eighteen feet long, with sloping sides and a canvas cover stretched over hoops. They were roomy enough to carry all the supplies a settler family needed. Typically they were pulled by four horses. During the heyday of Conestoga travel, tall, heavy horses, also called Conestogas, were bred especially to pull the wagons.

Pioneers bound for Oregon found the Conestogas too bulky. They preferred the smaller, lighter prairie schooners, also called *prairie clippers* or *prairie ships*. Mentions of prairie schooners begin in the 1830s. A stagecoach traveler near Chicago writes about the appropriateness of the name: "We met many large wagons, which well deserve their name of 'prairie schooners,' as their white covers show like sails at a distance."[12] The generic term *covered wagon* was in use by the mid-eighteenth century. *Wagon train* came in shortly afterward.

The beginning of the trail was called the *jumping-off place*. The term quickly acquired the added meaning of the farthest limit of civilization. A book about the exploits of Davy Crockett that was published in 1836 contains the following line about Natchez, Mississippi: "Where shall I find words suitable to describe the peculiarities of that unholy spot? 'Tis, in fact, the jumping-off place."[13]

The more daring pioneers attempted to shorten their journey by taking a *cutoff*, or shortcut to their destination. The word *cutoff* was in general use from the late eighteenth century. It could mean either a trail shortcut or a channel that cuts off a loop in a river.

As Americans went west, they faced new kinds of sometimes rugged terrain. Crossing the mountains, they passed through *gaps*—low passes—and over *divides*—ridges that divide two river valleys. The most notable divide in North America is the Continental Divide, which runs along the crest of the Rocky Mountains and separates the Atlantic and Pacific watersheds. Bartlett recorded *divide* in his 1877 edition, attributing its new meaning to western hunters and guides. Low-lying lands along the rivers were called *flats*. *Barren*, a word already in use, became more common because pine barrens—plains sparsely dotted with stunted pine trees and shrubs—were abundant on the Kentucky frontier.

Much of the land the settlers hoped to claim was covered with *brush*, overgrown thickets of bushes, saplings, vines, and other low-growing plants. Clearing the brush was the first task awaiting those who wanted to start cultivating their plot. Bartlett says the word is short for *brushwood* and applies not only to scrub but also to tree branches and any other wood that can't be chopped into cordwood. *Brush* led to *brush heap*, *brush fire*, and *underbrush*.

The frontier east of the Mississippi was also heavily wooded with what Americans called *timber*. In England, *timber* meant wood processed for building—American *lumber*. (In England, *lumber* means discarded furniture or other useless household objects, often stored in spare rooms called *lumber rooms*—yet another instance of meaning shift between the old country and the new.) *Timber* could refer to the trees themselves or more broadly to the forest or woodlands. Bartlett explains in 1877, "A man going into the woods will tell you he is going into the *timber*." Americans wrote about "timbered" land from at least the eighteenth century. Escaping into the forest was described as *heading for the tall timber*.

When settlers reached the frontier, their first order of business was to find a piece of land they could lay claim to. Ownership rights were confused and hard to enforce—the government owned part of the land, while other areas still belonged to the tribes, at least in theory—so many people simply became *squatters*, settling on a piece of property without benefit of title. The word *squatter* was first used in the late eighteenth century, but the practice and the word became more common as western lands opened up.

Americans had been setting and pulling up stakes since they first arrived on the continent. The vocabulary now expanded to include *stake a claim*, meaning to mark off the land you claimed with stakes. The plot of land someone owned was called a *lot*. In England, *lot* was an old word for property of any sort, especially an inheritance. In America, it narrowed to mean land, especially land for building on. The meaning might have come from the Massachusetts settlers' method of distributing parcels of land by drawing lots for them. *House lot* entered the language in the seventeenth century, *back lot* in the early eighteenth, and *corner lot* in the early nineteenth. To *go across lots* meant to go straight across, ignoring obstacles. The Mormon pioneer Brigham Young famously told his enemies to "go to hell across lots."[14]

Once settled, squatters began making *betterments*. They cleared ground, planted crops, and built log cabins (so-called since the eighteenth century) to establish their right to the land. Rickety cabins thrown up in a hurry might be stigmatized as *shanties*, from a French word for the temporary shacks that Canadian lumbermen built near where they were logging.

Another way to claim property was by carving your name and the date into a tree at one edge, known as getting *tomahawk rights*. *Tomahawk improvements* were minimal improvements to the land, such as clearing brush, that squatters judged would be enough to justify their possession of the property. Two centuries after John Smith first recorded the word *tomahawk*, it was a naturalized American English word. Expressions such as *bury the tomahawk* and *take up the tomahawk* (go to war) were familiar to most Americans.

Early examples of these expressions are literal. They describe symbolic actions that Algonquians and other tribes traditionally took when agreeing to a peace treaty or deciding to go to war. By the mid-nineteenth century, however, the phrases were often metaphorical, especially in the realm of politics. Bartlett notes that political speakers and writers used the expressions "with reference to the healing up of past disputes or breaking out of new ones."

Frontier people tended to settle close enough together that they could call on each other in times of need. Cooperative enterprises were known as *bees*, probably an allusion to the insect's communal industriousness. Activities called bees predate the frontier. As early as

1769, the *Boston Gazette* for October 16 announced, "Last Thursday about twenty young Ladies met at the house of Mr. L. on purpose for a Spinning Match; (or what is called in the Country a Bee)." Another type of bee that was mentioned starting in the eighteenth century was a *husking bee*, a social gathering for the purpose of husking recently harvested corn.

Almost any kind of work party could be called a bee. Raising bees raised the frame of a house or barn. Women gathered for quilting bees and men to split logs in chopping bees. Young people might get together for paring bees, also called apple bees—peeling and slicing apples for drying. Typically, these events were treated like social occasions, with the beneficiary providing food and drink. The one bee that most modern Americans have heard of—the spelling bee—didn't come into fashion until after the Civil War.

Settlers continued the habit of adopting Native American words as place names. Several states were named after tribes, such as Iowa, Kansas, Utah, and the Dakotas. Other place names were words in a native language—Oklahoma (Pawnee), Wisconsin (Algonquian, by way of French), Minnesota (Dakota), Omaha (Osage)—or the name of an individual, such as Seattle (Chief Si'ahl of the Suquamish tribe). Indiana and Sioux Falls are straightforward references to Indians. Native American terms for unfamiliar plants, animals, and other objects also kept trickling into the lexicon—*chipmunk*, *toboggan*, *potlatch*, and *abalone*, among others.

Besides contributing to the ongoing process of practical word invention, the old trans-Appalachian frontier was the birthplace of a flamboyant new way of talking. One feature was exaggeration. As Bartlett puts it in his introduction, "Our people, particularly those who belong to the West and South, are fond of using intensive and extravagant epithets, both as adjectives and adverbs, as *awful*, *powerful*, *monstrous*, *dreadful*, *mighty*, *almighty*, *all-fired*, etc."[15] Many of the words have the feel of purposely outlandish concoctions—*bodacious*, *rambunctious*, *highfalutin(g)*. In most cases, their origins are uncertain, but they were either coined or popularized in the western borderlands.

Dozens of expressions that captured frontier life started with literal meanings but soon evolved into metaphors—*eat crow*, *eat dirt*, *make the fur fly*, *paddle one's own canoe*, *be up the creek without a paddle*, *rope in*. The emphasis on hunting is reflected in the phrase *be loaded for bear* (ready for anything), and the importance of frontier people's guns in *lock, stock, and barrel*; *draw a bead*; and *flash in the pan*. Timber country inspired *easy as falling off a log* and *more than you can shake a stick at*. Offices set up to distribute government land gave rise to the expression *do a land-office business*.

The idea among Easterners that backwoodsmen were a lawless crowd led to the word *rowdy*, first a noun, defined by Bartlett as a "riotous, turbulent fellow." The origin of the word is uncertain, but it might come from *rowdy-dow*, a way of mimicking the sound of a beating drum. Some of the earliest examples of the word in print come from a British travel book titled *Memorable Days in America*. Recounting a story of a murder on the Kentucky frontier, the author says, "No legal inquiry took place, nor indeed ever takes place, amongst *Rowdies*, as the Back-woodsmen are called." The author later mentions "the Rowdies of Kentucky" and "Illinois Rowdies."[16]

Within a decade, the word spelled with a small *r* was being used to mean any noisy, violent troublemaker. By the 1830s, the word was an adjective and could apply to any boisterous person or group, such as rowdy children.

The idea that frontier folks owned a special vocabulary was widespread by the early nineteenth century. In 1823 the editor of the *Missouri Intelligencer* helpfully published a "Provincial Dictionary" for the benefit of new arrivals from the east. He describes a day's activities, with language samples that blend regional differences in word choice and pronunciation with nonstandard words and expressions. He tells readers that unlike Yankees, who call excursions away from home "outings," most Westerners would say they "had came" to the courthouse. On their way "thar," they met "a heap" of folks. These included working men who were "up and a doing" early, "toting" sacks of flour and meal to "whar" customers' wagons were parked. When asked, they "reckoned" that this year's "crap" of tobacco would be "tolerable."[17]

The Englishwoman Frances Trollope, who spent two wretched years in Ohio in the 1820s, took a less good-humored view of frontier speech habits. Like almost everything else that she found in America, they affronted her taste. In her 1832 book, *Domestic Manners of the Americans*, she writes, "I very seldom during my whole stay in the country heard a sentence elegantly turned, and correctly pronounced from the lips of an American. There is always something either in the expression or the accent that jars the feelings and shocks the taste."[18]

Fanny Trollope, mother of the Victorian novelist Anthony Trollope, arrived in the United States in 1828 with her two young daughters and her teenage son, Henry. (Anthony, another brother, and their father remained at home in England.) Like many others who traveled to the frontier, she was hoping to make her fortune—her barrister husband had squandered most of his money on bad investments in land. Trollope believed she could recoup some of their losses and give Henry a start in life by going into business in a place with fewer economic and social restrictions than London.

Trollope's original plan had been to join a Utopian community founded by a friend in the Tennessee backwoods. When she arrived, she discovered that the community consisted of a few unfinished cabins, so she fled with her children to Cincinnati. By the 1820s, the town was no longer exactly a frontier outpost. Ohio had been a state since 1803, and Cincinnati, with nearly twenty thousand inhabitants, was booming. Exports including whiskey, pork products, and various manufactured goods were shipped by steamboat from its bustling wharves. The town boasted a medical college, libraries, churches, schools, newspapers, and a theater.

Still, the place came as a shock to someone from London. Trollope describes the town as "an uninteresting mass of buildings" and as having "only just enough of the air of a city to make it noisy and bustling." Only the main street was paved. Garbage was disposed of by dumping it in the middle of the street and letting the free-roaming pigs help themselves. There were no gutters, so every rain shower washed detritus from the higher to the lower streets, where it collected in unpleasant mounds. Even the hills surrounding the town were devoid of shrubs and flowers.[19]

The Trollopes never really found their footing financially. After one or two unsuccessful attempts to earn money, they hit on the idea of presenting mechanical exhibits at the Western Museum, a natural history and antiquities museum. Their exhibit *The Infernal Regions,* portraying scenes from Dante's *Divine Comedy,* was very popular. They also presented theatrical performances in their home.

The Trollopes (encouraged by Trollope's husband, who briefly visited) overreached when they decided to build an enormous entertainment center that would have space for a theater, exhibitions, a lecture room, a coffeehouse, and commercial stalls. The Bazaar, an exotic-looking building modeled after the Egyptian Hall in London, cost a fortune to build. Once open, it steadily lost money. The final blow came when Trollope and her son both contracted malaria. The family abandoned their American project and began making their way east and finally home.[20]

Trollope took notes throughout her trip with the idea of writing a book. Back in England, still in a foul mood from her business losses, she settled down to compose *Domestic Manners of the Americans.* The book was a thorough indictment of the American character, way of life, and, not least, speech habits. Published in 1832, it was a runaway hit in on both sides of the Atlantic. On the English side, it reinforced the negative views that many people held of the United States. On the

American side, it inspired outrage but made for compulsive reading. Trollope had at last discovered a way to make money from Cincinnati.

The book is full of direct and indirect comments on American language use. Trollope was appalled by what she heard, but she had an excellent ear. Her quotations are full of striking words and expressions. Names for American baked goods that she records include *hot cake*, *hoe cake*, *johny cake*, *waffle cake*, and *dodger cake*. She notes that stores where bread is sold are called *bakeries*, rather than the *baker* or *bakeshop*, as in England. She also records the term *grocery store*, which the English would call a *grocer* or *grocer's shop*. (Bartlett doesn't mention bakeries but does list *grocery* as an Americanism.)

Like other English visitors, Trollope noticed Americans' expansive use of *fix*. A young woman explained that she was always fixed in her best when attending church. Trash was fixed into the middle of the street. Plucking and cleaning chickens was called fixing them. Trollope heard stories of people finding themselves in an unhandsome fix or an ugly fix.

Besides noting individual words, Trollope frequently quotes people to give a flavor of how they talked. She manages to illustrate several Americanisms at once with the speech of a man who congratulated her on having killed a copperhead snake during a walk. "My!" he exclaims, "If you have not got a copper. That's right down well done, they be darnation beasts."[21]

She made a more extended effort to illustrate American speech—at least her version of it—with "a fragment" of a play about a Cincinnati family, attached to the fifth edition of her book. In the play, Trollope indulges in a frenzy of Americanisms. The first line is reminiscent of David Humphreys's first line in *The Yankey in England*: "Come boys! up with ye! I wish I may be scorched if I don't send ye both east of sunrise if ye don't jump slick." The dialogue is packed with stereotypical Americanisms like *fix*, *reckon*, *calculate*, and *varmint*, as well as new words like *bakery* and provincialisms like *spry*. Trollope also provides an early example of the expression *live high on the hog*.[22]

The play's overload of Americanisms and nonstandard usages is probably not a very realistic representation of the language Trollope heard. Like earlier British critics of American speech, she showed her contempt for it by exaggerating its novelties. She also concentrated on its least educated speakers—people who said *comed* for *came*, *be* for *are*, and other nonstandard usages. Nonetheless, most of the words she makes her characters say are also recorded elsewhere. The 1859 edition of Bartlett's dictionary quotes Trollope for two Americanisms—*get along* meaning to get going, and *grave-yard*, an American variation on the English *church-yard*.

Of course American reviewers struck back at Trollope's portrayal of all Americans as crude, primitive people who didn't talk right. They pointed out an obvious shortcoming of the book—that she had spent nearly all her time in the United States among denizens of the Ohio frontier. What's more, they were not of the highest class. The prominent families of Cincinnati had refused to receive her.

A Cincinnati reviewer attributes this situation to her "singularly unladylike" air. He describes her as "a short, plump figure, with a ruddy, round Saxon face" and a "want of taste and female intelligence in regard to dress." She is a "a first-rate talker," he says. Then, using words she might have quoted herself as a sample of Ohio speech, he adds, "She went, as they say in the West, for quantity of that article." Other reviewers pointed out that she was a "greenhorn" who allowed the builders of the Bazaar to cheat her. Says one writer with false sympathy, "She might innocently look sour at a country where she lost 30,000 dols." About the only aspect of her commentary that everyone agreed with was her condemnation of the widespread male habit of chewing tobacco and spitting.[23]

In the end, Americans got their revenge in a particularly American way—by turning the author's name into a verb. A few years after Fanny Trollope's visit, the English writer Harriet Martineau also made a tour of the United States, although with a more positive attitude. She remarks in the resulting narrative that an American publisher who was interested in the book encouraged her to "Trollopize a bit" and so make her story more engaging. An American commentator complains about travelers who "come Trolloping over our country, to seek what blemishes they may descry."[24]

Around the same time that Fanny Trollope arrived in Ohio, Davy Crockett (or David, as he always called himself) arrived in Washington, DC, to represent the people of his rural Tennessee congressional district. Crockett swept into office on the same populist wave that put his friend Andrew Jackson in the White House. Fanny Trollope never met him, but with his inventive use of homegrown words and expressions, he would have made perfect fodder for her book.

Crockett was the apotheosis of the rugged American frontiersman—tough, bold, resourceful, and equally at home in the tall timber or the halls of Congress. A descendant of Scotch Irish settlers, he had grown up in extreme poverty. His education was minimal—he claims in his autobiography that he didn't learn to read until age fifteen. He was nonetheless astute enough to be elected to the Tennessee state legislature in 1821 and, seven years later, to the House of Representatives. What he lacked in polish he made up for in straight talk. His motto was "Be always sure you're right—then go ahead."[25]

When Crockett arrived in the more sedate East, he was an object of wonder—a genuine resident of a land that still seemed wild and strange to most Americans. Legends and tall tales soon grew up around him. During the 1830s, several books were written either purporting to be by "Davy" or using his voice. In 1834 he wrote an autobiography to set the record straight, but it was almost as full of amazing incidents and colorful language as the earlier fictional works.[26]

A big part of Crockett's larger-than-life persona was based on his way of talking—a kind of frontier speech writ large, full of fanciful word inventions, rural metaphors, and outsize boasts. *Davy Crockett's Almanack* for 1837, written by others after Crockett's death,

An engraving of "Colonel Crockett" by C. Stuart from an original portrait by J. G. Chapman. This picture shows Crockett as the ideal frontiersman, complete with buckskins, coonskin cap, and hunting dogs. *Prints and Photographs Division: Library of Congress, LC-DIG-pga-04179*

relies on all three. The *Almanack* is a collection of tall tales interspersed with more typical almanac material like weather predictions. It includes a story titled "A Tongeriferous Fight with an Alligator." In it, the narrator tells of the wild *rampoosings* of alligators on top of the house and Crockett's *rageriferous* wrestlings to get them down. In another piece, he describes Texas as a place where "the land is so rich, if you plant a crowbar at night it will sprout tenpenny nails before morning."[27]

Countrified vocabulary and nonstandard verbs abound. Two examples are "I was so wrothy I should have scun him alive" and "I div down in a slantidicular direction." Crockett chases off a "yankee peddler" by threatening, "If you ain't off in no time, I'll take off my neckcloth and swallow you whole." In the preface, he repeats his famous message to his constituents before the 1835 election, which he lost: "If they did not re-elect me, they might go to hell and I'd go to Texas." (The editor then goes on to explain that Crockett had indeed gone off to Texas to fight for independence.)[28]

Davy Crockett's books were responsible for popularizing several expressions that first arose in the trans-Appalachian West—*chip off the old block*, *a hard row to hoe*, *be stumped*, *go the whole hog*, *root hog or die* (work hard or lose out), *fire into the wrong flock* (mistake your target), and *bark up the wrong tree*. He often used the last expression when his hunting dogs were literally barking up the wrong tree—a tree other than the one that held the bear or raccoon he was chasing. He also used it figuratively. In a letter about the politics of the day, he writes, "Some people are going to try to hunt for themselves . . . but . . . seem to be barking up the wrong sapling."[29]

Crockett also popularized the word *blizzard*, which originally meant something like a violent blow or, figuratively, a noisy attack of words. In an anecdote about attending a dinner and being asked to give a toast, he says, "Not knowing whether he intended to compliment me . . . or have some fun at my expense, I concluded to go ahead, and give him and his likes a blizzard." He follows up with a hair-raising toast that begins, "Here's wishing the bones of tyrant kings may answer in hell."[30] Bartlett defines *blizzard* as "a poser" and says that the word is unknown in the East. The weather-related meaning of *blizzard* didn't begin to appear until the 1850s.

In 1830 the humorist J. K. Paulding wrote a play titled *The Lion of the West*, featuring a hero named Nimrod Wildfire who was clearly modeled on Crockett. Wildfire, a raw Kentuckian, writes to his aunt and uncle in New York to announce that he's on his way. His bombastic letter starts, "On my way I took a squint at my wild lands along by the Big Muddy . . . and had what I call a rael, roundabout catawumpus, clean through the d*ee*strict. If I hadn't I wish I may be *te-to-taciously ex-flunctified* [totally worn out]." He signs off, "Yours to the backbone."

Wildfire is partial to the exaggerated boast. He tells his uncle, "Let the fellers in New York know—I'm half horse, half alligator, a touch of the airth-quake, with a sprinkling of the steamboat!" Later he assures a new acquaintance, "I can jump higher—squat lower—dive deeper—stay longer under and come out drier! there's no back out in my breed—I go the whole hog."[31]

Lion of the West was performed regularly in New York for years and had a run of two or three months in London as well. It surely helped to cement Crockett's reputation as the most famous frontiersman of them all, even before his heroic death at the Alamo in 1836. Along with the books bearing his name, the play lifted him to an iconic status. At the same time, it introduced Americans in other parts of the country to the fabulous language of the western borderlands.

Western words and expressions quickly became an essential part of the American vernacular. The freewheeling speech of Crockett and his fellow frontier dwellers fired the imagination of anyone who used language for effect. It spiced up newspaper editorials and added a folksy touch to campaign speeches, even turning up occasionally in Congress. Politicians and newspaper writers would become the two widest conduits for western colloquialisms and slang and two of the richest sources for Bartlett's dictionary.

5

Slang-Whanging in Congress

THE GRAND EXPERIMENT of building a government from the ground up brought with it a flurry of new word coinages. Colonial forms of government typically took their terminology from England. For instance, the pre-Revolution Virginia legislature was known as the House of Burgesses. After independence, Americans wanted—and needed—terms of their own to match their newly invented institutions. Even words that were already part of English took on new meanings under the new system, and campaigning and speechmaking in the young republic carried language creation a step further. They inspired not only new words but also colorful and original new ways of talking.

One of the first preexisting English words to gain a specialized meaning was *constitution*. On May 25, 1787, fifty-five delegates convened in Philadelphia to overhaul the Articles of Confederation, the agreement that had held the states in a loose union since 1781. Once there, they decided to scrap the Articles and write a new agreement—or, as the preamble to the document states, a "Constitution for the United States of America." Their gathering is now known as the Constitutional Convention.

The word *constitution* had meant the makeup of some entity since the sixteenth century—for instance, the constitution of society or the constitution of the world. The word could also mean a body of rules or principles governing a nation or other organization, such as the Apostolic Constitutions of the early Christian church. Convention delegates had the second meaning in mind when they set out to write their document.

For Americans, *constitution* soon started to mean *the* Constitution—a specific document. *Constitutionality* and *unconstitutional*, also referring to that document, entered the language at about the same time. Webster's 1806 dictionary defines *constitutionality* as "the state of being agreeable to the Constitution"—that is, consistent with it. Pickering included the word in his dictionary of Americanisms, noting that it didn't exist in British dictionaries.

Other early political words have similar stories. *Senate*, which had referred to an appointive governing body since Roman times, took on the specific meaning of the upper house of Congress. *Congress* itself went from being a common noun with the meaning of a coming together or a meeting (for instance, sexual congress or a congress of scholars) to being the name of one branch of the government. Bartlett points out that Americans at first said "*the* Congress," but the word had since "acquired . . . the force of a proper name." Americans spoke of Congress the way the British spoke of Parliament.

The houses of Congress were named *chambers*. Americans also invented a new way of expressing a representative's right to speak in those chambers. In Parliament, members had "possession of the House," but in the United States, they had "the floor." Congressmen could get the floor, take the floor, or yield the floor to an esteemed colleague. Said Thomas Jefferson of John Adams, "He was a powerful advocate on the floor of Congress."[1]

The Constitution divides the government into three branches—*executive*, *legislative*, and *judicial*—adding three more specialized words to the political vocabulary. *Executive* first referred to the individual who held the office of president, but by the time Pickering was writing his 1816 dictionary, *the Executive*, short for *the Executive Power*, could cover that whole branch of government. To a lesser extent, *the Legislative* was used the same way. Pickering reports that the English, surprisingly, have accepted *Executive* and *Legislative* as appropriate American words, although without using them often.

Concern about the possibility that one branch of government would seize power and dominate the others led to the phrase *checks and balances*. Its first appearance in writing may be in an essay by Alexander Hamilton in the Federalist papers, where he proposes "the introduction of legislative balances and checks" as one way of avoiding some of the problems of a republican government.[2] After that initial appearance, the term flip-flopped to *checks and balances*. Early variations include *the doctrine of checks and balances, a check without a balance, the checked and balanced government*, and *checking and balancing one another*.

The power of the central government would be much stronger under the Constitution than it had been under the Articles of Confederation. Congress under the Articles couldn't levy taxes or declare war. Under the Constitution, it gained both these powers, plus many others. Advocates for this form of national government were called *Federalists*. Opponents of the Constitution, who preferred more autonomy for the states, were called *Anti-Federalists*.

The word *federal* with a lower-case *f* wasn't new. Based on a Latin word for *treaty*, it traditionally referred to any sort of compact. During the early days of forming a new government—a compact among the states—*federal* started to refer specifically to the national government. Participants in the Constitutional Convention called their meeting the Federal Convention. As the Constitution took shape, the word began to imply support for that document and for the stronger union that would result.

After the states ratified the Constitution, conflict over the role of the federal government remained. By the 1790s, two entrenched factions had emerged and the definition of *Federalist* shifted. The label now identified those who favored a strong central government run by "the rich and well-born," to use Alexander Hamilton's words.[3] Leading Federalists included Hamilton and John Adams. The Anti-Federalists, with Jefferson as their leader, believed in a more participatory "people's" government. As the two opposing factions grew into full-fledged political parties, the Jeffersonian party dropped the label of Anti-Federalist and named themselves Democratic-Republicans, or simply Republicans (unrelated to the modern party, which was founded in the 1850s). Both parties saw the other as a threat to the stability of the new nation.

Partisan clashes and language creation went hand in hand. Republicans considered Federalists *Monocrats*—democrats who were closet monarchists—because they wanted to maintain close ties with England. Federalists attacked Republicans as *disunionists* and *Jacobins*—the name for violent French radicals—because they were sympathetic to that country's recent revolution. When Jefferson ran for the presidency in 1800, his enemies labeled him a *Franco-maniac*, insinuating that he would bring French-style anarchy to the country.

The Anti-Federalist Philadelphia *Aurora* newspaper frequently ridiculed the *Anglo-federals* and their president, "Georgy" Washington. (Washington was opposed to political parties and tried to remain publicly neutral, but his tendencies were Federalist.) After the election of 1800 gave Jefferson the presidency, the *Aurora* observed on December 17, 1800, that "the Federal Jigg [jig] is up."

These two warring factions of the early republic are responsible for one of America's first and most enduring pieces of political slang. It came about through the machinations of Republicans in the 1812 Massachusetts legislature. Concerned that the number of Federalists in the legislature almost equaled that of Republicans, they hit on an idea for maximizing their potential gains in the upcoming election. They would creatively redraw the State Senate districts to squeeze most Federalist voters into a smaller number of districts with fewer representatives.

This tactic resulted in some tortuous boundary lines. One of the strangest divided Essex County into two voting districts—a compact circular district incorporating most pro-Federalist towns, and a larger Republican-heavy district that meandered all around the edge of the county. In spite of its questionable structure, the Republican governor, Elbridge Gerry, signed off on it.

At a gathering of Federalist sympathizers where a map of the newly apportioned districts was displayed, someone remarked that the Republican district only needed wings to look like a prehistoric monster. Artist Elkanah Tisdale immediately jumped up and sketched

"The Gerry-Mander," a political cartoon by Elkanah Tisdale, was originally published in the *Boston Gazette* for March 26, 1812. It soon appeared in other newspapers, along with the word it inspired. *Wikimedia Commons*

in wings, a head, and claws. "That will do for a salamander," he said. Another guest, possibly Benjamin Russell, the editor of Boston's *Columbian Centinel* newspaper, exclaimed, "Gerry-mander!" and a classic political slang word was born.[4]

The Federalist press lost no time in publicizing the artful blend of Gerry's name (pronounced like *Gary*, with a hard *g*) and *salamander*. Pictures of that strange political animal "the Gerry-mander" soon began appearing in Federalist newspapers, along with scandalized editorials denouncing the redistricting. If Gerry-mandering had failed to gain votes for Gerry's party, the new coinage might have disappeared after the 1812 election. In fact, it worked beautifully. Although more Federalists than Democratic-Republicans cast votes, causing Gerry himself to lose the governorship, the Republicans captured a comfortable majority of State Senate seats. The word and the practice were here to stay.

The redistricting law was revoked after a little more than a year, but by then the term had taken on a life of its own. At first it was capitalized and probably pronounced the way Gerry pronounced his name (*Gary-mander*), but after a few years, the memory of the word's origin began to fade. The spelling standardized as *gerrymander* and the word was pronounced with a soft *g*—the way *g* followed by *e* is typically pronounced in English (*gem*, *gesture*, *gentle*).

As early as December 3, 1812, the word was also being used as a verb. The *New York Post* for that date includes the sentence, "They attempted also to Gerrymander the State for the choice of Representatives to Congress." Forms like *gerrymandering* and *gerrymandered Senate* began appearing shortly afterward. In recent times, the *mander* part of the word has occasionally been used in new combinations. *Perrymander* was invented in 2003 as a reference to then governor of Texas Rick Perry's proposed redistricting plans.

The first elections brought more new words. One of the earliest was *ticket* to speak of the list of candidates, or, to use another early coinage, *office seekers*. One of the first examples comes from the *Gazette of the United States*, writing about the parties' slates of candidates on November 4, 1796. During the early nineteenth century, the terms *straight ticket* and *split ticket* came into the language. Those who voted for candidates of the other party might be called *bolters* or be said to be *bolting the party*.

Office seekers in the United States *ran* for their positions rather than *standing* for them, as British parliamentary candidates did. A party could also run a candidate. The *Aurora* announced in its December 5, 1800, edition, "General [Charles] Pinckney is no longer run as vice-president; it is the avowed object of the federal party to make him president." Candidates ran, or campaigned, on the party platform. *Platform* started to mean a statement of party principles beginning around 1803, when the *Massachusetts Spy* of April 27 wrote about "the platform of Federalism." By the 1830s, deciding on a platform was an integral part of party conventions. Individual principles of the platform were known as *planks*.

The party might choose to run a *favorite son*. This phrase was first used around 1789, when the *New York Daily Gazette* of May 1 described the newly elected George Washington as "the favourite son of liberty." By the nineteenth century, the meaning of *favorite son* had shifted to mean a candidate popular in his own state but not much regarded outside of it. President James Buchanan, for instance, was often described as the favorite son of Pennsylvania. Mostly unknown outside his home state, he tried for the Democratic presidential nomination several times before finally making the ticket in 1856. (The Democratic Party, an offshoot of the Democratic-Republicans, was founded in 1828 by Andrew Jackson and his supporters.)

In the early days of elections, campaigning in the modern sense was unheard of. To begin with, the vote was limited to male property owners, so broad-based public campaigns were pointless. Neither primaries nor open caucuses existed. Party officials were responsible for choosing nominees. The nominees themselves were expected to behave as though unconscious of the honor about to be conferred until the party invited them to run. Then they stayed out of the limelight while their supporters drummed up votes. To do otherwise would have been ungentlemanly.

Nonetheless, a certain amount of stealth campaigning went on, in the form of letters to the newspapers, barbecues thrown by supporters, backroom strategy sessions, and similar activities. These persuasive methods were called *electioneering*, possibly inspired by the British word *parliamenteering*. An *electioneer* could be a person (like an auctioneer or a puppeteer), but Americans used the term more often in the form *electioneering* or *to electioneer*. The newspaper the *Balance* for May 13, 1806, hints at a typical electioneering tactic when describing a popular new alcoholic drink: "It is vulgarly called bittered sling, and is supposed to be an excellent electioneering potion."[5]

It's doubtful if many people got elected without a little electioneering, but its acceptability was borderline. President Jefferson suggested that civil servants should be removed from office for "electioneering activity."[6] Others commented disapprovingly on the base business of electioneering or electioneering tricks.

A useful electioneering term that entered the language in the eighteenth century is *fellow countrymen*, meaning citizens of the same country as the speaker. This term was stigmatized as an inappropriate Americanism on the grounds that it was redundant. In his essay about problematic American usages, John Witherspoon declares, "You may say fellow citizens, fellow soldiers, fellow subjects, fellow christians, but not *fellow countrymen*." He admits, however, that the word is heard "in public orations from men of the first character."[7]

The problem was that to most people, the word *countryman* alone suggested a rural rustic. Bartlett notes in his 1859 dictionary entry for the term that "the want of a more definite expression has been felt in England as well as in this country." Because it filled a need, *fellow countrymen* not only persisted but also spread to Great Britain, in spite of language critics' protests. The phrase is echoed in *my fellow Americans*, used by President John Kennedy in his inaugural speech, and since then by others.

By the War of 1812, the government had acquired its own nickname—*Uncle Sam*. The *Troy Post* of September 7, 1813, features the first known appearance of the name. An editorial for that day exclaims, "Loss upon loss and no ill luck stiring [stirring] but what lights upon UNCLE SAM'S shoulders." A note at the bottom of the page explains that "this cant name for our government" is getting increasingly popular and speculates that it comes from "the letters U. S. on the government waggons."[8]

Like *Yankee*, *Uncle Sam* started out as a derisive nickname. Americans were bitterly divided over the War of 1812. Democratic-Republicans, including President James Madison, were eager to break free from English control once and for all, while opponents of the war, mainly Federalists, wanted to maintain peaceful relations with the old country. One way that opponents expressed their frustration was by assigning belittling nicknames to prowar politicians. Madison was variously known as Little Jemmy, King James, James the Great, and James the First Emperor of the Virginians and King of the United States.

Uncle Sam was another way for Federalists to vent their frustration. The name was first applied to tax collectors and customs-house employees, a way of protesting the new taxes that the war brought. An early example comes from the *Lansingburgh Gazette* of October 1, 1813. The paper describes a clash between "*Uncle Sam's Men*," meaning customs-house officers, and what the paper labels "*Men of New-York*." During the war, *Uncle Sam* was used almost exclusively by antiwar newspapers in sensational stories about military payroll scandals, tax collectors' overreach, and the like. Eventually, the name started to represent not only customs-house officials but also the government as a whole.

As with *Yankee*, the nickname was eventually embraced by the people it referred to. Anne Royall, writing about her experiences in the nation's capital, says, "It often happened while in Washington, that I met with 'Uncle Sam's men,' as they called themselves." After a trying encounter with an insolent civil servant who informs her that he works for Uncle Sam, she comments tartly, "No matter where you meet those understrappers, you may distinguish them by their unparalleled effrontery."[9]

I WANT YOU FOR U.S. ARMY. This famous World War I recruiting poster by James Montgomery Flagg is now the most familiar rendition of Uncle Sam.

Prints and Photographs Division: Library of Congress, LC-DIG-ppmsc-03521

By the time J. K. Paulding published a comic sketch titled "The History of Uncle Sam and His Boys: A Tale for Politicians" in 1831, the label had evolved into an affectionate one. Paulding describes Uncle Sam as "a famous squire, rich in lands and paper money," who is "a good, hearty fellow, about half horse half alligator."[10] Uncle Sam appeared in political cartoons throughout the nineteenth century, usually but not always with a goatee and top hat. His lasting image was established in 1917, when the artist James Montgomery Flagg produced his famous recruiting poster showing the now familiar version of Uncle Sam, over the legend I WANT YOU FOR U.S. ARMY.

Electioneering and its accompanying language heated up as western territories like Tennessee, Kentucky, Illinois, and Ohio entered the Union and their male citizens demanded the vote. The same independent spirit that drew settlers to the frontier made them believe they had a right to a voice in the government whether they met minimum property requirements or not. By the early nineteenth century, western states had given virtually all white men the vote and most of the thirteen original states had followed suit. Along with that expanded voter base came expanded campaigning.

The first presidential candidate to break free from the gentlemanly restrictions on campaigning was Andrew Jackson, who defeated the incumbent, John Quincy Adams, in a hard-fought 1828 contest. Jackson's background contrasted sharply with that of the first six presidents. Washington, Jefferson, Madison, and Monroe all came from prosperous plantation-owning families, and the Adamses were part of the New England establishment. Jackson was a backcountry Tennessean.

He was the perfect candidate for the new voters—a frontiersman like them, but one who had made good. Jackson rose from his lowly background to become a lawyer, major landowner, congressional representative, and, briefly, a senator. As a general during the War of

1812, he defeated the British at the Battle of New Orleans and earned the nickname Old Hickory for his toughness. Like his backcountry supporters, he believed in the rights of the individual and rejected the idea of government by the privileged few. Newspapers dubbed him the "People's Candidate."

While Adams held to the traditional ban against electioneering, Jackson threw himself into party organizing and getting out the vote. He opened the political season with a trip to New Orleans to celebrate the thirteenth anniversary of his great victory there, which had occurred on January 8. Although Jackson insisted that his attendance at the event had nothing to do with his presidential run, the tumultuous throngs who turned out to greet him must have gladdened the hearts of his campaign managers.

Jackson Democrats were enthusiastically committed to their man, and their language reflected that. A popular slogan that grew out of Jackson supporters' rural roots was "Jackson for president—Go the whole hog!" The Scottish traveler Thomas Hamilton reports seeing this unintelligible (to a Scot) expression on a campaign poster shortly after his arrival in New York. He records that his American friends define "going the whole hog" as going for radical government reform. The phrase, he says, "is used by the Democratic party to distinguish them from the Federalists, who are supposed to prefer less sweeping measures, and consequently *to go* only *a part* of the interesting quadruped in question."[11]

Hamilton's friends claimed that the expression originated in Virginia. When butchers there killed a pig, they supposedly asked customers if they were willing to "go the whole hog," or in other words, purchase the whole animal, which would make it cheaper per pound. The expression was no doubt current in other places as well. Killing a pig and salting it down for the winter was a common practice in nineteenth-century America. Bartlett later describes the term as a "Western vulgarism," but Americans in many regions would have understood its significance.

Faithful Jacksonians were called *whole-hog Democrats.* David Crockett, an early whole hogger, tells the story of how President Adams shook his hand when he arrived in Washington, "even though he know'd I went the whole hog for Jackson." (In the same book, he introduces himself to an Adams supporter with a version of the "half horse, half alligator" speech, saying, "I'm that same David Crockett, half horse, half alligator, . . . can wade the Mississippi, leap the Ohio, . . . hug a bear too close for comfort, and eat any man opposed to Jackson.")[12] Other enthusiasts used variations including *go the whole, go the entire animal, go the entire swine,* and *go the whole quadruped.*

Gradually the phrase lost its Jackson-specific reference and simply meant going to an extreme or fervently embracing a belief or activity.

"President's levee, or all Creation going to the White House." This aquatint by Robert Cruikshank shows a multitude of "whole-hog Democrats" mobbing the White House for the postinaugural festivities after Andrew Jackson's 1829 swearing-in. They later crowded inside, trampling the furniture and muddying the carpets. *Prints and Photographs Division: Library of Congress, LC-DIG-ppmsca-50970*

However, for most of the nineteenth century, it usually showed up in political contexts. A newspaper announcement of an 1842 political rally promises, "They will go the whole hog, and furnish brandy and hard cider after an unheard of fashion."[13]

In another reflection of rural places, loyal Democratic Party members were said to be *dyed in the wool.* Dyeing wool before it's woven into fabric ensures a more lasting color. Dyed-in-the-wool Democrats had a lasting commitment to their party that would never fade. Declared one congressman, "A Democrat of the Jeffersonian school, dyed in the wool, needed no clew to where he stood on the political chessboard. The people always knew where to find him."[14]

Campaigning among frontier residents called for stump speaking, or stumping—delivering a speech while standing slightly elevated on one of the stumps that were plentiful in recently cleared areas. The verb *stump* didn't originate with the Jackson campaign, but phrases such as *taking the stump*, *going on the stump*, *stump orator*, and *stumping the district* became much more familiar after 1828. After a while, *to stump* meant making a political speech from any sort of stage. Stump speaking was a questionable activity at first, a form of electioneering, but in time the term lost its stigma and became synonymous with campaigning.

In his determination to reward party members who went the whole hog for his cause, the newly elected Jackson put a new spin on an old word. *Spoils* traditionally meant plunder taken from defeated enemies, as in *the spoils of war.* During the Jackson administration, it meant the rewards of winning an election, or *the spoils of office.* Appointing friends to political posts was nothing new, but Jackson carried the practice to a whole new level. He fired hundreds of experienced civil servants, such as postmasters, from positions normally considered permanent and gave their jobs to party loyalists.

Sen. William Marcy explained how the system worked, speaking from the Senate floor. "When [politicians] are contending for victory," he said, "they avow their intention of enjoying the fruits of it. If they are defeated, they expect to retire from office. If they are successful, they claim, as a matter of right, the advantages of success. They see nothing wrong in the rule, that to the victor belong the spoils of the enemy."[15] The spoils system, as it was known, remained a well-entrenched political tradition for the rest of the century. President James Garfield's 1881 assassination by a disappointed office seeker finally led to calls for civil service reform and the reintroduction of merit-based hiring.

Nineteenth-century politics was the clearinghouse for all sorts of Americanisms and slang. In the introduction to his dictionary, Bartlett explains how new word inventions are channeled into politics and then into the larger culture. He writes, "Uneducated people invent words . . . and those words become permanent and provincial. They are seized upon by stump-speakers at political meetings, because they have an influence and are popular with the masses. Next we hear them on the floor of Congress and in our halls of legislation. Quoted by the newspapers, they become familiar to all."[16] This system went into high gear when the likes of Davy Crockett and other frontier politicians entered Congress.

The lively talk heard on the stump and on the floors of the House and Senate was known as *slang-whanging*. *Slang-whanger* was already an established "cant word" in 1816 when John Pickering wrote his dictionary of Americanisms. He notes in his entry for the word that it often applies to newspaper writers but also to "a noisy talker, who makes use of that sort of political or other cant, which amuses the rabble, and is called by the vulgar name of *slang*."[17]

The word *slang* itself had been part of the English language since at least the eighteenth century. It referred to any type of colloquial language or jargon. *Slang-whanging*, however, was an American invention and usually referenced political speech. For instance, a headline in the *Essex Register* of Massachusetts for May 20, 1809, reads, "Federal

Slang-whanging." Slang-whanging speech was contentious and inflammatory. The most incendiary slang-whangers were labeled *fire-eaters*.

Sticklers for correct language pointed to politicians as among the worst degraders of American English. One common complaint was their supposed penchant for freewheeling verb creation. *Affiliate*, *legislate*, *deputize*, and *itemize* are among the new verbs that appeared in congressional speeches. Congressmen were not above using the slang terms *skedaddle*, meaning to unceremoniously flee; *go it blind*, meaning to go ahead without the necessary information; or *demagogue*, meaning to make rabble-rousing speeches. One representative accused party leaders of "demagoguing upon the stump." Pickering notes that *proven* for *proved* and *stricken* for *struck* are often heard in congressional debates. He criticizes both as "antiquated" and no longer used in England.

Legislative work led to several terms that are still current. By the early nineteenth century, legislators called the enactment of a bill its *passage*, which Pickering describes as an American replacement for the British *passing*. By midcentury, a bill that combined different topics was being called an *omnibus bill*. The term *pocket veto*—the president's tactic of simply ignoring a bill that he didn't want to sign—was also in use by midcentury. The idea was that instead of vetoing the bill outright, he slipped it in his pocket and forgot about it.

Names of other legislative activities grew out of the American landscape. *Logrolling* is one example. Literally, it meant settlers' cooperative efforts to clear land by chopping down trees, which would either be rolled into a pile and burned or brought together to build a cabin. The figurative meaning of *logrolling* also indicated cooperation—in this case, legislators' mutual support for each others' bills. If a representative voted for his colleague's bill to fund road improvements back home, he expected his colleague to vote for his bill to build a local bridge.

Although the term *log-rolling* isn't much heard anymore—probably because the literal activity is obsolete—*sitting on the fence* is still a popular way to describe a wavering politician. This expression was known by the 1820s. Bartlett explains the point of balancing on a fence: "A man sitting on the top of a fence, can jump down on either side with equal facility." *Fence-men*, as they were sometimes called, were assumed to be lacking in strong principles. They waited to see where their advantage lay before choosing a side. Depending on where they landed, they might be said to *come down on the right side of the fence* or to *stay on the same side of the fence* as their party.

Another farm term that came in later in the century was *pork barrel spending.* Pork barrels were found in most, if not all, farmhouse kitchens, full of the salted pork that kept the family fed through the winter. For many legislators, Congress was a comparable source of largesse. One of the earliest uses comes from the *Defiance Democrat* of Ohio for September 13, 1873. The editor comments sharply on local politicians' "many previous visits to the pork barrel." The projects that resulted from representatives sandwiching juicy slices of local funding into larger spending bills came to be known as *pork barrel projects.*

Railing against pork barrel spending is still a good way to impress the folks back home. In the early nineteenth century, congressmen called remarks of this type *talking to Buncombe*—making a speech for the sake of letting your constituents know you're working hard. As the story goes, the phrase arose during an 1820 House debate, when the representative from Buncombe County, North Carolina, rose near the end of the day and began a meandering speech. His fellow legislators pleaded with him to wrap it up so they could leave. Unconcerned, he suggested that they go ahead if they wished. He wasn't speaking to them anyway—he was speaking to Buncombe. The unspoken idea was that he expected the people of Buncombe to notice and remember it at reelection time.[18]

Buncombe became a popular word for legislators who wanted to suggest that their colleagues were talking nonsense or making speeches just to hear themselves talk. During one debate, a representative accused his opponent of speaking "not for the purpose of bringing light to the House, but for Buncombe." Another representative conscientiously complained, "We spend the whole of our time in speechmaking to Buncombe, instead of practical action for the good of the country." Yet another assured his fellows that he would not "make a speech for Buncombe."[19]

Newspapers and political commentators picked up the term and began using it to criticize politicians with opposing views. As memories of the word's origin faded, the spelling was simplified to *bunkum*. In the twentieth century, the word was shortened to *bunk* and could refer to any sort of foolish or empty talk, not necessarily political. The word *debunk*—to remove the bunk from a statement—came into use in the 1920s.

When congressmen weren't talking to Buncombe, they might be listening instead. They met regularly with constituents or others who wanted something. Get-togethers between legislators and those hoping to influence them usually took place in the lobbies of the House and Senate, so asking for special favors from politicians became known as *lobbying*. The verb *to lobby* was common by the 1830s.

This unvarnished description by a British visitor reveals that lobbying took place at the state level as well: "A practice exists in the State capitals of the country, called 'lobbying,' which consists in this: A certain number of agents . . . are employed by public companies and private individuals, who have bills before the legislature. . . . These persons attend the lobby of the House daily, talk with members, form parties, invite them to dinner and suppers, . . . and . . . they usually succeed in corrupting a sufficient number of the members to effect their purpose."[20]

By the time Bartlett was writing his dictionary, the term *lobby-member* was current, and by the time of his 1859 edition, *a lobby* meant an organized group that worked on getting political favors. He quotes a reporter of the London *Times* who describes the "American Lobby" as a miscellaneous crowd of people whose influence may be "social, political, or local." The writer notes that many lobbyists are ex-members of Congress.

Occasionally, congressmen had to return to Buncombe for a visit. For this purpose, a tradition called *mileage* came into being. Mileage was being provided for legislative bodies before the Revolution. Benjamin Franklin makes one of the earliest mentions of it when outlining a 1754 plan for politically uniting the northern colonies through a "Grand Council." He suggests members be paid "shillings sterling per diem, during their sitting, and mileage for travelling expenses."[21]

When Franklin was writing, travel around the colonies was slow and onerous. Depending on how far away a meeting or assembly was, getting there could take several days. That meant spending money on food and lodging, as well as transportation costs. For those who were leaving behind farms or businesses, there was an additional hardship. They would need to travel back and forth occasionally to see to matters at home—a serious trek if your home was in Tennessee or Ohio. Mileage was a way to make the cost of government participation less prohibitive. Early comments on the practice indicate that mileage was paid to other groups as well, such as militia members and juries.

Constructive mileage was an extra benefit that accrued when a new president took office. Congress adjourned before he was sworn in but was called back the next day. In the meantime, members received mileage—as much as $1,500 for those in faraway states—to allow them to go home and return, although none actually did so. The *New-York Tribune* of May 2, 1848, editorializes about the amount of mileage being spent on congressmen who come from western states. Legislators from Texas receive "some $2,500 each every session," says the writer. He warns, "When we come to have Senators and Representatives from Oregon and California, we shall have to negotiate a loan expressly to pay the *mileage* of their members."

With the advent of automobiles, *mileage* started to mean the number of miles a driver could go on one gallon of gas. Representatives and senators still receive a travel allowance, but it's no longer called *mileage.*

Frontier politicians not only coined new words and expressions but also brought their ebullient, slangy way of talking onto the floor of Congress. Rep. Wick of Indiana must have been channeling his inner Crockett when he rose to participate in a debate over an appropriations bill. Questioning the point of attacks being made on the Van Buren administration, he asks, "Have we not heard it proclaimed . . . that the Administration is bodaciously used up, tetotaciously exflunctified? . . . Why, then, tomahawk the slain?"

In the same vein, Rep. Duncan of Ohio adopted one of Davy Crockett's favorite sayings during a speech in the House. "Instead of having treed their game," he cautions, "gentlemen will find themselves still 'barking up the wrong tree.'"[22]

It was not unusual for speechifying congressmen to indulge in casual word invention or popular slang and metaphors. A representative complaining about importunate office seekers called them "one of the most reckless and desperate hordes of camp followers that ever vexed an honest man, or disgraced God's footstool" (an evocative nickname for the planet). Declared a senator of his constituents, "Ours are a going-ahead sort of people." Another talked of taking "a snap judgment."[23]

During one debate, a senator prefaced his comments by comparing his performance to what can be seen onstage. "I have no highland fling to throw off," he admits, "No ground and lofty tumbling with which to amuse." *Ground and lofty tumbling* was a literal term that signified an acrobatic act performed both on the ground and aboveground with ropes. The phrase frequently appeared on posters advertising traveling circus acts. By the 1830s it was also a popular way to describe what now might be called political fancy footwork. For instance, a member engaged in a contentious debate ended his statement by wondering aloud, "How many Whigs will now take their turn upon the spring board and give us an example of ground and lofty tumbling."[24]

As a circus term, *ground and lofty tumbling* was especially appropriate for the Whigs. The Whig Party rose in the 1830s to oppose the Democrats. (The Federalists and the original Republicans had both disappeared by this time.) The Whig Party's name harked back to the name that pro-independence Americans adopted before the Revolutionary War because the English Whig Party was thought to be sympathetic to the revolutionaries. In 1836 the Whigs tried their hand against the Democratic presidential candidate, Martin Van Buren, who was Andrew Jackson's vice president. Unable to agree on a national candidate, they ran three regional candidates instead. Not surprisingly, Van Buren won. By 1840, when the Whigs were ready to challenge Van Buren again, they had learned a few tricks from their opponents for getting out the popular vote.

This time the Whigs nominated William Henry Harrison, a Virginian who had married a woman from Ohio and settled there when it was still part of the Northwest Territory. Superficially, he resembled the first frontier candidate, Andrew Jackson. However, while Jackson had grown up in poverty in the backwoods, Harrison came from a well-to-do eastern family and had received a good education. His move to the frontier came after college. Harrison's war record also couldn't begin to match Jackson's. His one claim to fame was leading forces against the Shawnee chief Tecumseh's confederation of Native Americans and defeating them in 1811 at the Battle of Tippecanoe.

Harrison had spent most of his time as a prosperous farmer and politician. He served as governor of the Indiana Territory and in Congress as a representative, and then a senator, from Ohio. When nominated, he was ensconced in a comfortable position as the clerk of courts for his county.

Harrison's hugely successful campaign theme was an accidental gift from a competitor. The *Baltimore Republican* reported that a friend of Henry Clay, a disappointed rival for the nomination, had this to say about Harrison: "Give him a barrel of Hard Cider, and settle a pension of $2,000 a year on him, and . . . he will sit the remainder of his days in his Log Cabin, by the side of a 'sea-coal' [soft coal] fire, and study moral philosophy."[25]

Clay's friend clearly meant the description as an insult, but Harrison supporters seized delightedly on this image of their candidate as just folks. (Drinking hard cider in Harrison's day was comparable to a modern candidate who chugs beer straight from the can.) Never mind that Harrison lived not in a log cabin but in a spacious house. Never mind that he earned an excellent income as the clerk of courts. Harrison was now the "Log-Cabin-and-Hard-Cider" candidate, a simple, rustic man of the people.

To strengthen the likeness to Jackson, the Whigs boosted Harrison as a military hero. They called him the Hero of Tippecanoe and Old Tip Harrison. When John Tyler of Virginia joined the campaign as the vice presidential candidate, they invented one of the most memorable campaign slogans of all time: "Tippecanoe and Tyler too." For good measure, they even gave Harrison the nickname Old Buckeye in a nod to the shade of Old Hickory. (The Democrats reacted by nicknaming Van Buren Old Kinderhook, for his New York place of birth. They called him O.K. for short, playing off a popular newspaper abbreviation and incidentally inspiring one of America's greatest linguistic inventions—but that's a story for chapter 6.)

With the election of 1840, full-bore carnival-style campaigning had arrived. Crowds, sometimes numbering in the thousands, gathered to listen to speeches adulating Harrison and to sing rowdy campaign songs. Party operatives threw lavish barbecues where hard cider flowed freely from bottomless barrels. Enterprising manufacturers churned out souvenirs of all kinds, from log cabin–shaped whiskey bottles to canes with miniature hard cider barrels for heads.

Campaign songs used language that reinforced Harrison's folksy frontier persona. One starts with the line, "Come, all you Log Cabin boys, we're going to have a raisin'," and goes on to describe how they'll finish the Whig cabin raising with "chinkin' and daubin'." Another one tells opponents, "Up the wrong tree you have long been barking." Lyrics of other songs made use of words like *botheration* and *tote* and expressions like *kick up a fuss*.[26]

The contest even spilled into the halls of Congress. In a sterling example of slang-whanging, Rep. Charles Ogle of Pennsylvania took advantage of a proposal for funding improvements to the White House to launch into a highly colored tirade against Van Buren. He portrayed the president as a snob who lived in luxury—the antithesis of Harrison. The speech was later published as a Whig campaign pamphlet titled *The Regal Splendor of the Presidential Palace*.

Ogle accused the president of living in a palace "as splendid as that of the Caesars, and as richly adorned as the proudest Asiatic mansion." He further accused Van Buren of turning up his nose at plain frontier fare like hog and hominy in favor of fancy French dinners. These were eaten off "massive gold plate and French sterling silver services."[27] And of course Van Buren accompanied these extravagant feasts with elitist French wine instead of working-man's hard cider.

Democrats labeled this grossly unfair portrait of life in the White House an "omnibus of lies" and responded with some tall talk of their own.[28] Rep. Duncan of Ohio took to the floor of the House to complain of campaign events that were more like "drunken orgies, that would have disgraced a Bacchanalian feast; . . . empty unmeaning pageants; ridiculous displays of log cabins," and other over-the-top displays that were "an insult to every understanding of morality and decency." He then read a poem that started, "What are the principles about which you prate? / I answer, log cabins and pickerel bait."

The Harrison campaign's most lasting linguistic contribution came from one of their circus-like activities. As an ongoing feature of the campaign trail, Whig Party loyalists walked from town to town, rolling ten-foot-high "parade balls" papered over with slogans. As they passed spectators along the road, they rallied the crowds to "keep the ball rolling for Harrison."

The Whigs didn't invent the expression *keep the ball rolling*—the point of the slogan would have been lost if people hadn't already understood its figurative meaning—but their antics ensured it a permanent place in the vocabulary. The most likely origin of the phrase is a game called shinny. Shinny was a popular colonial version of an old European game called bandy, in which a small ball was tossed back and forth or pushed to and fro on the ground (the inspiration for the old expression *to bandy words*). The American version was played with bent sticks, which players used to push a small ball over a frozen pond or field. The rules of shinny called for keeping the ball continuously moving.[29]

Although the popularity of shinny died down by the end of the eighteenth century, *keep the ball rolling* remained part of the American lexicon. By the time of the 1840 campaign, the phrase meant to keep a conversation going or to keep an idea or plan alive. The Harrison slogan alluded to this meaning. By keeping the parade ball rolling, the campaign was reminding voters to keep the momentum going for Harrison.

Parade balls, hard cider, and rousing campaign songs, along with a slumping economy, swept Harrison into the White House. His victory was short lived, however. After delivering a long inauguration speech in the rain, the sixty-eight-year-old Harrison contracted pneumonia and died a month later. The following four years, with the uninspiring John Tyler at the helm, were much quieter than the election had been. Nonetheless, high-voltage campaigning—complete with sensational language—was here to stay.

By the time of the 1840 campaign, the feedback loop that Bartlett noticed—the people to the politicians to the newspapers and back to the people—was well established. Slang and new coinages of all sorts often made their first in-print appearance in a newspaper, but much of the most striking language came from politics. This print megaphone would only get louder in the run-up to the Civil War.

6

American Words in the News

Okay, America's most famous word invention, started out as a newspaper joke. Sometime in 1838, Boston newspapers broke out in a rash of facetious abbreviations. One of the more popular was *s.p.* for *small potatoes*. The *Boston Morning Post*, a leader of the abbreviation fad, if not the instigator, used it frequently, as in "The proceedings were entered on the journal of the House, and reported with great pomposity in the whig papers. S.P. (small potatoes)."[1] Others included *n.g.* for *no go* and *o.f.m.*, a mildly satirical term for the Boston establishment that stood for *our first men*. The strings of letters could get quite elaborate, as in *g.t.d.h.d.—give the devil his due*.

It's hard to imagine finding this type of frivolity in a modern newspaper. Newspapers of the 1830s, however, were more idiosyncratic publications. They were written largely by the editor, who might also be the owner. Besides news items, they carried a mix of advertising, local announcements, political commentary, amusing or improving anecdotes, quirky stories culled from the police court, and whatever other material the editor felt like featuring.

Broad coverage was not a goal. Nor was objective reporting. Most newspapers were frankly committed to one political party or the other, and the editor felt free to put his slant on the news items, as the "small potatoes" remark shows. The founder and editor of the *Morning Post*, Charles G. Greene, was a loyal Democrat who took regular swipes at the Whigs. The built-in snark that came with absurd abbreviations was ideal for this purpose.

Abbreviations appeared most often in political contexts, but not always. For instance, names of cocktails were frequently abbreviated.

The Boston *Columbian Centinel* of June 13, 1838, includes the line, "The Major was in excellent spirits . . . on board the boat. He was refreshed with a G.C. [gin cocktail] on the passage." Common abbreviations like *o.f.m.* or the names of cocktails often appeared without a gloss. They were in-jokes between the editor of the paper and his readers. Less familiar or more intricate strings of letters usually came with an explanation. One example is this phrase from the *Morning Post* of October 1, 1838: "addressing secret circulars to the W.Y.M.O.N.Y. (whig young men of New York)."

Taking the joke a step further, some abbreviations represented comic misspellings meant to convey a nonstandard dialect, such as using *o.w.* to stand for *oll wright.* Humorously misspelled renditions of regional dialects were in vogue at the time. (A typical example comes from a humor essay in the *New York Enquirer* of April 22, 1828: "I'll be hang'd if yew evver ketch me in this kutthrote kuntry agin.") Misspelled abbreviations fit right in with this pattern.

In 1839 the abbreviations joke reached New York. Park Benjamin and Rufus Griswold, editors of the newly founded New York *Evening Tattler*, preferred the comically misspelled version. On July 27, 1839, the editors remarked, "A paper, printed on half a sheet, somewhere near the verge of creation in Illinois, requests us to exchange. K. G. (no go)." They mentioned the subject again on August 5: "A paper in Indiana inquires of us why we will not exchange. Answer K.Y. (no use)." (Newspapers often exchanged subscriptions to keep up with news in other parts of the country.)

Benjamin and Griswold discussed the fad for abbreviations in a commentary of July 1839. Their remarks indicate that the public had not only picked up on "initial language" but also was saying it out loud, just as people today say "lol." The editors explain, "This is a species of spoken short-hand, which is getting into very general use among loafers and gentlemen of the fancy, besides Editors, to whom it saves . . . much trouble in writing." They note that "Charley Greene of the Post always wrote O.F.M. [our first men]." They suggest that their own abbreviations, based on nonstandard spelling, are "more original, richer, and less comprehensible."[2]

Although Benjamin and Griswold apparently hadn't noticed it, Greene had his own nonstandard abbreviation, one that would prove to be much longer lasting than similar coinages in the *Tattler*. It had already appeared in print once or twice when the *Tattler* editors wrote their piece.

O.K., standing for *oll korrect*, made its first known appearance in banter between Greene and his opposite number at the Providence, Rhode Island, *Daily Journal*. The subject concerned the activities of the A.B.R.S., or Anti-Bell-Ringing Society, a spurious organization formed in 1838 to ridicule a Boston ordinance forbidding the ringing of dinner bells. The *Post* reported on the society's meetings, which were conducted by such officers as the "Lord High Chancellor, and Keeper of the Society's Conscience" and the "Chief Butler and Imperturbable Deliberator."

On March 21, 1839, the *Post* reported that the A.B.R.S. was planning to travel to New York for a convention. The following day the *Daily Journal* commented, "Quite an excitement was caused here yesterday, by an announcement in the Boston Post, that a deputation from the Boston A.B.R.S. would pass through the city. . . . The report proved unfounded however."

On March 23, the *Post* responded, "We said not a word about our deputation 'passing through the city' of Providence." However, the editor continued, "The 'Chairman of the Committee on Charity Lecture Bells' is one of the deputation, and perhaps if he should return to Boston, via Providence, he of the Journal . . . would have the *contribution box*, et ceteras, *o.k.*—all correct—and cause the corks to fly, like *sparks*, upward."

After this first appearance, the abbreviation showed up in the *Post* several more times. Two weeks later, in the same jocular vein, the April 10 edition announced, "Mr. Michael Hughes, better known here by his well earned office of 'Magnificent Punch Distiller for the

A.B.R.S.,' has opened a new hotel in New York. . . . It is hardly necessary to say to those who know Mr. Hughes, that his establishment will be found to be 'A. No. One'—that is, O.K.—all correct." On December 18, Greene used the abbreviation without a gloss: "Confucius Roundhead's communications are *all* 'O.K.,' and will appear in a short time." His use of the extra *all* (literally, *all all correct*) suggests that *O.K.* was already starting to be treated like a word in its own right.

Soon *O.K.* was in general circulation. Benjamin and Griswold used it on September 2, 1839, in the announcement of a lecture by British author Thomas Carlyle—"It is O K! all correct!" Papers started using it in nonjoking contexts as well. The theatrical weekly *Paul Pry*, reporting on a benefit for the family of a deceased actor on February 1, 1840, says, "The net proceeds was upward of $1,200, O.K."

By late 1839, the abbreviations craze had caught on around the country. In November of that year, the *Philadelphia Gazette* published a commentary about the "curious short-hand phraseology" circulating on Wall Street. The article lists the abbreviations "O.K.—all correct; I.S.B.D.—it shall be done; A.R. [presumably, all right]; N.S.M.G.—'nuff said 'mong gentlemen."[3] Papers in other cities, such as Chicago and New Orleans, also reported on the common use of abbreviations in writing and speech and noted original coinages like *O.D.V.* for *all done with* (*oll done vith*).

The 1830s were a heyday for lighthearted wordplay. Besides misspellings for comic effect, Americans also enjoyed silly puns ("Why is the city of Boston like a poultry-yard? Because the inhabitants are all City's hens [citizens]!"[4]) and outrageous word inventions like *exflunctify* and *blustiferous*. Most of these coinages, along with most abbreviations, disappeared a few years later when cultural fashions moved on. That would most likely have been the fate of *O.K.*, but politics stepped in.

One tactic of the uproarious 1840 presidential campaign between William Henry Harrison and Martin Van Buren was the creation of nicknames—flattering ones for your own candidate and insults for his opponent. The Whigs called Harrison Old Tip and Old Buckeye, but the Democrats called him Old Tip-ler, a slap at the hard cider theme, and Granny Harrison, the Petticoat General, an allusion to what they considered his less than impressive war service. (Harrison retired from the army before the War of 1812 ended.)

The Whigs retaliated by calling Van Buren Martin Van Ruin, because of his supposed extravagance; Little Matty, because of his short stature; and the Red Fox of Kinderhook, because of his red hair and reputed slyness. In another sneer at Van Buren's birthplace, the Whigs also named him the Kinderhook Cabbage Planter. The Democrats turned the tables by proudly emphasizing Van Buren's connection to the town with the nickname Old Kinderhook.

To further drum up enthusiasm, the Democrats organized pro–Van Buren social clubs. Probably at the suggestion of some alert campaign operative, the party took advantage of the coincidence between the slang term *O.K.* and the initial letters of Old Kinderhook and called them O.K. Clubs. A paid advertisement in the New York *New Era* for March 11, 1840, announced the first meeting: "The Democratic O.K. Club are hereby ordered to meet at the house of Jacob Colvin. . . . Punctual attendance is requested."

Democrats adopted the catchy new slogan enthusiastically. "Old Kinderhook is O.K.!" they cried. They marched with banners floating the letters *O.K.* and ran ads that said, "O.K. / Old Kinderhook / New York's favorite son." They published an O.K. songbook. The party encouraged voters to choose the Democratic ticket by asking, "Will you not say O.K.?" In the end, Old Kinderhook went down to defeat, but by that time, *O.K.* was a familiar term to all Americans.

In the decade or so after the 1840 election, *O.K.* made only sporadic appearances in print. Bartlett doesn't include it in any edition of his dictionary, which suggests that he didn't find it in the sources he reviewed or that he considered it too ephemeral for inclusion or, as an abbreviation, not suitable. Still, it continued to pop up here and there, usually in stories with a humorous slant. Gradually, it evolved from a joke abbreviation to an ordinary, if slangy, word.

This 1840 anti–Van Buren cartoon incorporates *OK* into a signpost pointing the president back to his hometown of Kinderhook, as former president Andrew Jackson pulls him toward the White House. Captioned A HARD ROW TO HOE, the cartoon also points out the obstacles in the way of Van Buren's reelection, including hard cider, log cabins, and a bundle of financial troubles labeled SUB TREASURY. *Prints and Photographs Division: Library of Congress, LC-USZ62-9463*

During the 1850s, the periods after each letter were often dropped, obscuring the word's origin. By the end of the nineteenth century, it was sometimes spelled *okay*, making it look even more like a regular English word. The adjective *okay*, as in *an okay time*, appeared in print in the 1870s, and the verb *to okay* was in use by the 1880s. The 1930s saw *okey-dokey* and the 1960s *A-OK*.[5]

By the twentieth century, even the English had adopted it, although not without the usual moans about Americanisms. Laments one letter to the editor in 1954, "'All right' has already virtually disappeared from our language, killed by the monstrosity 'O.K.'"[6] Complaints, as always, were in vain. As with other useful Americanisms, once *okay* gained a toehold, it was in the language to stay. Strict parents, teachers, and copyeditors on both sides of the Atlantic fought the battle for *all right* into the late twentieth century, but *okay* only gained in popularity. In fact, it's so handy as a casual affirmative that languages around the world have embraced it—a newsworthy achievement for a linguistic joke.

While *okay* is probably the only editorial creation that reached the status of worldwide icon, newspapers by the mid-nineteenth century were a hothouse for colloquial language and slang. Americans read newspapers right from the country's beginnings. During the 1790s around 260 newspapers were being printed, mostly weeklies.[7] Nearly every town of any size had at least one. Early newspapers didn't circulate very widely. They were sold by yearly subscription at a price that put them beyond the reach of most working-class people, who usually had to share a subscription or read the copies available at coffeehouses and taverns.

Nor were early newspapers geared to a mass audience. Many were primarily advertising vehicles. (The word *Advertiser* figures in the title of quite a few colonial papers.) Many others were founded as organs of one political faction or another and devoted much of their content to pushing the party line. Newspaper essays and letters to the editor were effective ways for early politicians to get out their message and for warring factions to hash out the issues of the day.

Aside from political feuds, early American papers tended to be on the staid side. Unlike today's newspapers, they didn't lead with breaking news—before the telegraph, word traveled too slowly for that. Whether "advertisers" or not, newspapers typically covered the first of their four oversize pages with brief classified ads. Their other content was equally dry and mainly of interest to businesspeople—for instance, announcements of ships' arrivals.

This situation changed dramatically with the advent of the penny papers. During the 1830s, advances in printing technology made high-volume newspaper printing feasible for the first time. The first successful penny paper was the New York *Sun*, founded in 1833 by a young printer named Benjamin Day. Unlike traditional papers, the *Sun* was published daily and it didn't require a subscription. Rather, a small army of vendors—mostly young boys called newsies—hawked it on the street for a penny a copy, about one-sixth of a traditional newspaper's price.

Day's inspired idea was to provide information that appealed to a broad range of readers. He printed a lively mix of brief news items, human interest stories, amusing facts, political scandals, and advertising directed to "every man." Items appeared in no particular order. Ads for elocution lessons or cure-all pills jostled against the activities of the state legislature, verbatim court reports, love poems, announcements of recent theater openings, and general-interest essays on topics such as the history of the pyramids. The *Sun*'s motto was IT SHINES FOR ALL.

Day's paper was an immediate success. Soon others were copying his formula. Cheap daily papers sprang up in all the large cities along the coast. By 1835, about twelve hundred newspapers were being printed around the country. By 1860 there were about three thousand, and circulation was booming.[8] One of the first to adopt Day's model was James Gordon Bennett, a Scottish immigrant with previous journalism experience, who founded the *New York Herald* in 1835. Bartlett relied heavily on the *Herald* when collecting Americanisms for his dictionary.

Bennett improved on Day's template by combining sensational news stories and titillating court cases with the kind of financial and political information that traditional newspaper readers wanted. He also sprinkled the paper with miscellaneous tidbits that amused casual readers. The *Herald* of September 17, 1835, includes the news that a boat race will take place that afternoon at Castle Garden; that the Colonization Society recently collected $10,000; that France is becoming "more despotic than it was under Napoleon"; and that yellow fever has broken out in Charleston, South Carolina. It also includes an appeal to "decent country newspapers" to quit printing stories about the recently unelected "zany Davy Crockett." Says the editor, "He is dished. Let him be forgot."

Bennett claimed to be committed to no party. Writing in an early issue, he declares his intention to "candidly express our opinion on every public question and every public man."[9] He hired reporters to cover Congress and send back daily reports. His sympathies tended to be with the Democrats, but he lambasted politicians of every stripe.

In this respect, he agreed with his rival, Horace Greeley of the *New-York Tribune*, which first hit the streets on April 10, 1841. Greeley got his start as the editor of William Henry Harrison's campaign paper, the *Log Cabin*. He insisted, however, that his paper would not be the mouthpiece of any party. His goal was to engage and enlighten his readers on the serious topics of the day, including abolition, the temperance movement, and other social issues. In order to sell papers, he also covered the same eyebrow-raising stories as the *Herald*. The *Tribune*, like the *Herald*, was important for Bartlett's word collecting.

The penny dailies favored a breezy tone and casual vocabulary. To connect with their mass audience, they made lavish use of punchy verbs like *back out*, *let up*, *go in for*, *cave in*, *chisel* (cheat), and *flummox* (confuse), and colloquialisms like *nary a one* and *not worth shucks*. Sometimes they made up words like *concededly* and *go-aheadativeness*. Journalists added snap to their articles with pithy expressions such as *make the fur fly*, *put the fat in the fire*, and *keep your eye peeled*. They adopted popular nonsense words, such as the now obsolete *absquatulate*, meaning to clear out in a hurry.

The *Sun*, the *Herald*, and other early penny papers pioneered this style, but papers around the country followed their lead. The *Cincinnati Daily Gazette* reached for sensational rhetoric when editorializing about conflict in Congress: "The *factious* and *revolutionary* action of the fifteen has . . . *fizzled out!*" The *New-York Commercial*

Advertiser reported that, owing to a bad storm, mail delivery had been "knocked into a cocked hat." Describing a weather disaster in Illinois, the *Chicago Tribune* told its readers that "the wind carried away the roof slick as a whistle." A headline in the *Oregon Weekly Times* asked, "The Music—Why Not Face It?"

The slang word *bogus* is one example of a word introduced to the general public through many newspaper mentions. The origin of the word is obscure, but its first known use is as a term for an apparatus that makes counterfeit coins. The earliest known mention is in the *Painesville Telegraph* of Ohio. Their July 6, 1827, edition includes the line, "He never procured the casting of a Bogus at one of our furnaces." The meaning of *bogus* shifted after a while to refer to the counterfeit money itself. Bartlett defines *bogus money* as "counterfeit silver coin" and notes that large quantities circulated in the West during the 1840s. Many early examples with this changed meaning also appeared in newspapers.

Gradually, the meaning of the word broadened to refer to anything fake or sham. It would have been in common circulation by the time the *Boston Daily Courier* of June 12, 1857, reported that a stiff-necked "learned Judge took occasion to manifest his abhorrence of the use of slang phrases . . . by saying that he did not know the meaning of 'bogus transactions.'"

The penny papers also introduced Wall Street jargon to a wider audience. They kept readers up to date on the highs and lows of the market, as well as investigating possible fraud and suspicious activities. Terms like *bulls* and *bears* (buyers and sellers), *lame ducks* (investors who can't pay for their losses), *fancy stocks* (stocks bought and sold blind), and *take a flier* (speculate on stocks) became familiar even to noninvestors once the dailies started reporting on them.

An Americanism that gained wider currency through frequent newspaper discussions was the term *corner*, meaning to gain control of a certain commodity or stock. For example, an exposé article in the *New York Herald* for August 31, 1835, draws attention to recent attempts to "corner the market" and questions their legality. *Corner* was used as both a noun and a verb. "The Erie Rail-road cornering has been a very unfortunate affair," commented the *Herald* on one occasion. As with *bogus*, the meaning of the word later expanded, so it's now possible to make a corner in all kinds of things, including abstract areas like knowledge.

Newspapers often took a jaunty tone with their Wall Street reporting, as they did with most subjects. The *New-York Tribune* complains that "every week-day morning, between 9 and 11, certain bulls and bears do congregate upon the sidewalk, on the northerly side of Wall street. . . . The prayer is 'that the nuisance may be abated.'"[10] This type of language was a far cry from the stuffy, unadorned business reporting provided by old-fashioned newspapers. Even people without the means or desire to "take a flier" could now get amusement out of the financial news.

For the first time, Americans could also catch up on pop culture by reading the papers. The fad for wearing bloomers—loose, billowing women's trousers that gathered at the ankle—would have been beneath the notice of traditional newspapers. For the penny papers, it made excellent copy. The *Boston Evening Transcript* gave a detailed description of a *bloomer suit* in the May 26, 1851, edition: "A young lady of 18 . . . made her appearance on Cambridge Street, accompanied with her father, dressed in a round hat, short dress, fitting tightly, and pink satin trousers." The *St. Louis Daily Morning Herald* of April 12, 1853, applied the new word to the wearer, saying, "A Bloomer was seen in Cleveland the other day. Her skirts were unusually short." (Early mentions usually capitalize the word because the outfit was named after Amelia Bloomer, editor of the magazine the *Lily*, which first featured illustrations of the new look.)

Much of the language of the penny dailies was borrowed from the frontier speech starting to drift back east. The papers picked up western slang like *get the drop on* and *sidewinder*. The *Charleston Mercury* sounded like Nimrod Wildfire when it reported, "In this debate, Mr. B. was 'catawamptiously chawed up.'"[11] Once words like *caterwaul* and *greased lightning* appeared in the papers, they became part of the national speech.

The newspapers got some of their best material from politics. Congressmen, stump speakers, and politicians generally were prone to colloquial speech. Many of the same slang words and expressions that are recorded in the *Congressional Globe* also appeared in the newspapers, giving them wider exposure among people who might be only casually interested in the machinations of government.

Both congressmen and newspaper writers talked about politicians *bolting*, or going against their party. Rep. Wentworth of Illinois was recorded in the February 4, 1847, *Congressional Globe* as declaring, "I said that I had never bolted a regular nomination of the Democratic Party." Both also referred to loyal Democrats as *dyed in the wool.* The *Herald* revealed on June 30, 1846, that Sen. Pickens of South Carolina was "a real red-hot Democrat, dyed in the wool."

Sometime around the 1830s the word *cahoot* started to appear in both places. According to Bartlett's dictionary, it was a western word that denoted "a company or union of men for a predatory excursion, and sometimes for a partnership in business." It may have come from *cohorte*, a French word for a group of people with a common purpose. Being *in cahoot* could be neutral—simply a partnership—but more often it was given the predatory meaning.

The term made one of its earliest appearances in the *Congressional Globe* of March 4, 1839, in the record of a speech by Rep. Duncan of Ohio. Duncan used it to suggest nefarious collusion on the part of two colleagues. "Only think of this!" he cried, "A rank Abolition Whig from the North in 'cahoot' with a rank anti-Abolition Whig from the South!"

A whiff of the negative hangs around most newspaper uses of the term as well. The May 28, 1846, *Oregon Spectator* paraphrased a stump speech as, "Who wants a parcel of low-flung barbarians to go in cahoot with us?" The *Herald* for May 20, 1857, used the word as a verb in the sentence, "They all agree to cahoot with the claims against Nicaragua and Costa Rica." In the late nineteenth century, the plural *cahoots* started to come into fashion.

The newspapers looked to current slang to express their opinions about political goings-on. A *Tribune* editor followed the American habit of softening "swear" words when he replaced the American coinage *cursed* with *cussed*, writing, "The Constitution is about to be used once more by the Democrats as a screen for pure cussedness." The paper used *gouge* in the newly invented sense of a figurative scooping out: "There is a clear, plain gouge out of the people's strong box." On a more positive note, the *Herald* thought that "General Cass is some pumpkins, and will do the needful in the office line, if he is elected."[12] *Some pumpkins* was a frivolous way of describing someone important or impressive—the opposite of *small potatoes*.

When Bartlett published his dictionary, the Civil War was still more than a decade in the future, but political battle lines were already being drawn. He collected several party or factional nicknames from the newspapers. Although now obsolete, they show how the popular papers shaped the language of the conflict. When Bartlett published his fourth edition in 1877, he added many more Civil War–related words.

During the 1830s and '40s, ardent abolitionists remained in a minority, but more Northerners opposed the spread of slavery into new states and territories. Southerners responded by becoming more implacably in favor of it. *Abolition*, meaning the process of doing away with something, had been an English word for centuries, but the meaning narrowed in the United States to mean doing away with slavery. The verb *abolitionize* was an American creation, appearing in congressional speeches and newspaper stories by the mid-1830s.

Whenever the United States acquired new territory, a fight broke out over whether or not slavery should be allowed there. The Missouri Compromise of 1820 had temporarily solved the problem by splitting the Louisiana Purchase into slave and free sections. However, as the country reached west and south beyond the borders of the

Louisiana Territory, the compromise didn't apply. By the end of the Mexican-American War in 1848, when Mexico ceded territory that would eventually be carved into several states, the issue had become highly inflammatory.

While Southern politicians were united in their commitment to slavery, political parties in the North split along various lines. Some of the offshoot parties acquired imaginative nicknames that were quickly taken up by the newspapers. The Democratic Party in the North divided into a progressive antislavery wing called *Barnburners* and a more conservative wing called *Old Hunkers*, or just *Hunkers*. The Barnburners were given their label by an old-fashioned Tammany Hall Democrat, who reportedly said, "These men are incendiaries; they are mad; they are like the farmer, who to get the rats out of his granary, sets fire to his own barn."[13]

The Barnburners responded by calling more conservative Democrats Old Hunkers. Hunkers were officially neutral on the slavery question and often voted with Southerners for the sake of party unity. *Hunker* may have been meant to suggest that the conservatives liked to hunker down and keep quiet for the sake of retaining their privileged positions in Congress. Another possibility is that the word came from the Dutch *honk*, the word for home base during a game of tag. Either derivation would have applied nicely to the Hunkers, who reached their congressional home base and hunkered down there.

Both parties petered out before the Civil War. However, the term *barn burner* has stayed around as a term for a sensational or exciting event—for instance, "The final game of the series was a real barn burner."

In the 1850s, the Barnburners and Hunkers morphed into the politically rigid Hardshells and the more moderate Softshells. Like Barnburners and Hunkers, Hardshells and Softshells lasted only until the eve of the war, but the terms have since been used to distinguish between extreme and moderate positions. One example is hard-shell and soft-shell Baptists, the latter being more socially liberal.

Other similar words occasionally appeared in the papers. *Doughface* was an insulting term for a Northerner who sympathized with slaveholders. A real "doughface" was a mask made of dough or papier-mâché that schoolchildren wore to scare each other on Halloween. During a debate over the 1820 Missouri Compromise, Virginia congressman John Randolph used the word while expressing his contempt for the Northern Democrats who voted with the South to make the compromise possible. "I knew these men would give way," sneered Randolph, "they were scared at their own dough-faces."[14]

The chivalry was a dismissive way of referring to Southern men, probably a reference to their supposed reverence for the "gentlemen's

President Abraham Lincoln was one of many politicians who wore stovepipe hats. This 1862 photograph by Alexander Gardner shows the president at Antietam, Maryland, with Allan Pinkerton (founder of the Pinkerton National Detective Agency) and Maj. Gen. John A. McClernand. *Prints and Photographs Division: Library of Congress, LC-DIG-cwpb-04326*

code" of behavior. *Stovepipe hats* were conventional members of any party. Literal stovepipe hats were top hats, so named for their resemblance to a length of stovepipe, the straight-sided pipe attached to a woodstove.

One Democratic faction was nicknamed directly by the newspapers. Around 1835, radical Democrats organized as the Equal Rights Party. Equal Righters were against monopolies and paper money and in favor of labor unions, hard currency, and equal rights for all Americans, which meant they were opposed to slavery. They inevitably clashed with the conservative Tammany Democrats.

On one memorable night in November 1835, New York Democrats converged on Tammany Hall to nominate candidates for an upcoming local election. Both sides arrived early, determined to fight for control of the meeting. As soon as the doors opened, a crowd of Equal Rights people rushed up the front stairs to the meeting room, while the Tammanies galloped up the back stairs. According to one witness, "a tumultuous and confused scene ensued." Amid the chaos, the gas lamps in the room were suddenly extinguished.

Either because such things had happened before or because they were forewarned, each Equal Righter had provided himself with a candle and a recently patented self-igniting match that went by the brand name *Loco-Foco*. The name may have been based on the Latin *locus focus*, meaning something like "fire in place," or the Spanish *loco fuego*, "crazy fire." The Equal Righters quickly lit the candles and were able to continue with the meeting. In the end, the Tammany slate won out, but not without a boisterous argument from their opponents.

The next day, when the story of the ruckus got out, two papers, the Whig *Courier and Enquirer* and the Democratic *Times*, immediately dubbed the Equal Rights Party *Locofocos*. Whatever the origin of the brand name, the coincidence between the first part of it and the Spanish word for *crazy* was too tempting to ignore. The Whigs then took the name a step further. They started calling all Democrats Locofocos, with the evident idea that they were all equally insane.[15]

The penny papers introduced the reading public to a slew of new Americanisms, including street slang and westernisms, which of course brought them under fire from language purists. Newspapers were being criticized for their word use even before the days of the popular press. John Pickering, who published his collection of Americanisms in 1816, considered newspapers vectors of bad English. Although Pickering doesn't address the issue directly, he frequently says that a word or usage is found only in the newspapers as a way of arguing that it's not an accepted word.

When he talks about the nonstandard use of *captivate* to mean *capture*, he says that a few British writers have pointed to it as an example of bad American usage, but he has never seen it in print, "even in our newspapers." Of the oddity *anxietude* (probably meaning *anxiety*), he says, "I never saw this word but once in any of our publications; and that was only in a newspaper." He points out that the American verb creation *notify* is mainly found in newspaper announcements.

Even Bartlett, who collected dozens, if not hundreds, of words from the newspapers, sometimes criticized the papers' casual way with English. He notes in his introduction that all newspapers use colloquial words and phrases, and admits that "there seems no other way of expressing certain ideas connected with passing events of every day life, with the requisite force and piquancy."[16] Yet, like Pickering, he points to newspaper use as evidence of a word's problematic status. He complains in his 1859 edition about *first* to mean a single one, as in "I won't pay you the first penny." He says it's "an absurd use . . . which has recently crept into the newspapers." He calls *stay put*, which appeared in the *New Orleans Picayune*, "a vulgar expression."

Later nineteenth-century language commentators also blamed the popular papers for the bad English that circulated. The language critic Edward Gould, author of *Good English*, writes, "Those who do the most mischief are . . . the men generally who write for the newspapers."

He proves his point by quoting from newspapers for at least half his examples of mistaken usage. Richard Grant White, who wrote the advice book *Words and Their Uses*, wrote for the newspapers himself. Nonetheless, he tells readers that to find examples of bad English, "we must go to the newspaper press."[17]

Newspaper writers, especially ad writers, used racy slang, such as *fork over* and *sound as a nut*. They also liked to shorten words for added zing. Two that critics frequently complained about are *pants* and *gents*. *Gents* was short for *gentlemen* but suggested men who really didn't deserve that title, as when the *Rocky Mountain News* for January 29, 1863, mentioned "gents about town." *Pants* was originally a shortening of *pantaloons*. During the 1830s, it started to mean trousers of any type. Several writers suggested that *gents* and *pants* went together—the one always wore the other.

Newspapers sometimes dropped whole words, such as saying *governments* when they meant *government securities*. They also chopped off words. They used *enthuse* to mean create enthusiasm and *donate* to mean make a donation. Bartlett comments in his entry for the word that it is "not in the dictionaries, but has only reached the newspapers and reviews."

Newspaper writers were also fond of that traditional American method of coining new words by adding *-ize*—for instance, *localize*, *itemize*, *deputize*. The word *jeopardize* was especially annoying to critics. Formed from the now obsolete verb *jeopard*, meaning to put at risk, it was rejected by traditionalists until the end of the nineteenth century. Pickering notes it in his collection of Americanisms and assigns blame to the unholy alliance of politicians and newspaper editors. He says, "This verb is often seen in the Debates of Congress, as they are reported in the newspapers."

Besides criticizing the popular press for their affinity with slang and off-the-cuff word creation, language sticklers disliked the pompous and extravagant vocabulary that journalists often indulged in. "We never eat, but always partake," writes one critic, "We never hear of a place; it is always a locality. . . . No man ever shows any feeling, but always evinces it."[18] White titled his chapter on newspaper English "Big Words for Small Thoughts." Newspapers used *inaugurate* for *start*, *lethal* for *deadly*, *commence* for *begin*, and *apprehend* for *think* or *believe*. They also employed euphemisms. They called a coffin a *casket*, legs *limbs*, and heaven *the place where all good men go when they die*.

Newspapers seemed to go out of their way to avoid straightforward language. Writing about a murder scene, one journalist reported that "a policeman went to [the culprit's] residence, and there secured the clothes that he wore when he committed the murderous deed." He found that "they were so smeared by blood as to incarnadine the water in which they were deposited."[19]

Bartlett offers some excellent examples of the purple prose favored by newspapers. He quotes a Springfield, Illinois, newspaper review of a singer who performed in that city: "Illumined by the lyric muse, she is magnificent. All nerve, all palpitation, her rounded form is the fittest setting for her diamond soul!" Borrowing a westernism from his own dictionary, Bartlett calls this style "highfaluten."[20]

Even as critics of the newspapers worried that American English was becoming adulterated beyond repair, others were working to give it greater respectability. Noah Webster was one such person. Undeterred by the hostile reception of his 1806 dictionary, he immediately started on a new and improved version. When it finally appeared in 1828, both the English and the Americans hailed it as an impressive achievement. At the same time, the books of Washington Irving were making Americans proud and helping convince the English that maybe the United States did have some literature worth reading.

7

American English Takes Its Station

Toward the end of October 1827, about a year before Noah Webster's second dictionary appeared, he had a conversation about American English with a British visitor named Basil Hall. Hall, a former officer of the Royal Navy from Scotland, was traveling around the eastern United States when the two were introduced at an evening party in New Haven. Because Hall knew that Webster was completing a dictionary, the talk turned to Americanisms.

Hall was surprised by Webster's insistence that Americans had both a right and a positive duty to create new words. While he accepted that a new word was occasionally required—say, *possum* or *tobacco*—he didn't think an Americanism should enter English if there was a preexisting term that meant the same thing. Webster countered by pointing out that it's nearly impossible to stop the progress of language. Drawing on a very American image, he said, "It is like the course of the Mississippi, the motion of which, at times, is scarcely perceptible, yet . . . quite irresistible. . . . Words and expressions will be forced into use, in spite of all the exertions of all the writers in the world." To him, Americanisms were a good thing but also inevitable.

Hall remained unconvinced. "Surely," he asked, "such innovations are to be deprecated?"

"I don't know that," replied Webster. "If a word become universally current in America, where English is spoken, why should it not take its station in the language?"

"Because," cried Hall, "there are words enough already."

Webster disagreed. He thought there was room in the language for "every English word in general use," he told Hall, whether originating in the new country or the old.[1]

Webster tactfully didn't mention that one of his main purposes in compiling a comprehensive record of American words was to free his fellow citizens from the straitjacket of British English. In the early days of the republic, he had championed a "Federal language." More

"Noah Webster." This portrait of Webster by Samuel F. B. Morse is undated but was probably completed in 1823, about five years before the publication of the *American Dictionary of the English Language*. *Courtesy of the Beinecke Rare Book and Manuscript Library, Yale University*

than thirty years later, he still believed that American speech standards should be based on the way Americans themselves talked.

As far as Webster was concerned, it was time for American words to take their station. With his second dictionary, he aimed to provide the most thorough, consistent, and accurate record of American English possible, a stunningly ambitious project that would take him the best part of twenty years to complete. When he finished, he would discover that the world had changed and views like Hall's were less common. The tide of linguistic opinion was shifting on both sides of the Atlantic. Webster's new dictionary added momentum to that trend.

One reason that the 1828 *American Dictionary of the English Language* took a long time to write was that Webster couldn't afford to spend all his time on scholarship. To earn an income for himself and his large family, he worked at a variety of jobs. He practiced law in Hartford for several years, edited a Federalist newspaper for a time, and wrote books and articles about topics other than American English, including a guide to infectious diseases. He was also active in politics.

A bigger reason why the work took so long to complete was the staggering amount of research involved. Shortly after beginning the dictionary, Webster decided that listing words and their definitions wasn't enough. He also needed to explore the origins of English to provide suitable word histories. His research on that topic took ten years—half the total time that he spent on the entire dictionary.

Webster's 1828 dictionary was a colossal achievement. It encompassed seventy thousand words, including twelve thousand not found in any previous dictionary, plus between thirty and forty thousand new definitions. (Webster may have been thinking about these numbers when he contradicted Hall's assertion that there were already enough words.) The front matter of the book included a history of the English language, a discussion of pronunciation, and the complete text of a grammar of English that Webster had written in 1807.[2]

In the preface, Webster reiterates his reasons for writing a comprehensive dictionary specifically for Americans. "It is not only important, but in a degree necessary," he says, "that the people of this country should have an *American Dictionary* of the English language; for, although the body of the language is the same as in England, . . . yet some differences must exist."[3] Americans lived in a different physical environment, besides having their own form of government and different laws and customs.

Webster gives several examples of institutional terms that aren't current in England or are used there with a different meaning—*land office, plantation, regent* (of a university). He thinks defining government words for Americans is especially important: "No person in this country will be satisfied with the English definitions of the words *congress, senate*, and *assembly*." Even when the words essentially refer to the same thing, as in *justice of the peace*, the definitions can't be exactly the same. In England, a justice is appointed by the king and has the title of *Lord*. The United States doesn't have a king or noble titles.

To emphasize his American perspective, Webster used American literary examples for his entries. He felt "pride and satisfaction" at being able to replace the names of Milton, Dryden, and other famous English authors (which Samuel Johnson's dictionary included) with those of Franklin, Adams, Jefferson, Washington Irving, and others.

The 1828 dictionary featured several of the same spelling innovations that had appeared in Webster's 1806 dictionary—simplifying *ck* to *c* in words like *musick*, dropping the *u* from words like *favour*, and flipping *re* to *er* in words like *centre*. All these were widely accepted by now. Webster also kept some of his more radical respellings, such as *aker* (*acre*), *tung* (*tongue*), *fether* (*feather*), and *ieland* (*island*).

Webster wrapped up the preface by imagining a time in the near future when the country would be populated with "*three hundred millions*" of English-speaking people—many more than in England. He wanted them to have a reliable record of the vernacular. He collected all the word creations, borrowings, changed meanings, and other linguistic remodelings that Americans had contributed to English and treated them like real words for the first time. Twenty years later, when Bartlett was finishing up his own dictionary, Webster remained the most complete source for American words.

Most of the earliest Americanisms found a place in Webster's *American Dictionary*—*raccoon, woodchuck, persimmon, moose, tomahawk.* (Strangely, *opossum* is not listed, although Webster used it in definitions—for example, in the entry for *marmot.*) Many of these and other Americanisms were carried over from the 1806 dictionary, but Webster added words as well. For instance, terms that his friend Samuel Latham Mitchill had pointed out were missing from the 1806 dictionary, such as *terrapin*, *yellow fever*, and *papoose* (spelled *pappoos*), are included in the 1828 edition. He also included the word *Americanism* itself, which he defines as both a pro-American feeling ("the love which American citizens have to their own country") and a word for "an American idiom." He also recorded *Americanize*, "to render American."

Words that mean something different in the United States and England are given both definitions. Under *bug*, Webster starts with the American usage: "In common language, the name of a vast multitude of insects." Then he goes on to note that in zoology, the word refers to the genus *Cimex*, or bedbugs—the British meaning. He provides a detailed description of the differences between a swamp in the United States and England. In England it applies to "boggy land" or "marshy ground," but in America it applies to "low, soft ground" that isn't covered with water. Webster also includes the verb *to swamp* and notes its figurative meaning of "plunge into difficulties."

The entries for *corn* take up almost two columns. Webster gives both the British sense—the seed of various grains—and the American sense—maize, or Indian corn. (*Indian corn* also gets its own entry.) American corn-related words that he lists include *corn blade, corn chandler* (a dealer in corn), *corn cutter*, *corn field*, *corn loft* (a granary), and *corn stalk*. He also includes *cob*, as in *corn cob*, and the now obsolete *bread corn*, corn used for making bread.

Powwow and *caucus* both occur in the dictionary, but only *caucus* has a political definition ("a meeting of citizens to agree upon candidates"). Webster says that the origin is unknown—its probable derivation from Algonquian wasn't recognized until later. *Powwow*, on the other hand, is defined only in its Native American meanings—"an Indian dance; also a priest." There is no mention of politicians holding powwows. Neither word is listed as a verb, although both were already being used that way.

Among other political words that took their place in the dictionary are *senate*, *congress*, *census* with its American meaning, and the new adjectives *congressional* and *governmental*. Webster gives all the political and nonpolitical definitions of *constitution* but specifically mentions the American form of government, writing, "In the United States, the legislature is created, and its powers designated, by the constitution." He also includes the new offshoots *constitutional* and *constitutionality*. He includes the new verbs *revolutionize*, *legislate*, and *electioneer*, as well as *electioneering*.

Many of the newly formed verbs ending in *-ize* or *-ate* that so annoyed British critics are found in the dictionary. These include *obligate*, *eventuate*, *appreciate* in the value sense, *advocate*, *deputize*, *antagonize*, and *citizenize*. Webster also includes *jeopardize*, although he obviously doesn't like it. In brackets he tells the reader, "This is a modern word, used by respectable writers in America, but synonymous with *jeopard* and therefore useless." Its use by respectable writers was enough to win it a place, regardless of Webster's personal feelings.

Other verbs found in Webster's dictionary include the Americanisms *to progress*, *to deed*, *to ambition*, *raise* in the agricultural sense, and *calculate* to mean reckon or guess. *Demoralize*, the word Webster claimed to have invented, is there with its original definition of weakening someone's morals but not with the later sense of undermining morale.

He gives the many American definitions of *fix*—"to put in order; to prepare; to adjust; to set or place in the manner desired . . . as to fix clothes or dress."

Belittle did not make it into the first edition of the dictionary, possibly because Webster thought it wasn't established enough. It does appear in later editions but is described as a rarely used word. It was apparently slow to catch on. Bartlett also treats the word as rare in the 1848 edition of his dictionary, but by the 1877 edition gives the modern definition of speaking of a person or thing "in a contemptuous way," along with several in-print examples.

Lengthy, the coinage that caused so much heartburn for both American and British language critics, is also listed. Webster says it applies "*mostly to moral subjects*, . . . as a *lengthy sermon*." He doesn't mention its iffy status. He gives several examples of its use, taken from both Americans (Washington) and English writers (Lord Byron), which seems to be an indirect rebuttal of the critics.

A handful of slang also ended up in the dictionary. Under *change*, Webster included the new phrase *change of heart*. He listed the vulgarisms *chaw* and *boost*, the jargon term *jail-bird*, and the New England regionalism *spry*. He allowed the expressions *let rip*, *clip someone over the head*, and *stump one's toe*. He also included *ain't*, spelled *ant*, but with a diacritic over the *a* indicating that it should be pronounced as a long vowel, like modern *ain't*. He describes the word as a contraction of some form of the verb *be* and *not* "in the vulgar dialect." He defends the form by saying that it is the "legitimate remains" of an Old English word.

Webster's scope went far beyond American words and usages. His dictionary offers a detailed portrait of the English language as it stood at the time. Most of the words Webster recorded weren't new, and many of the new terms weren't strictly Americanisms. He cast a wide research net, scooping up thousands of words that were used in both the United States and England but hadn't yet been captured in any other dictionary. By collecting words from a wide variety of sources, he provided a service to British as well as American English speakers.

One important category was technical and scientific terms. Webster says in his preface that one of his motivations for writing the dictionary was the "almost insuperable difficulties" he had when trying to understand the new words that appeared constantly in science books and journals. He included what he estimated to be no fewer than four thousand such terms not defined anywhere else. Although the majority are not Americanisms, thanks to Webster they were recorded in the United States first.

The results form a kind of verbal time capsule of scientific discovery and invention in the early nineteenth century. Many of the words he collected are now obsolete or rarely used because either science or the language has moved on. Examples include *siderite* (any of several plants with curative properties), *monogam* (a plant with a simple flower), *ichthyolite* (a fossil fish or the impression of one in rock), *conglutinant* (a medicine that heals wounds), *etherizing* (converting into ether), and *dynameter* (instrument for measuring the power of a telescope, also called a *dynamometer*).

Other words collected from the physical sciences are still familiar. These include *sulphuric*, *nitric*, *gaseous*, *phosphorescent*, *isomorph*, *disaggregate*, and *mineralogical*. Webster also recorded words for natural phenomena, like *iceberg* and *glacier*, and words for inventions, like *parachute* and *safety-valve*. New scientific verbs include *magnetize*, *oxidize*, and *quarantine*.

For some scientific words, Webster added new meanings that originated in the United States. For instance, *mammoth* first designated a large prehistoric animal found on the European continent. Webster added the information that it could also refer to the extinct North American mammal otherwise known as a mastodon. (He lists *mastodon* as well, a "mammiferous animal . . . known only by [its] fossil remains.")

In some cases, Webster added new forms to existing words. *Herpetology* and *taxidermy* were well-known English words, but Webster also recorded *herpetologist*, *herpetological*, and *taxidermist*. He noted that *lubricant* could be a noun as well as an adjective and added the meaning of *viable* that refers to a premature infant capable of surviving. He added *meteoric* in the literal sense of relating to meteors. Although the metaphorical sense (*a meteoric career*) appears in print beginning around 1800, it didn't make it into the dictionary.

Fittingly, he recorded the new word *lexicology*—meaning "the science of words"—culled from a scientific journal called the *Medical Repository*. He notes that the word comes from *lexicon*, Greek for a dictionary or word list. He also listed the older words *lexicography*, "the act of writing a lexicon or dictionary," and *lexicographer*, "the author of a lexicon or dictionary." (Webster resisted the temptation to make a joke, as Johnson had when he defined a lexicographer as a "harmless drudge.")

Webster also added a number of legal terms to the dictionary, and here he was helped by his legal training. He noticed that Johnson's dictionary confused certain terms, for instance the difference between *theft* and *robbery* and between *burglary* and *house-breaking*. Webster clarified the distinctions. He defines *theft* as the unlawful taking of another person's goods without the owner's knowledge. *Robbery*, by contrast, is the violent taking of someone's goods from his or her person. Likewise, *house-breaking* takes place during daylight hours, while *burglary* takes place at night. (Since Webster's day the definition of *burglary* has changed. It can now take place at any hour.) He also included up-to-date definitions for such words as *grand jury*, *indictment*, and *appeal* in the legal sense.[4]

Webster brought many older words up to date. In Johnson's 1755 dictionary, *notary* was defined as an officer who took notes, *investment* meant putting on clothes, and a *celebrity* was a splendid public ritual. Webster's dictionary added the modern definitions. Other words that changed their meaning between Johnson's dictionary and Webster's include *donation*, which now referred to the item given, as well as the act of giving; *speculate*, which had gained a financial sense; *muscular*, which could mean strong as well as referring to a muscle; and *original* to mean capable of new ideas as well as its earlier meaning of *first*.

Webster tried to make the entries as full as possible. Rather than simply listing synonyms, he gave detailed explanations, along with illustrative examples. The noun *disease*, for instance, lists five meanings. The main one is sickness or physical disorder, but he also gives the obsolete meaning of uneasiness (*dis* + *ease*) and the additional definitions of a disordered mental state, a moral vice, and political or civil disorder. (The last meaning relies on a quotation from James Madison, referring to "instability, injustice, and confusion" as "mortal diseases" of popular governments.)

The final word of Webster's dictionary is one last scientific term—*zygomatic*, "pertaining to a bone in the head." He finished writing that definition sometime in January 1825 while in Cambridge, England.[5] In his quest for thoroughness, Webster had traveled to England to consult the great libraries there and make sure the information in the dictionary was as up to date as possible. He also wanted to compare the American and British dialects. This trip reinforced his belief that Americans needed their own dictionary.

In June 1826, Webster returned to his home in New Haven. There he began the long process of editing and proofreading the enormous manuscript. He also searched for a publisher willing to take on the project of printing a work of over two thousand pages that included Greek, Hebrew, and other nonwestern scripts. Sherman Converse, editor of the New Haven *Connecticut Journal*, finally agreed to handle the publishing process. *An American Dictionary of the English Language* appeared in November 1828 in two hefty volumes. The first print run was twenty-five hundred copies. In 1832 an edition of three thousand copies was published in England after the word *American* was removed from the title. The contents of both versions were the same.[6]

When Webster had published his *Compendious Dictionary of the English Language* in 1806, critics insulted it in terms ranging from the comparatively mild "folly" to "a volume of foul and unclean things." American and English reviewers alike were outraged at the idea of preserving words that hadn't been vetted by Johnson or another authority. Webster's criticism of Johnson's dictionary infuriated them. They hated the spelling changes and called the inclusion of words like *lengthy* and *presidential* "a fault of most alarming enormity." The only praise came from a few of Webster's friends and acquaintances.

The reception of the *American Dictionary of the English Language* must therefore have come to Webster as a pleasant surprise.[7] Nearly all the reviews were overwhelmingly positive, especially in the United States. An early book notice announces, "This work is spoken of in the highest terms." Later reviews confirm that reaction. The *New-York Evening Post* reports on June 16, 1829, that a local organization of teachers and literary men appointed a committee to examine the new dictionary and it met with their "most unqualified approbation."

According to the *Post*, the committee thought the etymologies were superior to those of all former lexicographers. Committee members also praised the addition of new words, the very thing that had triggered so much disapproval of the 1806 dictionary. Their report states, "The committee consider the excellence and value of this work to be much enhanced by the addition of more than twelve thousand words . . . and among these are the technical terms of modern science."

Other reviewers also mentioned the addition of new words as a highlight of the dictionary. The *Western Recorder* of January 20, 1829, remarks, "The *vocabulary* is enlarged by the addition of many thousand words . . . not found in other dictionaries, and many of them the words for the precise meaning of which the general reader is most frequently at a loss." The April 1829 *North American Review* argues that a dictionary containing "a copious vocabulary . . . will be sought for by the greatest number of readers."

Even the idiosyncratic spellings didn't worry people too much. The learned committee agreed that "the orthography of words is sometimes mistaken" and could use correcting. The January 16, 1830, *Religious Intelligencer* approves of "several classes" of the orthography (likely the ones that were most accepted by the general public). The *North American Review* agrees with dropping the *u* in words like *favour* and the *k* in words like *publick* and commends Webster for trying to fix the problematic English spelling system.

The *North American Review* article, which examined Webster's dictionary in detail, illustrates how much attitudes had changed in twenty years. The reviewer begins by revisiting the claim that Johnson had covered the English language exhaustively. That argument "would probably now be urged by no one," he says. He points out that new words are entering the language all the time. Obviously, they need recording. He notes that a number of words may be thought "not sufficiently authorized" or "not English," as in the case of *lengthy*. However, he says, Webster has provided authorities for the word, so it must be accepted. Besides, the British use it at least as much as the Americans. The reviewer ends by predicting that Americans will soon come to appreciate the dictionary as a valuable linguistic aid.

Even more striking than the praise from American reviewers was the softened attitude of the British toward Webster's work. For one thing, they agreed with the *North American Review* that Johnson's dictionary no longer represented the peak of the lexicographer's art. It had, after all, been seventy years since that great work had been published. Although later scholars updated it from time to time, there were still large gaps in the vocabulary. In fact, some reviewers saw Webster's decision to retain most of Johnson's words as a fault.[8] The *Westminster Review* of January 1831 points out that dozens of Johnson's words are now obsolete and others, like *blood-boltered*, were only used once or twice in books and never became current. The reviewer thinks Webster would have done better to cut these out.

Most reviewers recommended the work, although they typically had a few nits to pick. The writer for the *Westminster Review*, for instance, finds the verb *to patent* offensive and claims never to have heard of the American term *fire-warden.* He nonetheless concludes that the dictionary "abounds in information adapted to the ordinary circumstances of life."

The British were impressed by Webster's scholarship. The *Dublin Literary Gazette* of April 17, 1830, says, "The introduction of technical and scientific terms is a very valuable addition to a general dictionary." The *Edinburgh New Philosophical Journal* remarks that the improvements in definitions appear to be "numerous and highly important." The March 13, 1830, *Edinburgh Literary Journal*, announcing the imminent publication of the British edition, says, "We do not doubt that the work . . . will be found an important addition to philology."

Even more remarkably, the work was seen as a positive reflection on the American people. The reviewer for the *Westminster Review* says that the interest shown in Webster's dictionary among Americans indicates that "the enlightened inhabitants of that country are anxious to prevent any wide deviation from purity of speech." He thinks that the dictionary will "certainly contribute much to this object." The reviewer for the *Dublin Literary Gazette* declares himself gratified to learn that the dictionary is being printed in England.

What happened between 1806 and 1828 to so radically change the minds of both homegrown and foreign critics? The idea of an American dictionary went from being an insult to Johnson's work, and even to the mother tongue itself, to being a timely rescue of both. Part of the explanation is in the changed attitudes of Americans toward their own culture and language. The War of 1812—the "second War of Independence"—helped Americans break away from the old country emotionally as well as politically. It seemed to prove that the United

States was an established political force, entitled to take its place on the world stage.

To add to that sense, the boundaries of the country kept expanding. By 1828, white settlement reached as far west as the recently admitted states of Illinois and Missouri, and areas of potential settlement stretched much deeper into the continent. Americans were setting their sights on Texas and the Oregon Territory. Webster's predicted population of "*three hundred millions*" of English speakers seemed like a real possibility.

As Americans felt more secure as a nation, they grew more comfortable with their own vernacular. The frontier language of the Appalachians and the West was increasingly familiar to Americans back east. Backcountry congressmen declaimed on the floors of the House and Senate using their own regionalisms and were later quoted in the newspapers, slang and all. Words that started out as oddities, such as *electioneer* and *citizenize*, were soon naturalized around the country.

At the same time, the British were coming to terms with American independence and starting to get used to American ways of talking. With little fanfare, once-offensive American terms were making their way into the everyday British vocabulary. Words like *obligate* and *legislate*, which Pickering had deprecated, appeared in British magazines without quotation marks. The *Quarterly Review* for October 1823 used the questionable *immigration*, noting that "the Americans have judiciously adopted this word from our old writers." The poet Samuel Taylor Coleridge, who was known to complain about Americanisms in British speech, adopted *presidential* and *reliable* in writing. Even *belittle* was starting to make headway.

Although *lengthy* was still occasionally singled out for notice, it often appeared without comment in British publications. "I must not be lengthy," writes the author of an 1823 review in the *New Monthly Magazine*. He doesn't even bother to bracket the word in scare quotes or mention that it comes from "our American friends."

Language purism was hardly dead. Americans who wanted to get ahead in life turned to traditional British, or at least British-style, grammar books to learn proper speech, and writers in both countries continued to complain about the linguistic shortcomings of Americans. The majority of the American population, on the other hand, enjoyed the color and liveliness of their own word inventions, including in popular literature. The English were beginning to soften toward certain American authors as well. That may have helped Webster's cause and the cause of American English generally.

The most popular American author in both countries was unquestionably Washington Irving. Irving's first book, the 1809 *History of New York* by Diedrich Knickerbocker, was the first American fiction to gain both critical appreciation and a large audience. It enjoyed immediate popularity in the United States. It was also read and admired in England, although unmentioned by reviewers until Irving's later books came out. When the first installment of *The Sketch Book* appeared in 1819, it too was enthusiastically received in both countries.[9]

Critics readily embraced Irving partly because he was considered an "English-style" writer. His language was polished and included few obvious Americanisms. British reviewers especially were struck by Irving's style. American reviewers might comment on his "pure English," but typically they concentrated on the content of his writing. British reviewers focused more on the amazing fact that Irving, an American, nonetheless wrote elegant prose.

The *Quarterly Review*, reviewing *The Sketch Book* in its April 1821 issue, gushes, "The author before us is the best writer of English . . . that America has produced since the era of her independence." *Blackwood's Edinburgh Magazine* of February 1820 calls the stories in *The Sketch Book* "very exquisite and classical pieces of writing." A writer in the August 1820 *Edinburgh Review* declares himself amazed at the level of Irving's writing, considering that he grew up and was educated in the United States. He admires Irving's "great purity and beauty of diction," which is comparable to the best English authors.

Reviewers in England might have been more willing to accept Irving because he was so clearly an Anglophile. He moved to England in 1815 partly to help his brother Peter revive the family's failing mercantile business but also because he found the old country a congenial place. It would remain his home base until 1832. Aside from the *History of New York*, most of his early stories were set in England. Although *The Sketch Book* is famous now for "Rip Van Winkle" and "The Legend of Sleepy Hollow," over half the pieces in that collection are about England and the English.

In fact, Irving's writing style and subject matter sometimes led otherwise friendly American reviewers to complain that he was a little too English. A writer for the July 1822 *North American Review* complains that *The Sketch Book* might just as well have been written by an Englishman. In the reviewer's opinion, Irving has missed the chance to write a book with a distinctly American point of view. He could have done so, says the reviewer, "without an allusion to a *caucus*, or the use either of *progressing* or *lengthy*." While the reviewer wanted more of an American slant, he apparently thought that Irving should try to achieve it without using American words and expressions.

If the *North American Review* writer and other reviewers had looked beyond Irving's high-toned style, they might have noticed that he did in fact use Americanisms in his writing. He provided the earliest, or nearly the earliest, in-print examples of a number of American words and expressions. Besides *bushwhacker* and *knickerbocker*, discussed in chapter 2, the *History of New York* also includes one of the first uses of the American word *cocktail*.

It occurs in a passage describing the "most formidable enemy" of the Dutch in New Netherland, the English colony of Maryland. The author crowds together not only *cocktail* but also several other terms for early American drinks. The name of the territory "was anciently written Merryland," he explains, "so called because the inhabitants were prone to make merry and get fuddled with mint-julep and apple toddy. . . . They lay claim to be the first inventors of those recondite beverages, cock-tail, stone-fence, and sherry-cobbler."[10] (Stone fences were a mix of rum and cider, while cobblers were made out of wine, sugar, and fruit juice.)

The origins of the word *cocktail* are obscure, although it's known to have originated in the United States. Both the drink and its name were around by the late eighteenth century. Probably the earliest use of the word in print comes from the May 13, 1806, issue of the *Balance, and Columbian Repository*, a Federalist newspaper in Hudson, New York. In reply to a reader's query, the editor explains that a cocktail is a mixture of spirits, water, sugar, and bitters. He adds, "It is supposed to be an excellent electioneering potion . . . of great use to a Democratic candidate [a Democratic-Republican] because a person, having swallowed a glass of it, is ready to swallow anything else."[11]

Both Irving and the *Balance* editor treat *cocktail* as though it refers to a specific drink. By the middle of the century, the word was being used more often as a cover term for any drink made with spirits and a mixer. Bartlett at first lists *cocktail* in the entry for *liquor*, along with numerous other names for alcoholic drinks, but by his 1859 edition, he gives *cocktail* its own entry. (Words for drinks and drinking are plentiful in the early American vocabulary. These will be explored more fully in chapter 8.)

Irving also contributed a lasting term on another subject dear to American hearts: the *almighty dollar*. The phrase occurs in a short story titled "The Creole Village," which appears in the November 1836 issue of *Knickerbocker* magazine. Describing a visit to a small, "dilapidated" Louisiana village, the narrator of the tale says, "The almighty dollar, that great object of universal devotion throughout our land, seems to have no genuine devotees in these peculiar villages."

Complaints that the expression insulted the American monetary system moved Irving to include a teasing footnote when the story was later reprinted in the 1855 collection *Wolfert's Roost and Miscellanies*. In it he assures his audience that he meant no disrespect to the dollar, "which, he is aware, is daily becoming more and more an object of worship."[12]

Like so many pungent American expressions, it was soon adopted by politicians. Rep. Butler of Connecticut, giving a speech in the House of Representatives on March 12, 1850, defended "that class of people, sneered at by the gentleman from North Carolina, but most invaluable, who seek the 'almighty dollar,' and the comforts and education it furnishes."

Other American terms that figure in Irving's early writing include the food items *hominy*, *hoecake*, *sauerkraut* (spelled *sour craut*), and *doughnuts*, the last two being favorites of his New Netherlanders. Irving's use of *doughnut* is one of the first recorded. He describes doughnuts in the *History of New York* as "balls of sweetened dough, fried in hog's fat."[13] These were more like what would now be called doughnut holes. The Dutch in New York called them *oliekoeks*, Dutch for *oil cakes*.

Irving also introduced the term *indignation meeting* and wrote about *bundling*, an old colonial custom that allowed young men visiting their fiancées to "bundle up" together, fully clothed, on a bed. (Bundling was a practical way to keep warm and get some privacy in tiny colonial cabins, but the British who read about it considered it more evidence of Americans' lack of refinement.) Irving also used the new American terms *squatter* and *squatting* in several places. He also used *nerve* with the American meaning of courage and *wilt* with the American meaning of wither. Bartlett later relied on Irving for examples of these and other early words.

Irving's writing got an infusion of American vocabulary when he returned to the United States after seventeen years abroad. After so long away, he was naturally eager to witness the changes in the country and especially to explore the western frontier territories that had burgeoned since he left. He spent several weeks reconnecting with family and friends but soon resumed his old traveling ways.

"Washington Irving." This photograph by Mathew Brady is from an original daguerreotype by John Plumbe, taken sometime between 1855 and Irving's death in 1859, about two decades after his travels in the West and publication of *A Tour on the Prairies*. *Prints and Photographs Division: Library of Congress, LC-USZ62-4238*

A chance meeting in August 1832 while crossing Lake Erie on a steamboat offered Irving an exciting opportunity for a western trip. He happened to meet Henry Leavitt Ellsworth, a young lawyer and the son of former chief justice Oliver Ellsworth. President Andrew Jackson had recently appointed him a commissioner to Indian Territory (approximately present-day Oklahoma and Kansas).

Ellsworth invited Irving to travel west with the commission and act as secretary. Irving jumped at the offer. He wrote to his brother that it would be an opportunity to see "the remnants of those great

Indian Tribes" and to visit "those fine countries of the 'far west,' while still in a state of pristine wildness, and behold herds of buffalo."[14] Irving's trip fulfilled his hopes. He met Osage, Creek, and other Native Americans. He also hunted buffalo, slept on the open range, witnessed a stampede of horses, and learned to appreciate skunk meat. All the while, he collected new American vocabulary.

The expedition started in September and lasted two months. The commission left from Cincinnati, traveling by steamboat to Louisville and eventually to St. Louis. From there, they switched to horseback and began their trek into Indian Territory. They reached the army outpost of Fort Gibson, Oklahoma, in early October. Using Fort Gibson as a base, they then looped into the Indian "hunting grounds" as far west as present-day Norman, returning from their explorations in early November.

Irving recounted his adventures in the 1835 *A Tour on the Prairies*. *A Tour* contradicts the notion that Irving avoided Americanisms in his writing. The book not only features numerous Americanisms but also adds new ones to the American word store. Many of the new terms in the book were making their first in-print appearance. Unlike the explorers Lewis and Clark, Irving didn't set out to record every aspect of the country he passed through. He simply noted whatever caught his interest. The landscapes and people he wrote about would have called for words that were new to him and his readers, simply because few Americans knew anything about life west of the Mississippi.

A term that would have been unfamiliar to many readers was *rolling country*. The word *rolling* to describe gently undulating hills had been used before, but the image was still novel for Americans living in the East. *Rolling* compared the landscape to the gentle swells of the ocean. Irving describes emerging upon "a grand prairie" after a long hike: "an immense extent of grassy, undulating, or, as it is termed, rolling country, with here and there a clump of trees, dimly seen in the distance like a ship at sea."[15] *Rolling prairie* and *rolling hills* were similar terms that were just starting to come into use.

Other landscape terms that would most likely have been new to anyone who hadn't visited the prairie are *sinkhole* and *cross timber*. A sinkhole is a depression in the earth where water runs in and is lost. A harrowing anecdote in Irving's book begins with a hunter falling into "one of those deep, funnel-shaped pits . . . known by the name of sink-holes."[16] Irving didn't invent the word, but like rolling prairies, sinkholes were exotic enough outside the West to make a detailed description necessary.

Cross timber, the name for belts of woodland found in Oklahoma, probably first appeared in print in Irving's book. He mentions cross timber several times. Sometimes he capitalizes the term, treating it like a specific entity (like the Mississippi or the Sierras). On one occasion he complains, "We still had to traverse many a weary mile of the 'Cross Timber.'"[17] Bartlett's definition of *cross timber* in the 1855 edition of his dictionary notes that it's "a marked feature" in the region where it's found.

Irving also contributed various words related to the wildlife of the region. These include two *buffalo* words—*buffalo camp*, the base for hunters of buffalo, and *buffalo prairie*, where the buffalo congregate. He writes about Osage hunters making trips to the buffalo prairie each autumn. Irving was also among the first to record the terms *deer bed* and *elk bed*, grassy spots where the animals slept.

Irving used *prairie* terms that were still unfamiliar to many people. When writing about the region that the commission traveled through he often named it with capital letters and quotation marks—"The Great Western Prairie" or "The Grand Prairie"—making it an entity like the Cross Timber. *Prairie dog* was a term from Lewis and Clark's journals, but Irving was the first to write about a *prairie dog village*. He also mentions the grouse-like *prairie hens*, another animal named by Lewis and Clark. A more recent term that appears several times in the book is *prairie fire*.

Irving was intrigued by the culture of the Native Americans he encountered during the trip and wrote about their activities, dress, and interactions with the commission. One less familiar term that he adopted is *braves*. He typically enclosed it in quotation marks, suggesting that he expected it to be new to readers. In one chapter, he writes about traditional hunting grounds, saying, "Their hunters and 'braves' repair thither . . . during the season of game."[18] French traders were the first to call young native men by this name, from the French *brave*, meaning courageous or intrepid.

Irving mentions *hunting grounds* in several places, sometimes with the name of a tribe, as in *Osage hunting grounds*. These were areas claimed by the various tribes for hunting forays but where there were no permanent tribal settlements. The expression *happy hunting grounds*, referencing supposed Indian beliefs about the afterlife, started to circulate around this time. Irving didn't use it in *A Tour on the Prairies*, but it does appear in his 1836 book *Astoria*. At first the phrase was only used in connection with Native Americans, but by the late nineteenth century, it was a broad euphemism for the hereafter.

A Tour on the Prairies was an instant success, both in England and the United States. "We found it impossible to lay down the volume until we had read every line of it," exclaims a *Dublin University Magazine* reviewer. The *Quarterly Review* names Irving "the only living classic of the United States." *Harvardiana* calls him a genius, and *Knickerbocker* magazine claims that the book "sustains his brilliant reputation." The reviews were notable as well for what they didn't mention. None remark on the unfamiliar vocabulary, and few comment on Irving's language use at all, except to praise his "polished style" and "expressive elegance."[19]

The author of a *North American Review* article referenced Irving's book to tweak Basil Hall (who thought English had "words enough already"). The reviewer assures Hall that if he will prepare himself by first perusing *The Sketch Book*, he might be able to master the language of *A Tour* "over the course of the summer"—at least "all but the hard places and the more outrageous Americanisms." As for the reviewer's own opinion, "We regard Washington Irving as the best living writer of English prose."

Together with Noah Webster, Washington Irving lifted the American language to a new level of respectability, while at the same time adding new words and expressions to the common vocabulary. Both men opened the door to a dictionary of Americanisms that would show the same respect for the American vernacular that they gave it in their work. And when Bartlett started compiling just such a work, he relied on the writings of both authors.

8

A Collection of Words "Peculiar to the United States"

SOMETIME DURING THE late 1830s, John Russell Bartlett traveled from his home in New York City to visit his father in Cape Vincent, a village by the side of Lake Ontario. He headed west from Utica by the leisurely method of canal boat. During this break from his busy life—Bartlett was a partner in a book dealership as well as a family man—he passed the time by reading "a late work in which the vulgar [colloquial] language of the United States abounded." His autobiography doesn't record which work it was. It might have been one of the humorous portrayals of typical "Yankees" that were popular at the time, or perhaps it was one of the plethora of recent works by or about Davy Crockett. Whichever it was, Bartlett enjoyed the book's "strange words and expressions" so much that he marked them in the margins.[1]

When Bartlett returned home, he discovered that his copy of Pickering's *Vocabulary* didn't include these idioms, so he wrote them in on the blank leaves of the book. He next went through all the Crockett books, "noted the particular idioms they contained," and wrote those down in Pickering too. By this time, Bartlett, an inveterate note taker and list maker, was hooked on his word project. "I now became greatly interested in my collection of words," he recalls.

Soon he had so many words that there was no room left in the blank spaces of the *Vocabulary*. In fact, he says, there were "sufficient to make a volume much larger than that of Mr. Pickering." He started fresh by transferring all his word lists to a large blank book. Then he "set vigorously to work" collecting even more words.

He whizzed through a series titled Carey & Hart's Library of Humorous American Works, gathering up all the "drolleries and quaint sayings." He read the *Herald* and the *Tribune* every day. Whenever a newspaper used a word or phrase "peculiarly American," or one that had a different meaning in England, he added it to his collection. He took to carrying around a small notebook so he could record any new words that he heard. Finally, to track down the origins of as many provincialisms as possible, he wrote to London booksellers and ordered all the books of British regionalisms that he could find.[2]

Bartlett also bought regular dictionaries, American and English, including Webster's. Of course he perused his copy of Pickering, as well as the essays by Witherspoon, the creator of the word *Americanism.* Like Pickering and Witherspoon, Bartlett was on the lookout for "all those words usually called provincial or vulgar," but not to condemn them.[3] Rather, he wanted to create a record of casual American speech. He was intrigued by the kinds of words and expressions that everyone knows but that never make it into formal writing or serious literature.

Bartlett didn't absolutely approve of every word or phrase that he collected. He labels many terms "low" or says that they're mostly used by the less educated. Critiquing the language wasn't his point, though. The low status of a word or expression is part of what made it interesting. Bartlett thought provincialisms and slang were worth preserving because they offered an unfiltered view of American speech—and by extension, American life—that couldn't be found in more conventional dictionaries. His *Dictionary of Americanisms: A Glossary of Words and Phrases Usually Regarded as Peculiar to the United States* was the next logical step after Webster.

Bartlett was the ideal person to compile a dictionary of this sort. Although he was a businessman, not a professional scholar, he zealously pursued a variety of intellectual interests. Ethnology, the study of human societies, especially absorbed him. He also had a serious

"John Russell Bartlett." This portrait of Bartlett was painted by John Nelson Arnold in 1871, six years before he published the final edition of the *Dictionary of Americanisms.* Bartlett was in his last year as secretary of state for Rhode Island and had been John Carter Brown's librarian for about fifteen years. *Courtesy of the Brown University Portrait Collection, Providence, Rhode Island*

bent for organization. Over the years, he would catalog and classify all sorts of materials, most significantly the library of book collector and philanthropist John Carter Brown, which later became the core of the Brown University library.

Bartlett was born in Providence, Rhode Island, in 1805. He spent most of his youth in Kingston, Ontario, but returned to Providence at the age of eighteen, a year after leaving school, to work in his uncle's dry goods store. After four years he made the move to banking. In 1831 the twenty-five-year-old Bartlett married Eliza Rhodes. He and his wife led an active social life, entertaining a large circle of friends at their Providence home. When he wasn't working or spending time with family and friends, he poured much of his considerable energy into pursuing the academic subjects he loved.

Shortly before he married, Bartlett helped found the Providence Athenaeum, a library and reading room meant to supplement the aging collection of the Providence Library. Bartlett was also active in the Franklin Society, a club for men interested in science, and the Rhode Island Historical Society. During what little was left of his leisure time, he drew and painted. He notes in his autobiography that nearly all the pictures by him that hang in his house were created during his time as a banker in Providence.

Founding the athenaeum gave Bartlett his first taste of acquiring and organizing books. He tells in his autobiography of traveling to New York to buy books for the library. Apparently he had a knack for encouraging donations for special items. He raised enough money to buy, among other titles, the twenty-three-volume *Description of Egypt* that had been commissioned by Napoleon and the "double elephant folio" edition of John James Audubon's *Birds of America*. Bartlett also prepared the library's first catalog.

Wherever Bartlett's business career took him, he got involved in scholarly and scientific societies. In 1836 he moved to New York City, where he spent the next thirteen years, first as a commission agent and then as a book dealer. Soon after he arrived, he was invited to join the New-York Historical Society, which hadn't actually met in several years and was virtually moribund. He set about rejuvenating it and building membership. Six years later, he founded the American Ethnological Society. Both organizations are still going strong.

Bartlett was inspired to start the Ethnological Society because of his abiding fascination with "Geography, Archaeology, Philology and . . . enquiries generally connected with the human race."[4] Bartlett's first book, *The Progress of Ethnology*, published just a year before his dictionary, started as a series of papers read before the Ethnological Society. In it he lists and describes archaeological, linguistic, and geographical research projects around the globe. The *Dictionary of Americanisms* fits into this pattern. It was another kind of cultural study, this time of his own culture.

Bartlett's instinct, when he discovered a subject that captured his interest, was to intensively collect and then organize whatever information he could find. An impressive example is his collection of Civil War material. Just as he patiently harvested slang from the daily papers for his dictionary, he carefully amassed news items during the war. According to his autobiography, he clipped and pasted items virtually every day—an average three hours of work a day for four years. In the end, he filled more than fifty scrapbooks with material relating to the war. Then, "with much labor," he produced a catalog of his finds.[5] The resulting bibliography, titled *The Literature of the Rebellion*, came in at 477 pages.

Each new turn in Bartlett's life led to collecting and classifying. Between 1850 and 1853, Bartlett was the US commissioner for the United States and Mexican Boundary Survey, charged with determining the boundary between the two countries after the Mexican-American War. Afterward, he wrote the two-volume *Personal Narrative of Explorations and Incidents in Texas, New Mexico, California, Sonora, and Chihuahua*—1,130 pages chock-full of detailed topographical and cultural information.

When Bartlett was elected secretary of state for Rhode Island in 1855, he decided to compile a "Bibliography of Rhode Island," a list of everything published about the state. Around the same time, he became private librarian to John Carter Brown, a position that he kept until his death in 1886. Over the years, he produced multiple printed catalogs of Brown's library.

By collecting material on subjects that he cared about, Bartlett was tapping into a common nineteenth-century trend. Those who had the time and means built collections of artworks, antiques, stamps, and other artifacts. As an ethnologist, Bartlett collected culture and history. The *Dictionary of Americanisms* was the outgrowth of his collecting impulse, combined with his scientific approach to human societies. He gathered all the linguistic bits and pieces that had accumulated since John Smith wrote about seeing his first "Covering of *Rahaughcums*" and arranged them into a unique display of American speech.

Not every Americanism made it into Bartlett's dictionary. He left out "cant" words that weren't part of the general vocabulary—the insider jargon of criminals and other closed groups—as well as "purely technical words" and "obscene and blasphemous words." As he explains in his introduction, he was looking for a certain type of language.

Bartlett skipped over many of the American words in Webster, scanning for the ones marked "low, or vulgar, or only to be heard in familiar conversation."[6] He also included terms that weren't necessarily low but were exotic. One such category is the contributions of the Dutch, Spanish, and French—*cookie*, *vamos* [*vamoose*], *bayou*. Another is words that were still limited to American use. He lists *corn* with the explanation that it's the name for *maize* "throughout the United States." Several *corn* terms follow, including *corn-cracker*, "the nickname for a native of Kentucky."

Certain terms read more like encyclopedia entries than straightforward definitions. Usually, these are capsule summaries of social and political trends. Although Bartlett's focus was on terminology, he was also painting a word picture of American society in the mid-nineteenth century. His entry for *Whigs and Democrats* discourses over two pages. He seems to view both parties with a jaundiced eye. Although he describes the distinctions between the two parties' platforms, he suggests that the main object of both is to gain and then keep the majority.

Some of Bartlett's entries are almost whimsical, giving a taste of the books he read while researching the dictionary. His entry on *hasty pudding*, a kind of cornmeal mush quickly made with boiling water and served with butter, milk, and sugar or molasses, includes one verse of a long poem on the subject by Joel Barlow. The first lines explain the name: "In haste the boiling cauldron o'er the blaze, / Receives and cooks the ready-powder'd maize." Bartlett says that hasty pudding is a favorite dish in every part of the United States, which would account for its mention in the second verse of "Yankee Doodle"—"there we saw the men and boys as thick as hasty pudding."[7]

Bartlett didn't spend much time on etymology, except for words of "purely American origin," such as *succotash*. His entry for that word includes the information that it comes from the Narragansett *msickquatash* (modern spelling *msiquatash*), meaning boiled corn. He also notes the origins of words from other languages that first appeared in America. He explains that *snoop* comes from the Dutch *snoepen* and *vamos* [*vamonos*] means *let us go* in Spanish. Sometimes he recounts the folklore of a word. In the entry for *bunkum*, he explains that it originated with "a tedious speaker in Congress."

Bartlett provided generous example quotations. While Webster took quotations mainly from American statesmen, Bartlett went to his "low" sources—newspapers, the *Congressional Globe*, descriptions in popular books by British visitors. He also took advantage of a new type of American writing. While he gathered plenty of words from Washington Irving, the most respected American author, he also rummaged through the comic writings that were just becoming popular in the 1830s. He explains in the introduction, "I have . . . attempted to illustrate by extract from American authors, whose writings relate to that class of people among which these words are chiefly found."[8]

Two writers that Bartlett relied on heavily were Seba Smith and Thomas Chandler Haliburton. Both men achieved their humorous effects with regional vocabulary and accents. Smith, a native of Maine, founded the weekly *Family Reader* and the *Portland Courier* (of Maine), both in 1830. He made the *Courier* and himself famous with his fictional letters, written "to" the *Courier* under the name of Major Jack Downing. Major Downing satirized partisan politics in a "down-east" dialect. Reporting, for example, on the doings of the

Maine state legislature, he writes, "In the arternoon, the legislater they call the Sinnet got stuck, and in trying to make it go, it rather seemed to crack a little."[9]

Haliburton was a judge living in Nova Scotia. His most famous character, Samuel Slick, also appeared first in a newspaper, the *Novascotian*, and was later immortalized in the 1836 book *The Clockmaker; or, the Sayings and Doings of Samuel Slick, of Slickville* and three later volumes. Sam Slick was a Yankee clockmaker who traveled through the countryside with a narrator known as the Squire. Sam often escaped from tight spots through Yankee ingenuity and fast talking. Describing how he tricks people into buying clocks, Slick tells the Squire, "We trust to '*soft sawder*' [flattery] to get [the clocks] into the house, and to '*human natur*' that they never come out of it."[10]

The language of these books was a large part of what made them appealing, although there were dissenters. One reviewer remarks sourly that "the Jack Downing and David Crockett taste . . . vulgarizes us at home . . . and brings ridicule and disgrace . . . abroad," and another complains that Sam Slick's so-called dialect is a "ridiculous compound" of provincialisms and made-up expressions.[11] However, most reviewers enjoyed the characters' extravagant speech.

Connecting Jack Downing and David Crockett (as the first reviewer did) makes sense. Even though the Downing character was a New Englander and Crockett hailed from the western frontier, they both used similar rustic expressions. Among the examples that Bartlett took from the Jack Downing letters are *knock into a cocked hat*, *clear out*, *gone goose*, *know what's what*, *chock-full*, and *see how the cat will jump*. Some of these phrases appeared in the Crockett books, and all of them sound as though they could have.

Examples from Crockett and Sam Slick also overlap. Crockett describes meeting "true chips of [off] the old block"—his way of describing patriotic young men—while traveling in Boston. Sam Slick's father tells him, "You're a chip of the old block, my boy." Both Slick and Crockett use *the clean thing*, which Bartlett defines as "a low expression denoting propriety, or what is honorable." Slick also uses casual expressions like *cut and run*, *no two ways about it*, and *go the whole figure*, a variant on the Crockettesque *go the whole hog*.

Both Seba Smith and Thomas Haliburton were popular in England as well as the United States. No doubt part of their appeal was that they made fun of Americans, but they were also appreciated at a deeper level. An article in the *London and Westminster Review* says, "These books show that American literature has ceased to be exclusively imitative. A few writers have appeared in the United States who, instead of being European and English in their styles of thought and diction, are American—who therefore produce original sounds instead of far-off echoes."[12]

Bartlett collected words and expressions from every region. From the South came the verbs *disremember*, *cotton to* (also common in the West), and *done* with a verb, as in *done did it*, *done come*, and *done gone*. New Englandisms include *admire to*, "very absurdly used" in expressions like "I should admire to see the president"; *yank* to mean a sharp tug; and old-fashioned verb forms such as *boughten* and *hain't*. He also includes the regional *to conduct* for *to conduct oneself*, in spite of considering it "an offensive barbarism," because it has received "the tacit sanction of Dr. Webster." The westernisms are mostly of the Davy Crockett sort—*bark up the wrong tree*, *go the whole hog*, *fire into the wrong flock* (mistake your target), *shake a stick at*.

Bartlett records some examples of unusual pronunciations and nonstandard syntax. In the West, people say *bar* for *bear* and *at* for *in* ("at the North"). Southerners say *holp* for *help* and *used to could*. New Englanders say *hull* for *whole*. They also say *farziner* (as far as I know) and *fortiner* (for aught I know). Bartlett comments of the latter, "This remarkable specimen of clipping and condensing a phrase approaches the Indian method of forming words." He was referring to the fact that most Native American languages incorporate into a single word meanings that would be expressed by several words in English.

He also noted the emphatic adjectives that were popular in the South and West—*powerful, monstrous, dreadful, almighty, all-fired,* and similar words. These often amounted to euphemistic expletives. Early nineteenth-century Americans were known for their excessive verbal delicacy. European visitors fell afoul of their American hosts by using such unrefined words as *leg* instead of *limb* and *woman* instead of *female*. Fanny Trollope, in *Domestic Manners of the Americans,* tells of a young German man who offended one of Cincinnati's prominent families by pronouncing the word *corset* in front of the young ladies.

Bartlett was aware of this trend. In the introduction to his 1859 edition, he explains, "Among some of the Western people there are strange ideas regarding the use of certain words. . . . The essentially English word *bull* is refined beyond the mountains . . . into *cow-creature, male-cow,* and even *gentleman-cow*!"[13] Other animals suffered the same treatment. Some examples are *male sheep, male hog,* and *he biddy,* a replacement for *rooster,* which itself replaced the older *cock*.

One outgrowth of that squeamishness was the substitution of various profanities with much milder recastings. Bartlett's dictionary lists a number of watered-down swear words. These include the New Englandisms *by gosh* ("an inoffensive oath"), *darned* (a substitute for *damned,* "generally called a Yankeeism"), and *I swan* ("a euphemistic pronunciation of the word *swear*"). Other versions are *I swow, I swamp it,* and *I dad,* popular in the West. He also lists *darnation* and *tarnation*. These could be adjectives as well as nouns, as in *tarnation strange*.

Under *goodness,* Bartlett says, "This inoffensive word is much used in a variety of ways by people of all classes." He gives *Oh, my goodness* as an example of a phrase favored by "old ladies." *Goodness me, goodness gracious,* and *goodness sake* are also common. He gives examples from a couple of publications. The *New-York Commercial Advertiser,* quoting a businessman who fears that the railroads will all begin raising their rates, says, "Goodness knows where he will find himself landed." Bartlett admits that expressions like *goodness me* are also used in England. However, the American emphasis on polite speech makes them even more characteristic of the United States.

Bartlett collected words and expressions from several other important facets of American life. One example is alcohol consumption. Early Americans knocked back an eye-watering amount of beer, hard cider, spirits, and, if wealthy, imported wine. Drinking plain water was considered unhealthy (as it could be in the days before water treatment plants). Although drunkenness was frowned on, most Americans over the age of fifteen imbibed a certain amount of alcohol every day, starting at breakfast.

Between 1800 and 1830, the annual per capita consumption of distilled spirits exceeded five gallons. This amount was in addition to the beer and cider that most people drank with meals. Whiskey was treated like a food staple. Soldiers received a daily whiskey ration, and a typical laborer drank four ounces of spirits a day. Even women, who often felt that swilling whiskey was low class, downed a fair amount of distilled alcohol in the form of cordials or alcohol-based medicines. The notion that a shot of liquor was good for your health was widespread.[14]

Long before Bartlett began collecting for his dictionary, an article titled "The Drinker's Dictionary" appeared in the January 6, 1737, *Pennsylvania Gazette*. This list of over two hundred slang words and expressions for being drunk was unsigned but is often attributed to Benjamin Franklin. Some of the terms on the list are still familiar. These include *tipsy*, *boozy*, *fuddled*, *intoxicated*, *oiled*, and *stewed*. Others have disappeared, such as *cherubimical*, *nimtopsical*, *double-tongued*, and *jambled*.[15]

The article also lists some colorful metaphors—*loose in the hilts*, *got on his little hat*, *going to Jerusalem*, *dizzy as a goose*, and *stiff as a ring-bolt*. Only a few of the terms on the list made it into Bartlett's dictionary—*soak*, *fuddled*, and *boozy* (spelled *boosy*). Most would have been obsolete by the 1830s.

The usual spirit in colonial America was rum, made from molasses imported from the British West Indies. One of Bartlett's terms is the now obsolete *rum-bud*. Rum-buds were red blotches on the nose and face associated with excessive drinking. Bartlett gives the synonym *grog blossom*, the term commonly used in England. (Grog, the usual tipple of sailors and soldiers, was a mixture of spirits and water, with the spirit usually being rum.)

With the advent of the Revolutionary War, molasses imports were severely restricted, so Americans had to find something else to distill. At first they tried wheat and rye—both Jefferson and Washington owned rye distilleries—but eventually settled on the quintessentially American grain, corn. The end product is now known as *bourbon*, but that term didn't appear until the mid-nineteenth century. Bourbon probably acquired that name because much of it was produced in Bourbon County, Kentucky (named for the French royal family, the Bourbons). At first, however, the drink was simply called *corn whiskey*, *corn juice*, or *corn squeezings*.[16]

Bartlett doesn't list *corn whiskey* but gives the slang word *corned* for drunk, as well as *corn juice*, which he claims is a western term. He also includes the expression *acknowledge the corn*, now sadly obsolete.[17] Acknowledging the corn meant admitting that you were drunk or, more broadly, taking responsibility for your actions. Bartlett calls it "an expression of recent origin, which has now become very common."

Newspapers often used the phrase. The St. Louis *Daily Pennant* for July 14, 1850, reports that "David Johnson acknowledged the corn, and said that he was drunk." The Philadelphia *Spirit of the Times* for March 16, 1842, used another version of the term. The paper reported that a reveler, brought up before a judge, freely admitted his guilt, saying, "Your honor, I confess the corn. I was royally drunk." The more general meaning of confessing guilt was also in common use. The *New York Herald* for June 27, 1846, says of a rival paper, "The Evening Mirror very naively comes out and acknowledges the corn, admits that a demand was made, &c."

Bartlett takes note of the American cocktail habit under the heading "Liquor." He says, "Many and very singular names" have been given to the mixtures served up in "fashionable bar-rooms." A list of sixty cocktail names follows, including the word *cocktail* itself. Virtually all of the names are unfamiliar now. Bartlett lists several versions of *juleps*—peach, pineapple, strawberry, mint—which would have included spirits, sugar, and ice. He also lists *flips*—a hot, sweetened mix of beer and spirit—and *slings*, made from spirits, sugar, and water.

More colorfully named drinks include the *deadbeat*, a mixture of ginger soda and whiskey, "taken by hard drinkers after a night's carousal," and *chain-lightning*, a brand of raw whiskey. Imaginatively named drinks with ingredients that are now mysterious include *slip ticket*, *Virginia fancy*, *Knickerbocker*, *pig and whistle*, *epicure's punch*, and *ching-ching*. A mixture that must have been invented for the rollicking 1840 election is called *Tip and Ty*. Presumably, it included hard cider.

Bartlett also lists a number of drinking terms separately. These include *in liquor* and *liquor(ed) up*, both references to drunkenness, as is the southern expression *shot in the neck*. *Apple brandy*, with its variant *apple jack*, gets a separate heading. So do *bitters* and *schnapps*, which Bartlett describes as a New York word for Dutch gin. Applejack might have been taken as a *nightcap*—a glass of something before bed. Bartlett suggests a *hot toddy* or *gin sling* as two other nightcap possibilities. A second glass was called *a string to tie it with*.

Tee-total—"a modern cant word" formed by reduplication (repeating the initial sound)—also appeared in the dictionary. The word was actually invented in the north of England. It was popularized by Richard Turner, a working man who used *tee-total* in an 1833 speech to emphasize his high level of commitment to avoiding all alcoholic beverages. (To many people of the time, abstinence meant avoiding hard liquor but not necessarily beer or cider.) "I have signed the tee, tee-total pledge," Turner declared.[18]

The temperance movement in the United States was gearing up at the time and quickly adopted the word. *Tee-totaller* and *tee-totally* were also common. Although *tee-total* became a naturalized Americanism soon after its invention, Bartlett must have decided that it wasn't American enough because he removed it from later editions of the dictionary. However, he kept *teetotally*, which Americans also used as an emphatic way of saying *totally*. In *The Attaché; or, Sam Slick in England*, for example, Slick remarks that the "meetin' houses" in England are "teetotally different" from those across the water.[19]

Bartlett also added the American invention *teetotaciously*—"a strange Western term, meaning a little more than *teetotally*, if such a thing be possible." Logically, it might not be possible to be more than teetotally for or against something, but it was that extra level of intensity that gave the word its typically western spin. Bartlett's example comes from the New York *Spirit of the Times* ("If he wasn't, I hope to be teetotaciously chawed up!"). He might just as easily, however, have quoted J. K. Paulding's character Nimrod Wildfire or the Indiana congressman Wick (see chapters 4 and 5).

On the flip side of the vocabulary from such racy subjects as liquor and swearing was the language of religion and preaching. In his introduction, Bartlett singles out the clergy as the casual creators of many "strange and barbarous words." They were especially prolific with new verbs. Bartlett mentions as examples "*to fellowship*, *to difficult*, *to eventuate*, *to doxologize*, *to happify*, *to donate*, &c., &c." Words like *to difficult* (to have some difficulty) and *to happify* (make happy) are not especially religious, although they sprang from the pulpit. Other word inventions had specifically religious meanings.

To fellowship (still current in some circles) means to come together for fellowship and worship with people who hold compatible beliefs. Pickering also included it in his list of Americanisms, so it had been around for a while. The term was used most often to explain why members of one group could not fellowship with another group. *To doxologize* meant to give glory to God, created from the noun *doxology*, a short prayer praising God. (*Doxology* itself comes from a Greek word meaning to utter praise.)

Bartlett also recorded the verb *inheaven*, meaning to raise to heaven, either literally or figuratively. Bartlett claims the word was invented by the Boston Transcendentalists. His example—"the one circumflows and inheavens us"—is taken from the novel *Margaret* by Unitarian minister Sylvester Judd, published in 1845. Other words that he captured include *angelology* (the doctrine of angels), *christianization*, and *come-outers* (people who were former members of some Christian denomination but who now believed that institutionalizing religion was sinful and so had "come out").

Bartlett also included the term *Transcendentalism*, although his definition is singularly unenlightening: "the state or quality of being transcendental." Transcendentalism originated in New England in 1836, when the Boston philosopher and essayist Ralph Waldo Emerson, along with Henry David Thoreau and several others, founded the Transcendental Club. The Transcendentalist movement combined religious, philosophical, and social aspects. Transcendentalists believed in the essential goodness of human beings and the primacy of the individual. Bartlett's failure to provide these details in his definition might indicate that he considered the movement a minor trend. The entry for it disappears altogether from later editions.

During the decade when Bartlett was compiling his dictionary, the United States was nearing the tail end of a Protestant religious revival known as the Second Great Awakening. The movement began around the turn of the nineteenth century, reached a peak in the 1820s and '30s, and didn't completely fade until midcentury. Traveling preachers held tent revivals that drew thousands and sometimes lasted for days or weeks. The evangelical movement started with conventional denominations like the Methodists and Baptists, but it eventually inspired new religions.

The epicenter of the revivalist movement was western New York. Religious fervor burned so hot in this region that it got to be called the *Burned-Over District*. The name was popularized by the prominent evangelical preacher Charles Grandison Finney, who declared that the fires of the spirit had consumed so many people in this area that there were few left to convert. It was as if a wildfire had flattened everything in its path.

Bartlett recognized the importance of the New York religious resurgence by providing long entries for three of the major movements that originated there—the Millerites, the Mormons, and the Shakers. He gives detailed explanations of each religion's doctrines—all three believed, among other things, that the Second Coming was imminent—plus details of its founding and present situation. Bartlett's descriptions and comments give a sense of how Americans viewed these religions just after they were founded, when their activities were still news rather than history.[20]

Bartlett seems to take a skeptical view of the Millerites, named for their founder William Miller. He describes their belief in a "first judgment," when Jesus will return to Earth to raise up the saints and burn the bodies of the wicked. One thousand years later a second judgment will take place. The Millerites were so convinced that the first judgment would happen sometime in 1843 that they "disposed of all their worldly treasures, provided themselves with 'ascension robes,' and waited . . . for the sounding of the last trumpet." However, Bartlett says, because of repeated disappointments, "the sect has happily dwindled down to an insignificant number." The Seventh-Day Adventists, founded in 1863, grew out of the Millerite movement.

Bartlett is more in sympathy with the Mormons. After explaining that they derive their name from the Book of Mormon, published in 1830, he goes on to describe the history of the church's founding by Joseph Smith and his followers' major beliefs. He notes in passing that they are also called "Latter-Day Saints." (Officially, they are the Church of Jesus Christ of Latter-Day Saints.)

Bartlett recounts the Mormons' search for a place to settle, first in Missouri, then in Nauvoo, Illinois. He includes a detailed description of the Nauvoo temple. Then Bartlett tells how "persecution followed these poor people in Illinois" and forced them to flee west. He reports that they finally settled near the Great Salt Lake, "where some 20,000 of them are now forming a settlement." In the 1859 edition, Bartlett claims that "some 40,000" are settled in "the Territory of Utah."

Bartlett also gives the Shakers, a sect that started in England, a long entry. He includes them because a group of the faithful settled in Watervliet, near Albany, in 1776. He reports that the society "still exists" and now possesses "2000 acres of good land." The official name of the sect is the United Society of Believers in Christ's Second Appearing, but soon after their founding they were nicknamed the Shaking Quakers, in Bartlett's words, "from the shaking of their bodies in religious exercises." The phrase was later shortened to Shakers.

Shakers were known for their herbal medicines, and Bartlett mentions them under several American plant names, including *cow parsnip*, *flea-bane*, *frostwort*, *Oswego tea*, and *thimble weed*. Membership reached its peak in the mid-nineteenth century and then began to dwindle, partly because the Shakers' practice of celibacy meant that membership could only grow through converts. By the 1859 edition, Bartlett had dropped the entry, no doubt reflecting the group's miniscule numbers.

Bartlett also covered money. In an encyclopedic entry headed "Federal currency," he names the types of coins in use when he was writing and describes the evolution of the monetary system in the earlier United States. In Bartlett's time, the coins were a gold ten-dollar piece called an *eagle*, half and quarter eagles, the silver dollar, half and quarter dollars, a silver dime and half-dime, and a copper cent. Bartlett mentions that half-cent pieces were once coined, but not in recent years. Five-cent coins called *nickels*, made of nickel alloy, would not go into circulation until after the Civil War. Paper money—called a *bank-bill* or sometimes a *bank-note*—was issued by individual banks rather than the government.

Money in the United States took a while to standardize. As English citizens, colonial Americans naturally used the British system of pounds, shillings, and pence. Besides English money, coins from other countries circulated throughout the colonies. The most common was the Spanish *peso* from Mexico, called a *piece of eight* because it was worth eight *reales*, the basic unit of Spanish money. (One *real* was worth approximately twelve and half cents in most places.) *Peso* coins were also known as Spanish dollars. The word *dollar* had come into English centuries earlier, adapted from a German word for a large silver coin.

After the war, Thomas Jefferson among others argued for basing American money on the dollar. In Jefferson's words, it was "a known coin, and the most familiar of all, to the minds of the people. It is already adopted from south to north."[21] He suggested that the denominations be a gold ten-dollar piece, a silver dollar, a silver tenth of a dollar, and a copper hundredth of a dollar. He pointed out that dividing the dollar into tenths would result in monetary values similar to the coins that were already in circulation. That way, people could estimate what the new coins were worth without having to do too much calculating.

Because of a chronic silver shortage in the United States, Mexican coins continued to circulate alongside American money until the middle of the nineteenth century. The old terminology also lingered. In colonial times, a *real* was called by different nicknames in different regions, reflecting the fact that it was worth varying amounts. In New England, a *real* was worth nine cents, so it was familiarly known as *ninepence*. In Pennsylvania it was called *elevenpence*, or *levy* for short. New Yorkers called it a *shilling,* and in many of the southern states it was known as a *bit.*

Bit was the only term that stuck, usually in the plural—*two bits, four bits*, or *six bits*. These terms were especially common in the West. One 1907 word collector claimed, "On the Pacific coast the man who says a quarter, or twenty-five cents, is sized up for a tenderfoot. The Forty-niners and their descendants would say two bits."[22]

Bartlett also recorded other general money-related terms. He notes the adjective *monetary*, "pertaining to money," saying that it is a recent invention, found in Webster but not other dictionaries. He also gives an early definition of *hard money*, which meant silver and gold, as opposed to paper money (bank bills). A variation was *hard cash*. The term has evolved over time. By the late nineteenth century, it meant money in any form, including paper money, rather than credit. In the twentieth century, *hard money* in the context of politics started to mean direct contributions to an individual campaign. Hard money is regulated by election laws, while soft money—donated to a party for general "party-building" purposes—is not.

The year of the dictionary's publication, 1848, was an eventful time for the country. The last of the founding generation had passed with the death of the eighty-year-old John Quincy Adams early that year. Politics had entered a new era, and new movements were gaining momentum. The abolitionists, once part of the radical fringe, had become a political force. The newly formed antislavery Free Soil Party felt strong enough to run their own presidential candidate, former president Martin Van Buren. Van Buren won about 14 percent of the northern vote, enough to encourage the party to run candidates again in 1852.[23]

Inspired partly by the abolitionist movement, women were also organizing to demand civil and political rights. On July 19 and 20, 1848, women's rights activists led by Elizabeth Cady Stanton and Lucretia Mott held a convention at Seneca Falls, New York. The participants issued a Declaration of Sentiments, calling for "admission to all the rights and privileges" that belong to citizens of the United States, including the right to vote. In another forward step for women that year, the Boston Female Medical College opened its doors for its first term on November 1.

Nationalist pride was also on the rise. The most memorable public event for the majority of Americans that year would have been the signing of the Treaty of Guadalupe Hidalgo on February 2, ending the two-year Mexican-American War. The conflict had started four years earlier, when James K. Polk was elected president with the slogan "All of Texas, all of Oregon." (The snappier "Fifty-four forty or fight!" alluding to the proposed northern boundary for Oregon was invented after the election.)

Polk was playing on the increasingly powerful belief among Americans that they were inevitably fated to establish democracy across the entire continent. American settlers were steadily trickling into Oregon, even though Great Britain also claimed title to the area. Thousands more had settled in Texas. Initially invited there by the Mexican government to help fill out the skimpy population, Americans soon outnumbered Mexicans by a large margin. In 1836 Texans declared independence from Mexico and were now intent on becoming a state.

The term *Manifest Destiny*—the idea that American dominance of the continent was both a good thing and a foregone conclusion—was first used by John L. O'Sullivan, editor of the *United States Magazine and Democratic Review*. O'Sullivan was a fierce proponent of bringing both Texas and Oregon into the Union. He used the term several times but most prominently in a *New York Morning News* column for December 27, 1845. He argued that Oregon should belong to the United States "by the right of our manifest destiny to possess and overspread the continent which Providence has given us for the development of the great experiment of liberty."

The phrase quickly spread. Rep. Winthrop of Massachusetts appropriated it for a speech about Oregon on January 3, 1846. Whatever the legal agreements, he insisted, Americans had a moral right to claim the region. Obviously paraphrasing O'Sullivan, he declared that "our best and strongest title" was "the right of our manifest destiny to spread over this whole continent."[24]

Bartlett didn't include the term in his dictionary—he might have felt that it didn't fit into his definition of what constituted an Americanism—but he must have been aware of it. By the 1850s, it was common enough for army wife Teresa Viele to use it when

"American Progress." An alternative title for this 1872 painting by John Gast is "Westward ho! Manifest Destiny." It depicts the inevitable westward movement of Americans by horse, covered wagon, stagecoach, and train, while Columbia, the female personification of the United States, leads the way. Exiting the scene to the left are Native Americans and buffalo. *Prints and Photographs Division: Library of Congress, LC-DIG-ppmsca-09855*

describing the settlement at Fort Brown, Texas. She says in her travel narrative, "Buildings of every description bore the marks of inevitable progress, or go-aheadativeness, otherwise called 'manifest destiny.'"[25]

After the election, Polk moved forward with cross-continental expansion. He negotiated a compromise treaty with the British that gave the United States Oregon up to the forty-ninth parallel. He also annexed Texas, including territory between the Nueces River and Rio Grande that was claimed by Mexico. Fighting broke out over the disputed territory, leading to the war and eventual treaty negotiations.

The Treaty of Guadalupe Hidalgo affirmed that the Rio Grande formed the southern border of Texas. Mexico also agreed to cede California to the United States, along with an area covering present-day New Mexico, Arizona, Utah, and Nevada, in exchange for $15 million. Suddenly, the United States had expanded by about half a million square miles. Manifest Destiny seemed on the way to being fulfilled. At the end of the year, Americans showed their approval by electing a Mexican-American War hero, Zachary Taylor, to be the next president.

The prevailing nationalist spirit is evident in some of the reviews of the *Dictionary of Americanisms*. The *Southern Literary Messenger* opens ebulliently with, "We are a great people. . . . From the night when the tea was thrown overboard from the ships in Boston harbor, we have been *progressing* (a good word, in spite of the lexicographers) until this day." The *Christian Register* strikes a similar note. The reviewer declares the dictionary "a work . . . whose usefulness will be co-extensive with our vast territory, and as acceptable in the far West or the remote South, as in New York or New England."[26]

A few of the comments show that concerns about linguistic purity weren't entirely dead. The *Literary Messenger* is anxious to point out that *to progress* and other supposed American novelties are actually found in Shakespeare. *Littell's Living Age* makes the same point: "If you have flap-jacks for breakfast, call them flap-jacks," says their reviewer, for "that's what Shakespeare called them." The *Literary Messenger* worries that Bartlett is preserving "mere blackguardisms"—low, coarse usages that might otherwise disappear.

The overwhelming tone, however, is celebratory. The *Literary Messenger* says, "We have read his book with great pleasure and we consider it a most acceptable contribution to literature." The reviewer for the *North American Review* concludes, "Mr. Bartlett has certainly made a very entertaining book for a winter evening." He finds the political definitions especially amusing. The *Christian Register* says the book is "replete with amusement as well as instruction." *Littell's*

Living Age agrees. "The whole book," says the reviewer, "furnishes a fund of fun to entertain any winter circle of true-bred Americans."

The dictionary was Bartlett's greatest writing success. Bartlett reports in his autobiography that the first print run of 750 copies "met with a ready sale."[27] Not only reviewers but also readers were enthusiastic. He continued to expand and improve on the dictionary for most of the rest of his life, bringing out new editions in 1859, 1861, and 1877. As the country changed and new word inventions sprang up, Bartlett kept pace—and his work formed a solid foundation for the American dictionaries that followed. Slang and jargon are ephemeral by their nature. If not for Bartlett, much of the popular speech of early America might have been lost.

The *Dictionary of Americanisms* came at a pivotal moment for American culture. In 1848 Americans were finally ready to celebrate their vernacular. Bartlett, with his collector's passion, gave them that chance.

9

The Words Keep Coming

THE 1848 *Dictionary of Americanisms* was just the beginning of Bartlett's word collecting. New words and phrases continued to crowd into the language and Bartlett snapped them up for future editions. The next version of the dictionary, brought out in 1859, contained around twice as many entries—in spite of the fact that Bartlett removed nearly eight hundred words after deciding that they weren't "pure Americanisms" because they were also common in England. When the fourth edition appeared in 1877, the dictionary had grown again to encompass, in Bartlett's estimation, about one-third more words. "Since the last revision," he writes in the preface, "the vocabulary of our colloquial language has had large additions."[1]

Bartlett's preface touches on some of the events that contributed to the growing vocabulary. Much had changed in the country since he published the first version of his dictionary, but American language creation still flowed mainly from the same bountiful sources. Politics was still a laboratory for imaginative new coinages, and the "late civil war" had furnished a host of new terms. So had ongoing western settlement, especially during the 1849 gold rush. Business, commerce, new inventions, and the latest fads added their share. As always, the newspapers were often the first to pick up on the new vocabulary, using it to enliven their reports on all these topics.

In Bartlett's opinion, the preponderance of fresh entries came from slang. He divides this category into "respectable slang"—the jargon of Wall Street, for instance—and the slang of closed groups like college students and politicians, as well as the street slang of "rowdies and roughs." Some of these latter words, says Bartlett, "after a struggle, become engrafted on our language, and finally obtain places in 'Webster's Unabridged.'"[2] Critics objected to the inclusion of such terms on the ground that it perpetuated their use, but Bartlett disagreed. Slang usually disappears as suddenly as it appeared. He believed that in the meantime, a work such as his helped people understand what they read in the paper and heard in conversation.

Most of the street slang that Bartlett collected has long disappeared, but some of it has "become engrafted" as he predicted. Expressions that are still heard include *fizzle*, *skedaddle*, *fork over*, *have a screw loose*, *let something slide*, and *take someone down a peg*. *Shut up* as a command was just coming in. Bartlett calls it "a vulgar expression," but it's had remarkable staying power. Lately the word has lost its sting in certain situations and can be used to express surprise or admiration, similar to *you're kidding* ("You made that yourself? Shut up!").

Words related to rowdies and roughs include the word *rowdy* itself, meaning boisterous and noisy; *to spot*, first used by police to mean keeping tabs on a criminal; and from the world of boxing, *let up* and *throw up the sponge*. (The now more common *throw in the towel* first appeared in the early twentieth century.)

Two new words for idlers were *loafer* and *bum*. *Bum* is a shortened form of *bummer*, from the German *bummerl* with the same meaning. Bartlett explains that *bummer*, meaning "an idle, worthless fellow" was a common term among soldiers in the Civil War. It was often used to insult someone of high rank with a soft job who was thought to have achieved his position through influence with the War Department. A May 2, 1876, *New York Herald* article claims that former army bummers, too stupid to earn an honest living at any profession paying real money, now get along as congressional lobbyists.

Part of the reason why Bartlett's 1877 dictionary was a heftier volume was that it covered American topics more completely. Bartlett included not just low words but also some that were so widely accepted they were hardly considered Americanisms. He left many of these out of the first edition. For instance, in 1848 Bartlett recorded the expression *play possum*, but he didn't list *possum* itself. He included *buffalo chips* and *buffalo grass* but not *buffalo* (except as the common name of a freshwater fish found in the Mississippi). The 1877 book has both of the omitted words, plus more *buffalo* words, including *buffalo berry*, *buffalo grass*, *buffalo robe*, and *buffalo wallow* (a mud hole created by heavy rains on the prairie). *Buffalo* is also cross-referenced with *bison*.

Bartlett included new kinds of America-related information, such as state nicknames (*Buckeye State*: Ohio; *Palmetto State*: South Carolina), and offered various cultural notes. For instance, he lists *Stars and Stripes*, together with an explanation of how the design for the original flag was decided on. (It was adopted by act of Congress on June 14, 1777.) He also includes *Star-spangled Banner*, explaining that Francis Scott Key invented the term while writing the song of that name. Bartlett mentions that the song has become a "national" one. It was officially named as the national anthem in 1931 but was regularly performed on public occasions long before then.

Bartlett also added holidays like Independence Day and Thanksgiving. He defines *Independence Day* as "the day on which the Congress of the United States renounced their subjection to Great Britain." *Thanksgiving Day* is "a day set aside once a year (usually in the month of November), by the Governors of States," to thank God for blessings enjoyed. Bartlett remarks that it has "almost wholly usurped" Christmas as the occasion of family gatherings.

Americans had been celebrating days of thanksgiving since the Pilgrims invited Massasoit and his people to a three-day harvest festival in 1621. In the early United States, Congress or the president proclaimed national thanksgiving days from time to time. Not until 1863, however, did President Lincoln formally declare the last Thursday of November an annual day of thanksgiving. Surprisingly, Bartlett doesn't mention this fact. His definition suggests that the specifics of the celebration were still fluid in the 1870s.

Some of Bartlett's new entries reveal a fast-moving technological world. These include *telegram*, *cablegram*, and *telephone*. Telegraphs had been around since the 1830s, but the words *telegram* and *cablegram* were recent inventions. Bartlett tells readers that the word *telegram* was introduced by the *Albany Evening Journal* of April 6, 1852. A correspondent to the newspaper suggested it as a replacement for the clunkier *telegraphic dispatch* or *telegraphic communication*. *Cablegram*, a message sent by underwater cable, was first used in the 1860s. The word *telephone* had been around for decades as a name for earlier acoustic devices, but the modern telephone was a recent invention of Alexander Graham Bell, as Bartlett explains in his entry for the word.

Advances in train travel gave Bartlett another category to explore. Trains weren't new in the 1870s—the first rail lines had been built fifty years earlier. However, early trains ran only short distances. Although people traveled on them, they were mainly built with shipping in mind, either to compete with the extensive system of canals that crisscrossed the eastern states or to supplement it. One of the first lines was the Mohawk and Hudson, which connected the Mohawk River at Schenectady, New York, with the Hudson River at Albany. The only line to reach as far west as the Ohio River in the first part of the century was the Baltimore and Ohio. The B&O, when completed in 1852, ran from Baltimore to Wheeling, West Virginia, where it connected with the Ohio River.

As American territory expanded, the government began to see the military and commercial advantages of a cross-country railroad. After much haggling over the route, Congress finally authorized construction of a railroad along the forty-second parallel. Work on the first transcontinental railroad started in 1863. Two companies built it. The Union Pacific Railroad laid 1,086 miles of track west from Omaha, and the Central Pacific Railroad started in San Francisco and went east for 689 miles. The two lines were joined on May 10, 1869, at Promontory Summit, Utah, with a ceremonial hammering-in of a golden spike.[3]

The new transcontinental rail line ushered in a travel boom, carrying thousands of people into the far West. Although slow and miserably uncomfortable by modern standards, train travel was an immeasurable improvement over stagecoaches and covered wagons. Trains also gave the postwar economy a boost, as crops and cattle were shipped from the farms and ranches of the West to waiting consumers in eastern cities.

The importance of shipping is reflected in two Bartlett entries, *freight train* and *cattle train*. He also includes different types of passenger cars, such as *sleeping car*, *baggage car*, and *smoking car*. Most trains had a *mail-car* attached. A *palace car* was an unusually luxurious (and presumably more expensive) passenger car, sometimes called a *drawing-room car*. The original name for drawing-room cars had been *Pullman car*, after their manufacturer, the Pullman Company of Chicago.

Bartlett also lists the word *car* itself—"the carriages that compose a railway train"—because it's an Americanism in the context of trains. The British call passenger cars *carriages*. The English travel by rail, says Bartlett, but Americans go by the cars. One term that's missing is *dining car*. Some trains provided meals in transit, but it was still more common to carry your own food or eat at stops along the way. Another important feature of trains was the *cow-catcher*, a guard built onto the front of the train that swept aside meandering cattle and kept them from derailing the train.

Bartlett includes an entry for "Railroad Nomenclature" that lists other differences between British and American terms. For instance, Americans say *railroad depot*, but the English say *railway station*, Americans say *track* instead of *line*, and American tracks have *switches* rather than *points*. Bartlett also lists other terms, such as *conductor* and *engineer* and the now obsolete *duster*. Early travelers wore these brown linen coats to keep off the dust and grime that the train churned up as it clacked along. The term for someone with extra train tickets to sell was *scalper*. The broader meaning of the word—a speculator who sells tickets to an event at more than their face value—was just starting to come in when Bartlett's fourth edition went to press.

Bartlett also took note of new social trends. He includes, for instance, *Woman's Rights*, defining it as "involving the political, industrial, educational, and general social status of women, and their legal rights and disabilities." He explains that the movement grew out of the antislavery movement. Another new entry is *spiritualism*, which he says "has recently gained numerous converts." Spiritualism arose in the 1840s, in the same Burned-Over District where new religions sprang up during the Second Great Awakening. Bartlett also lists the terms *medium*, *spirit rappings* (knocking sounds supposedly produced by "disembodied spirits"), and *spiritual funeral*, a funeral where the spirit of the dead person may speak with mourners.

He further lists all the ways that the dead convey messages through the medium—rapping, table turning, speaking, and writing. Holding séances where the spirits were called forth was a thrilling new after-dinner pastime when Bartlett was compiling his fourth edition. Famous mediums such as Cora Scott also drew large crowds with their public demonstrations.

Dime novels were another recent fad. These were, according to Bartlett, "cheap, trashy novels sold for a dime." Dime novels (which in fact sold for anything from a nickel to a quarter) were the literary equivalent of penny newspapers. Like penny papers, they were designed for a mass audience and priced accordingly. The first dime novels were published during the 1860s and the most popular sold in the tens of thousands. Genres included westerns, detective stories, and boys' adventure stories. Bartlett dismisses dime novels as cheap and trashy, but they would have been worth his time for at least one reason. They were excellent sources of slang. For example, that might be where Bartlett found the expression *cheese it*—"what bad boys exclaim to one another when a policeman is seen coming, i.e., run, scamper."

Bartlett was one of the first word historians to collect college slang.[4] Nothing recognizable as a youth culture existed in the United States until the Jazz Age of the 1920s. The closest approximation was the almost entirely male world of college students. Like all youth slang, many of the college students' words that Bartlett collected were local and ephemeral. Several that he lists, however, are still around. He lists *haze*, which originally meant something like to frolic, or alternatively, to harass or punish someone. The college-related definition, "the treatment which Freshmen sometimes receive from the higher classes," is closer to the second meaning. By the time Bartlett was writing, hazing was apparently a well-established custom.

Other college slang that hasn't completely died out includes *flunk*, *feel one's oats*, *pill* meaning a bore, and *hunky-dory* (possibly from *hunk*, the Dutch word for home base). Bartlett also noted *sheepskin* as slang for a diploma (because sheepskin was once used to make parchment), *valedictorian*, and *sophomore*. Bartlett says that the last is "generally considered an American barbarism," but in fact originated at the University of Cambridge in England before catching on in Cambridge, Massachusetts, at Harvard.

Besides covering new developments, Bartlett added to some topics that were part of the 1848 book. In the religion category, he cross-referenced *Millerite* with *Adventist*, a name for the group now called *Seventh-Day Adventists* that was beginning to be used. Under *Saints*, he explains that it's "a title which Mormons often apply to themselves" as shorthand for the Church of Jesus Christ of Latter-Day Saints. He also includes *Gentile*, the Mormon designation for nonbelievers, and *Deseret*, their name for the territory of Utah, from an ancient Egyptian word meaning honeybee that's found in the Book of Mormon. (Although the federal government rejected *Deseret* as a state name in favor of *Utah*, after the Ute tribe, it's used in local names, such as Salt Lake City's *Deseret News*. The state nickname is the *Beehive State*.)

More Wall Street terms entered the everyday vocabulary after the war, reflecting growing investment opportunities. The stock market was booming. Bartlett explains the workings of the market under the heading "Stocks." He also records *margin* (money deposited with a broker as security), *sell short* (sell stocks you don't yet own), *spill stock* (dump stock on the market), *buyer's option*, *seller's option*, and several other common terms.

One that was current until the end of the nineteenth century is *curbstone broker*. Curbstone brokers were seat-of-the-pants operators who ran their brokerage businesses on the curb, or in other words, literally right on Wall Street. They were particularly fond of "all the different methods of doing a large business on a small capital." These included *puts* (an agreement to sell an asset on or before a certain date) and *calls* (an option to buy an asset at an agreed-upon price by a certain date).

Liquor was still a popular topic in late nineteenth-century America, although the temperance movement was going full swing. (Bartlett doesn't include *temperance* as an entry, but it appears in several example sentences, so it was on people's minds.) Bartlett's list of drink names has at least doubled since the first edition. It now includes several types of cocktail—brandy, champagne, gin, japanese, jersey—and several types of flips, toddies, and sours. Bartlett also gives *bourbon* its own entry and adds the words *damaged* for drunk and *sample room*, a euphemistic name for a place where liquor is sold by the glass.

The "Liquor" entry features a "Toddy Time-table" that Bartlett discovered in a magazine. The timetable for drinking starts at 6:00 AM with an *eye-opener* and ends at 12:00 PM with a *nightcap*. In between are such creative excuses to lift a glass as the 10:00 AM *refresher* and the 4:00 PM *social drink*.

By far the most significant category of political words and phrases to swell the vocabulary between 1848 and 1877 was Civil War terms.

Bartlett's copious collection of material about "the late rebellion," as he called it, assured that he had plenty of terminology to choose from when updating his dictionary. He added buzzwords that were current before the conflict (*peculiar institution* as a euphemism for slavery), *slave* words (*slave driver*, *slave state*, *slave power*, a term for the political strength of the Southern states), and sectional names (*Confederate states*, *North and South*), among other entries. Taken together, they reveal the outlines of the conflict. The wording of many of Bartlett's definitions also makes clear that he was a loyal Northerner.

The country exploded into war on April 12, 1861, when Confederate forces fired on the federal garrison of Fort Sumter, but the tensions leading up to that moment had been building for decades. They were already obvious in some of the terms that Bartlett featured in his 1848 dictionary, such as the nicknames of factions—*Barnburners* (progressive and antislavery), *Old Hunkers* (conservative and neutral on slavery), and *Locofocos* (the radical antislavery Equal Rights Party). He carried these over to his 1877 edition, even though they had only historical interest by that time.

He also carried over *doughface*, which took on a more expansive meaning as the two sides grew more hardened in their positions. Originally, Bartlett defined it as a nickname for "northern favorers and abettors" of slavery. Closer to the war, the word took on the more general meaning of an unprincipled politician ready to put his own self-interest first, or more specifically, someone who wasn't committed enough to the party line. As Bartlett bluntly explains, the word applies to Southerners who "are false to the principles of slavery, as Northern dough-faces are to the principles of freedom."

When the war started, Northerners with Southern sympathies got a new nickname—*Copperheads*—after a venomous snake that's common in the eastern United States. Bartlett is equally severe in the wording of this definition. After giving the literal meaning of a "poisonous serpent," he adds the figurative meaning of "a venomous biped of northern birth and southern tendencies." He gives the word an additional gloss of "disloyal person." Unlike modern professional lexicographers, Bartlett didn't feel the need to define his entries using neutral language. His attitude about a term, or what it refers to, is often evident from his definitions.

Missouri Compromise was among a handful of terms that Bartlett added that could be classified as indirect causes of the war. He also lists *Mason and Dixon's Line* (usually called *the Mason-Dixon Line*) and the still familiar term *states' rights*. The Mason-Dixon Line was named after the two surveyors who drew it in the 1760s. It marked the border between Pennsylvania and Maryland but later became a way of referring to the boundary between free and slave states. He defines *states' rights* as "the rights of the several States, as opposed to the authority of the federal government." Before the Civil War, the concept of states' rights was used as an argument against federal interference in the rights of slave states. Since then, it has been given as a reason to resist federal initiatives such as the push for voting rights.

Although these terms were current long before the war, Bartlett omitted them from his original dictionary. That might be because his definition of an Americanism was narrower at the time. It's likely, though, that at least part of his reason for deciding to add them to the fourth edition is that they took on a significance in retrospect that wasn't obvious until war came.

Another term that was known before 1848 is *Underground Railroad*. Bartlett succinctly defines it as the "means of conveyance" by which fugitive slaves formerly escaped to the North or Canada. The Underground Railroad was not a specific means of conveyance. Rather, it was a widespread network of secret routes and safe houses that abolitionists, including free blacks, used to help runaway slaves escape from the South. According to most estimates, about one thousand a year made their way to freedom.[5]

It's not clear exactly when the term *Underground Railroad* first arose. The system had been in existence in some form since the late eighteenth century, long before train terminology was part of the popular culture. An early account of the Underground Railroad claims the term was first used in an 1839 newspaper story describing the escape route as a railroad that "went underground all the way to Boston."[6] The term made another early appearance in the *New York Semi-Weekly Express* for September 28, 1842, which quoted an abolitionist's report that twenty-six slaves had been sent to "the land of freedom" the previous week, all by "the underground railroad."

Bartlett continued to track the evolution of political parties through the 1850s. By the eve of the war, the Whigs had collapsed, torn apart by conflicts over slavery. Southern Whigs started voting with the Democrats, and Northern Whigs joined the new *Republican Party*, organized in 1856. The main plank of the Republican platform, in Bartlett's words, was "opposition to the extension of slavery to new territories." Their first presidential candidate was John C. Frémont, a former army major who was instrumental in wresting California from Mexico.

Frémont lost to Democrat James Buchanan, mainly because of a third party that had sprung up in recent years calling themselves the *Native American Party*. Their enemies named them the *Know-Nothings* because of their secretive ways. Members were instructed that when questioned about their meetings, they were to respond, "I know nothing." The major purpose of the Know-Nothings was to combat what they saw as the twin threats of cheap labor and Catholicism from recent German and Irish immigrants. They hoped to pass laws clamping down on future immigration.

Know-nothing as a general term for an ignoramus had been current since the early nineteenth century. Although the term is still in popular use, the party of that name was short lived. They ran former president Millard Fillmore in the 1856 election, garnering about 21 percent of the popular vote and causing Frémont to lose, but folded soon afterward. Like the Whigs, they were sharply divided on the issue of slavery.

The second Republican candidate, Abraham Lincoln, had better luck than Frémont, thanks in part to an organization of energetic young supporters known as *Wide-Awakes*, who marched around singing campaign songs. The club got its start, according to Bartlett, when a group of young Republicans held a torchlight procession in Hartford, Connecticut. Finding that the oil from the torches tended to drip onto their clothes, they outfitted themselves with oilcloth caps and capes. The procession was so successful that Wide-Awake Clubs soon mushroomed around the Northeast, all wearing the same caps and capes. Their name might have referred to their headgear, which resembled a soft wide-brimmed hat called a *wide-awake*. It could also have come from the figurative meaning of *wide awake*, fully alert.

Bartlett began compiling the fourth edition of his dictionary during the post–Civil War Reconstruction period. He didn't include this term in the dictionary, but he did record related postwar terms that are still heard. A *carpetbagger* (or *carpet-bagger*) was a Northern opportunist who went South looking to make a profit from the postwar chaos. Carpetbaggers got their name from their alleged habit of arriving in the South with all their belongings carried in a soft-sided traveling bag made of carpet. Republican legislatures in the South were sometimes referred to as *carpet-bag governments*.

Bartlett calls carpetbaggers "unprincipled adventurers." Modern opinions vary on how legitimate their activities were, with some pointing to their part in helping newly freed African Americans get elected to state legislatures, but the word still has negative connotations. In modern times, *carpetbagger* is occasionally applied to a politician who relocates from out of state with the intention of establishing residency and running for office.

The Southern counterpart of the carpetbagger was the *scalawag*. Originally, *scalawag* was western slang for cattle that were so scrawny and unhealthy they weren't worth butchering. Before the war, it had the added meaning of a scoundrel. It could still mean that after the war—Bartlett defines a scalawag as "a scamp, a scapegrace"—but the word eventually narrowed to describe a Southerner who cooperated with Reconstruction forces for the sake of getting his hands on some government cash. *Carpetbagger* and *scalawag* were often paired.

Bartlett also recorded the emergence of the Ku Klux Klan. He defines the term in trenchant language. "Originally a secret political organization in some of the Southern States," he writes, "but which subsequently laid aside all connection with politics, and resorted to murder to carry out their purposes." The Klan was organized shortly after the war. *Ku-Klux*, the name members went by at first, most likely comes from a Greek word for *circle*. *Klan* (an alternative spelling of *clan*) was tacked on later. Both indicate the closed, secretive nature of the organization. Bartlett describes the group in the past tense. When he was writing, the original Ku-Klux had almost disappeared, put down by federal troops. New iterations have arisen at different times, such as during the 1920s and at the beginning of the twentieth-century civil rights movement.

Two entries unconnected with the war give a worrisome picture of the state of electoral politics in the 1870s. The first is *ballot-box stuffing*—"a new name for a new crime," according to Bartlett. He says the practice requires a ballot box with a false bottom and secret compartments. The party in charge of the box can insert as many spurious ballots as it likes, to be counted along with the genuine ballots when the voting is over. Bartlett says, "The most outrageous frauds have been committed by this means." The first instances of the phrase appear in print during the 1850s. When electronic voting came in, the meaning expanded to cover any attempt to affect the outcome of an election by casting, or getting others to cast, more than one vote.

The other new word is *filibuster*. The original filibusters were seventeenth-century pirates who harried the Spanish colonies of the West Indies. The word comes from the Dutch *vrijbuiter* (*freebooter*—one who makes off with booty or ill-gotten gains), by way of the Spanish *filibustero*. In the 1850s, the label was applied to a new class of troublemakers, Americans who mounted freelance expeditions to

Central America to foment revolution. Bartlett gives this definition of *filibuster*, also listing the verb *to filibuster*.

Then he mentions a new meaning that's just coming in. "This word is now (1877) much used in politics, particularly in Congress," he says, "and means the sharp maneuvering of one political party to get an advantage over an opponent." Just as filibustering adventurers overturned Central American governments, rogue senators commandeered the legislative process. The more specific meaning of blocking a vote in the Senate by refusing to end the debate didn't evolve until later in the century. The first known mention of the word with that meaning occurs in the *Congressional Record* for February 11, 1890, in comments by Rep. Payson of Illinois: "A filibuster was indulged in which lasted . . . for nine continuous calendar days."

Although the word *filibuster* was new, congressmen had employed the tactic of obstructing legislation through continuous talking since the early nineteenth century. At first, legislators in both houses used it, but by the time Payson gave his speech, filibusters were only possible in the Senate. The House had already passed rules limiting debate.

The West remained a major source of material for Bartlett's dictionary. He added the names of new plants and landscape features found only west of the Mississippi. The example quotations he uses indicate that he found many of these words and their definitions in the books of travel and exploration that poured from the region in a steady stream. He encountered other words, and the items that they name, while traveling through the Southwest from 1850 to 1853 as the commissioner of the United States and Mexican Boundary Survey.

Some terms are straightforwardly descriptive. Bartlett lists *alkali desert*, a stretch of desert covered with alkaline soil, found in areas like Colorado and Nevada, and *salt prairie*, a tract of land covered with an efflorescence of salt, often seen in Texas and New Mexico. *Big tree*, a redwood of California, carries its definition in the name, as does the clumping *bunch grass*. *Hog back*, a steep mountain ridge, and *badlands*, the word for the broken, rocky terrain found mainly in the Dakotas, are more imaginative terms. By the late nineteenth century, *badlands* could apply to any dangerous region.

Buttes are another topographical feature found mainly in the far West. These isolated hills with a rounded top were named by French trappers with the French word for a mound. The buttes of Monument Valley, straddling the Utah-Arizona border, are the iconic examples of this landscape feature. They figure in the background of several movies by the director John Ford, for instance the 1939 *Stagecoach*.

Bartlett added several terms that were invented or first recorded by Lewis and Clark. Although Lewis and Clark's expedition took place at the beginning of the nineteenth century, the parts of their diaries dealing with plants and animals were slow to be published, so Bartlett may have only recently become aware of them. Entries include *mule deer*, *turkey buzzard*, *Oregon grape*, *pronghorn antelope*, and *medicine* as a Native American term. Bartlett's explanation of this word—"anything mysterious, supernatural, sacred"—echoes the definition in Lewis's diary—"whatever is mysterious or unintelligible." Bartlett gives as examples *medicine man*, *medicine bag*, *medicine feast*, *medicine hut*, and *medicine pipe*.

Because so much of the new territory west of the Mississippi had previously belonged to Mexico, a number of the words Bartlett collected came from Spanish. *Canyon*, *chaparral* (dense brushwood), *arroyo* (a steep gully), *mesa* (a flat, elevated plain), *mesquite* (a thorny shrub), *pinion* (a pine tree), and *sierra* (a saw-toothed mountain range, such as the Sierra Nevada) are some examples. He also records several cultural words, such as *frijoles* (beans), *tortilla*, *chili*, *adobe*, and *serape*. To illustrate the use of *serape*, the multicolored blankets worn by Mexican men, Bartlett quotes from his own travel narrative: "Our escort, who put on their gaudy serapes, made a very picturesque appearance."[7]

Bartlett included a few terms from western tribes—*tepee* is a Dakota word and *totem* probably came from Ojibwe. Three other new terms give a stark picture of relations between Native Americans and western settlers. *Indian liquor* is watered-down whiskey sold to Indians. An *Indian reservation* is, in Bartlett's words, "a tract of land reserved for the use of Indians." By 1877, most tribes were confined on reservations. A broad term for native clothing was *blanket*, and Indians who were reluctant to abandon their traditional ways were disparaged as *blanket Indians* or still *wearing the blanket*. Bartlett also added an explanation of *Indian* as a name for Native Americans, citing Christopher Columbus as the originator of the term.

Bartlett included *Pueblo Indians* as a separate entry, describing them as "Catholic Indian villager[s] of New Mexico." Pueblo Indians (*pueblo* means *village* in Spanish) were different from the tribes that Americans had encountered before. They lived in multistory dwellings, usually made of adobe. Bartlett met inhabitants of the pueblos while traveling with the boundary commission.

Cattle ranching was another new topic that came to Americans' attention after Mexico ceded its western lands. Cattle had long been raised in the eastern United States—the first livestock were imported to Jamestown shortly after its settlement—but western cattle raising was on a much grander scale. The vast tracts of open grassland found in California, Texas, and other areas of the Southwest made it relatively easy to run thousands of head. The Mexican government had encouraged the development of cattle raising in California by granting certain families large tracts of land. This arrangement was known as the *rancho* system.

The Spanish word *rancho* originally meant a hut or small, simple building where soldiers, travelers, or herdsmen could take shelter overnight. Bartlett defines the word as "a rude hut" where herdsmen or farm laborers sleep. He also lists *ranchero*, "a person who lives in a rancho," and the more recent *ranchman*, "an owner . . . of a ranch." The anglicized *ranch*, meaning a large estate for raising livestock, didn't become common until the mid- or late nineteenth century. Bartlett lists as a separate entry *cattle-ranch,* "a plantation or farm where cattle are raised on a large scale," as well as *sheep-ranch. Ranch house,* meaning a one-story house, was first heard around the 1950s.

Other Spanish cattle-ranching words that were Americanized are *lasso* and *lariat.* They carry similar definitions—a rope or cord used for catching wild horses or cattle—although a lariat can also mean a rope used to secure an animal to the ground to keep it from wandering. *Lasso* had entered the language by the late eighteenth century, but *lariat* didn't become widely known until Washington Irving used it in his *Tour on the Prairies.* He describes lariats as "noosed cords" used to rope in a wild horse. *Bronco,* a half-wild horse, also comes from Spanish. The adoption of *bronco* in the 1860s was followed by the word coinage *broncobuster* in the 1880s.

Before the word *cowboy* conjured up romantic images of square-jawed, steely-eyed men riding the range, it literally meant a boy who tended cows, or a herder. During the Revolution, it was slang for violent Tory partisans whose treatment of their opponents was "exceedingly barbarous." Bartlett includes this now obsolete meaning, as well as the more recent meaning of "ranch hand and drover," which didn't arise until the 1850s. That use probably didn't become widespread until after the Civil War. It was then that the cattle industry grew into a big business, drawing scores of rootless young men west—especially veterans of the Confederate army, but also African Americans, Mexicans, Native Americans, and European immigrants.

Other words relating to cattle include *range, corral* (another Spanish term), and *drive.* Bartlett defines a drive as an annual gathering of large herds of cattle for the purpose of branding. Driving cattle also meant herding them along trails that led to railroad depots, where they could be loaded onto cattle cars and shipped east.

Bartlett also wrote about the very recent word *maverick,* an unbranded yearling. Mavericks were named after Samuel Augustus Maverick, a Texas politician and owner of a cattle ranch, who couldn't be troubled to brand his multitude of livestock. Unbranded cattle roaming loose got to be called mavericks. A Colorado statute of 1885 declares that "all neat stock found running at large in this State . . . upon which there is neither mark nor brand, shall be deemed a maverick, and shall be sold to the highest bidder for cash."[8] (Ranchers whose land abutted Maverick's usually got mavericks by the more direct method of corralling and branding any stray cattle at the first opportunity.)

The word *maverick* took on its figurative meaning of an independent-minded nonconformist, especially in politics, by the end of the nineteenth century. The *Galveston Daily News* of August 19, 1880, declares ferociously, "We . . . will crush radicals . . . and all other foes of democracy, especially those independent gentlemen, those mavericks." In recent times, *maverick* has been popular as a name for sports teams, rock bands, and a variety of consumer products, as well as the title of a popular mid-twentieth-century television show about cardsharps in the Wild West.

After the war, cattle ranching and a craving for land brought thousands west, but before that the biggest draw was gold. In January 1848, gold flakes were discovered in the American River near Coloma, California, where a Swiss immigrant named John Sutter was building a sawmill. When the news got out, it triggered a wild scramble to the West Coast. Tens of thousands of *forty-niners*, so-called for the year the first ones arrived, descended on Sutter's mill hoping to get rich quick. The majority were Americans, but treasure seekers traveled from as far away as China, Latin America, and western Europe. The California gold rush was on.

Bartlett didn't include *forty-niner* or *gold rush* in his dictionary—neither term was widespread at first—but he listed several mining words invented by those who succumbed to *gold fever*. Much of the mining in gold rush California was *placer mining* (from Spanish *placer*, a deposit of sand). Placer mining entailed sifting through the sand or gravel of a riverbed, looking for nuggets of gold. This process was simple and cheap—miners only needed a shallow pan. They used the pan to scoop up soil and water from the river, then gave it a good shake. The soil washed out with the water, while any bits of gold sank to the bottom of the pan. This technique was also known as *gulch mining*, *panning for gold*, or *panning out*. The figurative use of *pan out* to mean work out successfully was current by the 1870s.

The place where people dug for gold was called *diggings*. The word was first used as slang for lead mines, but in California it meant the riverbed, or wherever the gold was found. Prospectors dug for likely veins of ore in the earth as well as panning in the rivers. *Pocket diggings* were hollow places where gold collected, worked by *pocket miners*. Some holes were called *coyote diggings* because they looked like the small burrows dug by that animal. *Diggings* could also mean lodgings or someone's neighborhood. By the end of the nineteenth century, the word with this meaning was shortened to *digs*.

Specialized words that Bartlett listed include *sluice*, a wooden trough used to separate gold from dirt, and the verb *to sluice*; *rocker*, a similar device that looked like a cradle; and *tailings*, the leftover earth after the gold was washed out. The miner's fervent hope was to strike *pay dirt*—dirt that yielded gold. A rich vein of gold was a *bonanza*, from a Spanish word for prosperity. *Bonanza* was familiar enough back east to be adopted as a figurative expression by the 1880s—*Harper's Magazine* for November 1883 wrote about an Oregon company that had proved "a bonanza to its stockholders." *Pay dirt* to mean profit or success of any kind was in use by the start of the twentieth century.

Besides the words of their trade, western miners evolved their own "peculiar idiom," as Bartlett puts it. In his introduction, he tells readers, "In the mining districts of California and Nevada, many strange words and expressions have sprung into existence which have so taken root that they are heard in the colloquial language of the towns and cities."[9] He recommends Mark Twain to anyone who wants to appreciate the full richness of this jargon.

When Bartlett was writing, Twain was several years away from producing *The Adventures of Huckleberry Finn*, the book that would give him lasting fame. He was best known at the time for his stories about the West. Born Samuel Langhorne Clemens in Florida, Missouri, in 1835, Twain started his working life as a printer's apprentice and later worked as a newspaper correspondent. In 1857, when he was twenty-one, he fulfilled his youthful dream of becoming a Mississippi riverboat pilot. He worked at this trade until the Civil War curtailed river traffic. He would later take his pen name from the depth-sounding cry of "mark twain," meaning that the water measured two fathoms deep.

In 1861 Twain moved west with his brother Orion, who had been appointed secretary to the governor of the Nevada Territory. There he started writing for the Virginia City newspaper, the *Territorial Enterprise*. His time in the West inspired his first nationally successful short story, "The Celebrated Jumping Frog of Calaveras County," published in the *Saturday Press* in 1865. His experiences also led to the 1872 book *Roughing It*, which recounts his journey west by stagecoach and his time as an unsuccessful prospector in the silver mines of Nevada.

Roughing It is a bonanza of western language. Along with descriptive terms—*sagebrush*, *alkali desert*, *adobe*—and common mining words—*strike gold*, *pan*, *pocket miner*—the book gives lavish examples of the "strange words and expressions" that made up the miners' daily speech. Twain believed that the mixture of nationalities and regions made mining slang "the richest and most infinitely varied and copious that had ever existed anywhere in the world," except possibly among the prospectors of California. He adds, "It was hard to preach a sermon without it, and be understood."[10]

That was a lesson that the new preacher in town learned when a miner named Buck Fanshaw came to see him about a funeral for his friend Scotty Briggs. Buck starts out by asking this "new fledgling" from an eastern seminary, "Are you the duck that runs the gospel mill next door?" When the puzzled minister finally manages to interpret Buck's question, he replies, "I am the shepherd in charge of the flock whose fold is next door," a response that leaves the miner flummoxed. The two men are obviously destined for misunderstanding.

In his attempts to get his message across, Buck relies heavily on poker slang. Poker was a new game that first gained popularity in gold rush boomtowns, where card games were a popular way to fill the hours that couldn't be spent at the mine. When Buck can't make out what the preacher is saying at first, he admits defeat by offering to "ante and pass the buck," meaning that he'll let the other man take a turn at deciphering. After another round of frustrating back-and-forth, he says, "I'll have to pass. . . . I can't neither trump nor follow suit."[11]

Passing the buck was a routine part of frontier poker games. It meant to pass some object to whoever was in line to deal the next hand. The exact nature of the buck that passed from player to player varied. Some word historians think that it was originally a knife with a buckhorn handle. Accounts of early poker games often say that the buck was a pocketknife, but other items are also mentioned, such as pencils. By the early twentieth century, the phrase *pass the buck* had the figurative meaning of taking responsibility. President Truman famously kept a plaque on his desk with the motto THE BUCK STOPS HERE.

After a *power of trouble*, Buck at last makes the preacher understand that his friend Scotty has *passed in his checks* (another way of cashing in his chips), *gone up the flume*, *thrown up the sponge*, and *kicked the bucket*. When enlightenment dawns, the *gospel-sharp* readily agrees to give the dead man *a good send-off*. "I think you're a square man," cries Buck, energetically shaking the parson's hand, "Put it *there*!"

Bartlett's *Dictionary of Americanisms* blazed the trail for American word collectors. After Bartlett, students of the language who wanted to delve into the history and use of Americanisms no longer had to trot out the excuse that they were educating people about what not to say. Nor did they feel any pressure to apologize for preserving colloquialisms, slang, and other "low" language in print. Bartlett had explained the rationale for collecting and preserving American English, and it was now deemed self-evident.

In 1872, five years before Bartlett's final edition of his book came out, a modern languages professor named Maximilian Schele de Vere published *Americanisms: The English of the New World.* Schele de Vere explains in his introduction that the years since the beginning of the Civil War have been an unusually productive time for language creation. He undertook his project because it's important for those words and expressions to be recorded before they either disappear or their origins are lost. To him, it was a given that the American language—"a faithful mirror" of our national life—deserved attention and respect.[12]

Schele de Vere, a Swedish immigrant who taught at the University of Virginia, took a different approach from Bartlett. His book is organized into a series of discursive essays that skip from word to word in no obvious order. For instance, he begins his chapter on political language by listing political nicknames (for instance, *Rail-splitter* for Abraham Lincoln, a reference to his rural background). He moves from there to terms like *gubernatorial* and *Congress* and then to slang like *gerrymander* and *bunkum.*

Schele de Vere's book is a very different reading experience from Bartlett's, but Schele de Vere looks to the same areas of American life for his vocabulary—Native Americans, immigrants, politics, the West. He also relies on Bartlett heavily for Americanisms that entered the language before 1859 (the date of Bartlett's second edition). Most of the earlier Americanisms that he includes were recorded by Bartlett first. He writes in his introduction, "Mr. Bartlett's admirable and exhausting work naturally supplied many words."[13] He quotes Bartlett's definitions and example sentences (and credits him) in almost every chapter, from early Americanisms like *raccoon* and *breadstuff* to political terms like *platform*; words from the West such as *chaparral*, *mesa*, and *butte*; and slang like *acknowledge the corn* and *dyed in the wool.*

Schele de Vere would not be the last to take advantage of Bartlett's copious example sentences. They were a boon to all future dictionary makers, from the *Oxford English Dictionary* to twentieth-century dictionaries of American English. The *Oxford English Dictionary* features over six hundred quotations from Bartlett's dictionary, fifty of which represent the earliest example found for that term.

In 1889, three years after Bartlett's death, a group of twenty-eight language scholars and enthusiasts took American word collection to the next level by founding the American Dialect Society. Their purpose was the "investigation of the English dialects in America, with regard to pronunciation, grammar, vocabulary, phraseology, and geographical distribution." A society circular published that same year states, "The real life of language is found only in the folk dialects . . . the native and natural growths" of American English.[14] It was a sentiment that Bartlett might well have agreed with.

A large part of the American Dialect Society's work in the early days was collecting word lists from all over the country. The first volume of the society's journal *Dialect Notes* includes lists from New England, Ohio, Tennessee, New Jersey, Texas, Kentucky, Louisiana, and Missouri. Society members went about their task with a Bartlett-like energy. They pored over crumbling official documents, long-forgotten novels, newspapers, diaries, and letters. They sent out questionnaires and called on interested members of the public to note down any likely words and expressions they heard and pass them on. They also studied their Bartlett.

A number of the words and phrases the society collected—many of them as they were about to slip away—were items that Bartlett had collected first. The list makers often cited Bartlett as an authority.

Some entries, like the one for *cahoot*, begin with the statement "see Bartlett." A list of Kentucky words and phrases references Bartlett under *corn-dodger*, *flummox*, *git through*, *fotch*, and *dubersome*, among others. The entry for *some*, meaning a lot, gives the example *some pumpkins* with the information that "Bartlett reports the phrase from the South and West." An essay on gathering material for a possible future dictionary remarks, "Of course a complete investigation of the subject would require treatment of all the words in Bartlett."[15]

Besides the founding of the American Dialect Society, the year 1889 also brought the publication of another dictionary of Americanisms: *Americanisms, Old and New* by John S. Farmer. The most remarkable aspect of this text is that its author was British. A lexicographer best known for coauthoring a seven-volume work titled *Slang and Its Analogues*, Farmer viewed American English with an expert's detachment. Americanisms, he says, "have long been a bugbear to purists." To the student of language, however, most of the words and phrases in question, "which at first sight seem novel, uncouth, and obscure," turn out on closer examination to be the products of regular processes of word creation or to have grown out of American history and culture.[16]

The influence of American speech on British English is "daily gaining ground," says Farmer. Scores of books and magazines, even American newspapers, circulate throughout the country, and they are popularizing Americanisms to an extent that would once have been thought incredible. Farmer doesn't consider this state of affairs a cause for worry. On the contrary—American linguistic innovation is "indicative of the vitality and creative vigor still enshrined in our speech," he says.[17] Language is never static. It changes its shape constantly and, in Farmer's view, that's a good thing. He expects the American linguistic influence to grow as time goes on and is looking forward to seeing which new words and phrases turn up next. In Farmer's list of sources, Bartlett's dictionary is one of a small handful that he marked with a star to indicate their exceptional value.

British acceptance of American speech had come a long way since the eighteenth-century critic who wrung his hands in despair over *belittle*. Over a couple hundred years, American habits of speech and language creation went from being a fringe element of English, viewed with disquiet even by educated Americans, to being an indicator of linguistic "vitality." Or to put it in words that will certainly show up in some future slang dictionary, Americanisms went from being a bug to a feature. Bartlett deserves a generous slice of the credit for that shift.

Epilogue

The American Way with Words

ALMOST TWO HUNDRED years after the *Dictionary of Americanisms* first appeared, words are still flowing into the American language from the same bottomless sources that inspired Bartlett. Words still arrive regularly from the West, although not from the worlds of miners, ranchers, or cowboys. In the early twentieth century, the West Coast meant Hollywood. The movie industry contributed many new terms, including the word *movie* itself—short for *moving picture*. Some, like *newsreel*, have disappeared as times changed. Others have stayed current through the decades—*star*, *fan*, *extras*, *flop*, *close-up*, *fade out*, and *back lot*, among others.

California continued to represent the cultural frontier right through the century. The jargon of surfers—*wipeout*, *gnarly*, *stoked*—filtered out to the rest of the country, including their most valuable contribution, *dude*. The trendy young girls of the San Fernando Valley also enjoyed a brief moment of linguistic fame. Most of their slang—*grody to the max*, *gag me with a spoon*—didn't last, but their habit of using *like* as both a hedge word and a substitute for *say* ("I was like, gag with me a spoon!") is apparently here to stay.

The next wave of vocabulary came from Silicon Valley. Besides the countless technical terms that all computer users learn—*bit*, *byte*, *hard drive*, *firewall*, *server*—a number of cyberwords have taken on a broader meaning and joined the general vocabulary. These include *hackers*, *geeks*, *multitasking*, *networking*, *spam*, and *google* as a verb. Social media has contributed the verbs *friend* and *unfriend* and a whole collection of new abbreviations like *lol* and *imho*.

Politics also still churns out a seemingly endless flow of slang and catch words. Every era provides a few terms of lasting value. As in the past, most first gained currency by appearing in newspaper articles. President Theodore Roosevelt, a talented word coiner, kicked off the twentieth century with *muckrakers*, *lunatic fringe*, *parlor pink* (since morphed into *armchair leftist*), and the recently repopularized *malefactors of great wealth*. A sampling from later decades includes *boondoggle* (originally a word for a gadget), *fellow travelers*, *credibility gap*, *dirty tricks campaign*, *October surprise*, and *throw someone under the bus*. The 1970s Watergate scandal triggered a long list of *-gate* words to name every large and small public scandal. One recent example is *servergate*, alluding to 2016 presidential candidate Hillary Clinton's use of a private email server while secretary of state.

The 2016 presidential race inspired other buzzwords as well. A few that gained traction include *dumpster fire*, *deplorables*, *Bernie bros*, *snowflake*, and *surrogate* applied to someone who speaks for a candidate.

Events since the election have given us *tweetstorm*, *woke*, and *fake news*, among other terms. The scandal over alleged Russian interference in the election added yet another *-gate*, *Russiagate*, as well as bringing to the fore such spy words as *cutout* (an intermediary) and *kompromat* (damaging information about a public figure). The 2018 midterms triggered a resurgence of the term *wave election*.

It's not hard to imagine a latter-day Bartlett studying the newspapers and skimming Twitter to collect these latest examples of popular slang for a future dictionary. Like all such words, they add to the ever-evolving story of American speech.

Notes

Prologue: American Talk

1. *"those who would speak* correct English*"*: Pickering, *Vocabulary*, 18.
2. *"big words for small thoughts"*: White, *Words and Their Uses*, 28.
3. *"remarkable for their elegance"*: Bartlett, *Dictionary of Americanisms* [1848], xviii, xix.
4. *most people were enthusiastic*: See chapter 8 for a discussion of Bartlett's reviews.
5. *Early British commenters*: Chapters 2 and 3 talk in more detail about British attacks on American English.

Chapter 1: One English Becomes Two

1. *"uppon a Bedstead"*: Smith, "A True Relation" [1608], in *Works*, 19. All Smith quotations are from this edition of *Works*.
2. *"The Empereur Powhatan"*: Smith, "True Relation," 23; "a beast they call *Aroughcun*" comes from "A Map of Virginia" [1612], in *Works*, 59; the spelling *Rarowcun* is from *A Generall Historie of Virginia* [1624], in *Works*, 400.
3. *a large language family*: Modern Algonquian languages cover a large area of the United States and Canada and include Ojibwe, Cheyenne, Cree, Blackfoot, and Mi'kmaq. Many of the languages spoken along the East Coast in the seventeenth century, including Virginia Algonquian, are now extinct. The meaning of Powhatan's name comes from J. Hammond Trumbull, *The Composition of Indian Geographical Names, Illustrated from the Algonkin Languages* (Hartford, CN: Case, Lockwood & Brainard, 1870), 10.
4. *"heaven and earth"*: Smith, "Map of Virginia," 48.
5. *"The* Opassom*"*: Smith, *Generall Historie*, 355; "The *Putchamin*" is from *Generall Historie*, 353.
6. hominy, muskrat: Smith, "A Description of New England" [1616], in *Works*, 207.
7. *"are governed by the Priests"*: Smith, "Map of Virginia," 51.
8. *"Hee promised to give me Corne"* and *"Your kind visitation"*: Smith, "True Relation," 20, 25.

9. *"the great kinge"*: Smith, "Map of Virginia," 102.
10. *Several Powhatan made the voyage east*: Alden T. Vaughn, "Powhatans Abroad: Virginia Indians in England," in *Envisioning an English Empire: Jamestown and the Making of the North Atlantic World*, ed. Robert Appelbaum and John Sweet (Philadelphia: University of Pennsylvania Press, 2005), 49–51.
11. *"So they lefte that goodly and pleasant citie"*: Bradford, *Plymouth Plantation* [1630], 79.
12. *Except for quotations*: The Puritan leader Cotton Mather, for instance, said, "They found that they must live like strangers and pilgrims," in *Magnalia Christi Americana* [1702] (Hartford: Silas Andrus, 1820), 1:101.
13. *"our Pilgrim Fathers"*: Daniel Webster, *Great Speeches and Orations of Daniel Webster* (Boston: Little, Brown, 1886), 27.
14. *"call . . . their kings there abouts* Sachems*"*: Smith, *Generall Historie*, 767.
15. *"Before they came to the English"*: Bradford, *Plymouth Plantation*, 114.
16. *"The Indians . . . had a powwow"* and *"They powwow often"*: John Oldmixon, *The British Empire in America* (London: 1708), 395.
17. *"She hath a bagge"*: Smith, "Map of Virginia," 59; the Bradford quotation is from *Plymouth Plantation*, 210.
18. *"the Indians losse"*: Smith, "True Relation," 8.
19. *"their freinds of the Company"*: Bradford, *Plymouth Plantation*, 207; the Smith quotation is from *Generall Historie*, 642.
20. *"they would have eate it up"* and *"this being the first"*: Bradford, *Plymouth Plantation*, 99, 138.
21. *"In the upper countrey"*: *A Relation of Maryland* [1635] (New York: Joseph Sabin, 1865), 23.
22. *"A Counterblaste to Tobacco"*: (London: 1604), 27. Tobacco figures are taken from Foner, *Give Me Liberty!*, 59.
23. *at least forty thousand gentry*: Fischer, *Albion's Seed*, 226.
24. *"there are so many sofisticating Tobaco-mungers"*: Smith, *Generall Historie*, 541.
25. *"an Herb called James-town-weed"*: Clayton, quoted in Metcalf and Barnhart, *So Many Words*, 38.
26. *"For we must consider"*: Robert C. Winthrop, *Life and Letters of John Winthrop* (Boston: Ticknor & Fields, 1867), 19.
27. *more than twenty thousand settlers*: Lamont, *Forty Years*, 226.
28. *"the drawling, whining cant"*: Webster, *Dissertations*, 108.
29. *"Some small Marshes"*: Smith, *Generall Historie*, 610; "course Hay" is mentioned in William Penn, *A Further Account of the Province of Pennsylvania and Its Improvements* (London, 1685), 7.
30. *"I am loath to hear of a stay"*: Quoted in Bartlett, *Dictionary of Americanisms*, 4th ed., 503.

31. *"I aime at Americanizeing"*: William Penn, Sep. 21, 1686, quoted in *Pennsylvania Magazine of History and Biography* 80 (1956): 240.
32. *"an able bad Man"*: William Penn, *Some Fruits of Solitude* [1682] (London: Freemantle, 1901), 55.
33. *"Their entertainment was a green Seat"*: William Penn, *William Penn's Own Account of the Lenni Lenape or Delaware Indians* [1683], rev. ed. (Moorestown, NJ: Middle Atlantic Press, 1970), 35.
34. *"It stands upon the flat of a Hill"*: Francis Moore, *A Voyage to Georgia* (London: Jacob Robinson, 1744), 23–24.
35. *"This treatise"*: Johnson, quoted in Read, "British Recognition," 317.
36. *"the words, figures, and forms of speech"*: Quoted in Read, "British Recognition," 314.

Chapter 2: The Two Englishes Part Ways

1. *"Went a ducking"*: All examples of Washington's usage are taken from *The Diaries of George Washington, 1748–1799,* edited by John C. Fitzpatrick (Boston: Houghton Mifflin, 1925).
2. *"In England, and particularly in London"*: John Walker, *A Critical Pronouncing Dictionary, and Expositor of the English Language* [1791] (Philadelphia: Budd and Bartram, 1803), xc.
3. *a population of well over two million*: Foner, *Give Me Liberty!*, 107.
4. *"We lay still"*: Almira Larkin White, *Genealogy of the Descendants of John White* (Haverhill, MA: Chase Bros., 1900), 36.
5. *"so great growing a population"*: Thomas Jefferson to John Waldo, Aug. 16, 1813, in *The Works of Thomas Jefferson*, vol. 6 (New York: Townsend Mac Coun., 1884), 185, 189.
6. *"the tendency of nature to belittle"*: Thomas Jefferson, *Notes on the State of Virginia* [1787] (Boston: Lilly and Wait, 1832), 67.
7. "Belittle!": *European Magazine and London Review* 12 (1787): 114.
8. *"Washington was a great man"*: Anthony Trollope, *North America*, vol. 2 [1862] (Philadelphia: J. B. Lippincott, 1863), 22.
9. *"Ran-away"* and *"a native Irish servant"*: These newspaper advertisements are quoted in Read, "Assimilation of the Speech," 75.
10. *"occasionally betrayed his lineage"* through *"there never was seen"*: Parton, *Life of Andrew Jackson*, 1:47.
11. *"so mangled" the English language*: Royall, *Sketches of History*, 58; the Bartlett quote comes from *Dictionary of Americanisms* [1848], xxiv.
12. *"When they would say* pretence*"*: Royall, *Sketches of History*, 58.
13. *"the language of Shakespeare"*: An early argument for the so-called Elizabethan hypothesis is found in Calvin S. Brown, Jr., "Dialectal Survivals in Tennessee,"

Modern Language Notes 4 (Nov. 1889): 205–9. An article that helped popularize the idea is William Goodell Frost, "Our Contemporary Ancestors in the Southern Mountains," *Atlantic Monthly*, Mar. 1899, 311–20. Modern linguists have concluded that evidence for Elizabethan survivals in these places amounts to a handful of vocabulary words, some of which aren't specific to that region. For a recent take, see Michael Montgomery, "In the Appalachians They Speak like Shakespeare," in *Language Myths*, ed. Laurie Bauer and Peter Trudgill (New York: Penguin, 1998), 66–76.

14. *around nine thousand Europeans*: The population figure is taken from Foner, *Give Me Liberty!*, 88.
15. *"the Dutch dialect"*: William Smith, *The History of the Province of New York from the First Discovery to the Year MDCCXXII* (London: Thomas Wilcox, 1757), 210. The Webster quotation is taken from Webster, *Notes on the Life*, 1:156.
16. *"Here arrived . . . one Gardner"*: John Winthrop, *History of New England from 1630 to 1649*, with notes by James Savage (Boston: Phelps and Farnham, 1825), 174.
17. *"gallant bushwhackers"*: Irving, *History of New York*, 311.
18. *"to give the home stamp"*: Irving, 14.
19. *"My posts are now so fortified"*: James Wolfe to Major-General Amherst, June 19, 1758, quoted in Beckles Willson, *The Life and Letters of James Wolfe* (London: Heinemann, 1909), 376.
20. *"Yankee Doodle came to town"*: Much research has gone into trying to ascertain the exact origin and original lyrics of "Yankee Doodle." One early source of information is Elias Nason, *A Monogram on Our National Song* (Albany: Joel Munsell, 1869). The verse from the Battle of Lexington appears on page 24. A thorough examination of the song's history is included in Sonneck, *Report*.
21. *"a kind of roots"*: Richard Hakluyt, *The Principal Navigations, Voyages, Traffiques & Discoveries of the English Nation* [1589] (Glasgow: James Maclehose, 1904), 6:457.
22. *some people found them eerie*: The region where hoodoos appear is referred to as Goblin Land in several nineteenth-century sources. For example, Walt Whitman, writing in *Specimen Days in America* (London: Walter Scott, 1887), says, "I had wanted to go to the Yellowstone River region . . . to see . . . the 'hoodoo' or goblin land" (229).
23. *"one may travel for miles"*: Bartlett, *Dictionary of Americanisms* [1848], xvii.
24. *"propriety of Language"*: Lord Adam Gordon, "Journal of an Officer Who Travelled in America and the West Indies in 1764 and 1765," quoted in Read, "British Recognition," 322. The William Eddis letter is quoted in Read, 323.
25. *"in general speak better English"*: Cresswell, *Journal*, 271.
26. *"The dialect of the citizens"*: Royall, *Sketches of History*, 58, 229.

27. *"almost omit the sound"*: Webster, *Dissertations*, 103ff.
28. *"Taylor threatened to tar and feather me"*: Cresswell, *Journal*, 74.
29. *"The verb 'to fix' is universal"*: Captain Marryat, *A Diary in America*, vol. 2 (Philadelphia: Carey & Hart, 1839), 35, 32. The quotation in the following paragraph ("It is remarkable how very debased the language has become") is found on page 30 of the *Diary*.

Chapter 3: An American Tongue

1. *Philological Society of New York*: The announcement of the society's founding is quoted in Read, "Philological Society," 131. Some discussion of suggestions for other national languages is found in Mencken, *American Language*, 79–80.
2. *Grand Procession*: A detailed description of the Grand Procession can be found in Martha Joanna Lamb, *History of the City of New York*, vol. 2 (New York: A. S. Barnes, 1880), 321–27. The number of participants and length of the procession are from Webster, *Notes on the Life*, 2:464. The description of the Philological Society's display, attributed to Noah Webster, is quoted in Read, "Philological Society," 133–34.
3. *"As an independent nation"*: Noah Webster's thoughts on a national language are taken from Dissertations I and II of his book *Dissertations*, 17–130. Webster's set of textbooks first appeared between 1783 and 1785 with the title *A Grammatical Institute of the English Language* (Hartford, CT: Hudson & Goodwin). Volume 1, the speller, was later published as *The American Spelling Book* and became one of the country's first bestsellers. Volumes 2 and 3 were a grammar book and a book of practice readings.
4. *"correct, enrich and refine it"*: *Royal American Magazine* 1 (Jan. 1774), 6–7.
5. *"public institution" for "correcting, improving, and ascertaining"*: John Adams to the President of Congress, Sep. 5, 1780, quoted in Read, "American Projects," 1144; "After Congress shall have done it" comes from John Adams to Edmund Jenings, Sep. 30, 1788, quoted in Krapp, *English Language*, 1:7.
6. *"Nothing can obstruct American improvement"*: Quotations are taken from Cairns, *British Criticisms*, 21, 22.
7. *"The Americans have been gradually making"*: Quoted in Neil G. Grill, "The *New Monthly Magazine* and American English, 1814–24," *American Speech* 47 (Autumn/Winter 1972): 257–58.
8. *"the language of Milton and Shakespeare"*: Hamilton, *Men and Manners*, 232–35.
9. *"We wish well"*: *Quarterly Review* 25 (Apr. 1821): 53, 66.
10. *"We have often heard it reported"*: Quoted in Leon Howard, "A Historical Note on American English," *American Speech* 2 (Sep. 1927): 497.
11. "pleasant or amiable": Hamilton, *Men and Manners*, 233.

12. *"A native of England"*: Royall Tyler, *The Yankey in London*, vol. 1 (New York: Isaac Riley, 1809), 104–5. It's unclear where Tyler's views of British English come from. He never traveled to London (or anywhere in England) and *The Yankey in London* is a work of fiction.
13. *"In America, authors are to be found"*: "A Political Sketch of America," *Monthly Review*, May 1808, 104.
14. *"We shall at all times"*: The attacks on *lengthy* are quotations are from "Report of the Secretary of the Treasury of the United States, on the Subject of Manufactures," *British Critic*, Nov. 1793, 286; John Davis, *Travels of Four Years and a Half in the United States of America* (London: R. Edwards, 1803), 202; *New-England Palladium*, 1801, quoted in Thornton, *American Glossary*, 1:531.
15. *"words of our own invention"*: *Analectic Magazine*, May 1814, 406, 408.
16. *"phrases, or terms, or a construction of sentences"*: Witherspoon's essays appeared under the title "The Druid" in the *Pennsylvania Journal and Weekly Advertiser* of Philadelphia for May 9, 16, 23, and 30, 1781. They are reprinted in Mathews, *Beginnings of American English*, 14–30.
17. *The blowback started in 1800*: Quotations are taken from Bergen Evans, "Noah Webster Had the Same Troubles," *New York Times Magazine*, May 13, 1962, 11, 77.
18. *"as Mr. Webster's dictionary"*: "Reflections on the Plan of a New Dictionary," *Port Folio*, Nov. 21, 1807, 323–24.
19. *"has commenced . . . with . . . indiscriminate"*: Review of "A Letter to Dr. David Ramsay of Charleston, S. C.," *Monthly Anthology and Boston Review*, Dec. 1, 1807, 670; review of *A Compendious Dictionary*, *Monthly Anthology*, Oct. 1, 1809, 251.
20. *Several of his simplifications*: Spelling reform was a popular cause in the postwar republic. Webster and Franklin corresponded about it, and Franklin went so far as to send Webster a type font for his Reformed Alphabet. Webster declined to use it, saying that he thought the system was impractical since it included new letters. Franklin, a linguistic conservative, also wrote to Webster to object to certain new verbs, including *notify* and *advocate*, which he hoped Webster would help suppress. Instead, they were included in his dictionary.
21. *"injudicious and impracticable"*: *Monthly Anthology and Boston Review*, Oct. 1, 1809, 251.
22. *"by far the most complete"*: Webster, *Compendious Dictionary*, xxii–xxiii.
23. *"The fault of most alarming enormity"*: *Monthly Anthology and Boston Review*, Oct. 1, 1809, 264.
24. *Webster defended his choices*: Noah Webster to Thomas Dawes, Aug. 5, 1809, reprinted in the *Monthly Anthology and Boston Review*, Sep. 1, 1809, 209.

25. *"Where we have invented"*: Adams and Mitchill are quoted in Webster, *Notes on the Life*, 2:9, 2:21. The *Panoplist* quotation is from May 1806, 554.
26. *"Had that darned old vessel"*: David Humphreys, *The Yankey in England*, 1815, 19.
27. *"I'll be even with you"* and *"We wan't brought up"*: Humphreys, *Yankey in England*, 55, 33.
28. *Only one performance is on record*: Francis Hodge, *Yankee Theatre* (Austin: University of Texas Press, 1964), 54.
29. "for which there is no authority": John Pickering to Timothy Pickering, May 9, 1800, quoted in Read, "Collections for Pickering's," 271.
30. *"they must in write in a language"*: Quotations are taken from Pickering, "Essay," in *Vocabulary*, 9–23.
31. *"I cannot help indulging"*: Dudley Atkins Tyng to John Pickering, Aug. 20, 1813, quoted in Read, "Collections for Pickering's," 272.
32. *"With great pleasure we acknowledge"*: *North American Review and Miscellaneous Journal*, Sep. 1816, 355.
33. *"I found in it many things"*: *A Letter to the Honorable John Pickering: On the Subject of His Vocabulary* (Boston: West and Richardson, 1817), 3.

Chapter 4: Words from the West

1. *Organized as an army unit*: The list of members comes from Elliott Coues, *History of the Expedition Under the Command of Lewis and Clark*, vol. 1 (New York: Francis P. Harper, 1893), 3, 253–56. French Canadian boatmen and army privates assigned to accompany the party for the first part of the trip temporarily swelled the numbers to forty-five.
2. *"a small French village"*: All quotations from Lewis and Clark's journals can be located by date. The most recent edition of the journals is *The Journals of the Lewis and Clark Expedition*, edited by Gary E. Moulton, available both in print and online at https://lewisandclarkjournals.unl.edu. An earlier standard edition is *Original Journals of the Lewis and Clark Expedition 1804–1806*, edited by Reuben Gold Thwaites.
3. *"with great pains and accuracy"*: Thomas Jefferson to Meriwether Lewis, June 20, 1803, reprinted in Barth, *Lewis and Clark Expedition*, 18–22.
4. *black woodpecker*: Lewis first noted what he calls a black woodpecker in his journal entry for July 20, 1805. The bird was later named Lewis's woodpecker (*Melanerpes lewis*) by the ornithologist Alexander Wilson. Wilson also gave *Nucifraga columbiana*, a bird that Clark first described in his journal entry for August 22, 1805, the common name of Clark's nutcracker.
5. *"Capt. Lewis . . . had killed a Whiteish bair"*: Quoted in Criswell, *Lewis and Clark*, 12.

6. *"who has been at St. Louis"*: William Clark to Major Will Croghan, May 21, 1804, in Lewis et al., *Original Journals*, 7:301.
7. *"They say, 'I spent'"*: *New Monthly Magazine*, Dec. 1, 1820, 630.
8. *more than two hundred thousand settlers*: John Mack Faragher, *Daniel Boone: The Life and Legend of an American Pioneer* (New York: Henry Holt, 1992), 351.
9. *4.5 million settlers*: Foner, *Give Me Liberty!*, 309.
10. *"The intent of sending men hither"*: George Washington to Major David Lewis, Oct. 18, 1756, in *The Writings of George Washington*, vol. 1, ed. John C. Fitzpatrick (Washington, DC: Government Printing Office, 1931), 482.
11. *census officials defined the frontier*: Mitford M. Mathews, *A Dictionary of Americanisms on Historical Principles*, vol. 1 (Chicago: University of Chicago Press, 1951), 670. The classic work on the meaning of the frontier for Americans is Frederick Jackson Turner, *The Frontier in American History* (New York: Holt, 1947).
12. *"We met many large wagons"*: "A Prairie Voyage," *Western Messenger*, Oct. 1837, 107.
13. *"Where shall I find words"*: [Richard Penn Smith], *Col. Crockett's Adventures and Exploits in Texas . . . Written by Himself* (Philadelphia: T. K. and P. G. Collins, 1837), 98. Although claiming to be written by Davy Crockett, the book was in fact the work of Philadelphia playwright Richard Penn Smith. It first appeared in 1836, the year that Crockett died at the Alamo.
14. *"go to hell across lots"*: Brigham Young, *Journal of Discourses*, vol. 1 (Liverpool: F. D. and S. W. Richards, 1854), 83.
15. *"Our people, particularly those who belong to the West and South"*: Bartlett, *Dictionary of Americanisms*, 2nd ed., xxiv. By Bartlett's day, the West extended much farther out than Kentucky and Tennessee, which might have been the area that he was referring to as "the South." Kentucky and Tennessee were part of what's now referred to as the Old Southwest, before settlement moved into Texas and the current Southwest.
16. *"No legal inquiry took place"*: W. Faux, *Memorable Days in America* (London: Simpkin and Marshall, 1823), 179.
17. *"Provincial Dictionary"*: (Franklin) *Missouri Intelligencer*, Mar. 4, 1823, quoted in Christopher Phillips, *The Rivers Ran Backward* (Oxford: Oxford University Press, 2016), 23.
18. *"I very seldom during my whole stay"*: Trollope, *Domestic Manners*, 40. All Trollope quotations are taken from this edition.
19. *"an uninteresting mass of buildings"*: Trollope's trenchant description of Cincinnati in 1828 is found in *Domestic Manners*, chapter 4. The population figure is from the introduction by Pamela Neville-Sington, xiv.

20. *The family abandoned their American project*: Trollope's efforts to make money in Cincinnati are detailed in the introduction to *Domestic Manners*, vii–xliii. The Bazaar stood for a number of years but was eventually knocked down and replaced by another building.
21. *"My! . . . If you have not got a copper"*: Trollope, *Domestic Manners*, 196.
22. *"Come boys! up with ye!"*: "A Fragment" appears in the above edition of *Domestic Manners*, appendix C, 332–38.
23. *"singularly unladylike"*: T. Flint, "Some Notice of Mrs. Trollope," *Literary Journal and Weekly Register of Science and the Arts*, Oct. 26, 1833, 162; *Cincinnati Mirror*, Aug. 18, 1832, 188.
24. *"Trollopize a bit"*: Harriet Martineau, *Retrospect of Western Travel*, vol. 3 (London: Saunders & Otley, 1838), 219; DeBow's *Review* 5 (1848): 283, quoted in James B. McMillan, "New American Lexical Evidence," *American Speech* 20 (Feb. 1945): 38.
25. *he didn't learn to read*: Crockett, *Narrative of the Life*, 19.
26. *he wrote an autobiography*: Books supposedly by Davy Crockett, but actually written by others, include *Sketches and Eccentricities of Col. David Crockett* (1834); *The Life of Martin Van Buren* (1835); *Col. Crockett's Exploits and Adventures in Texas* (1836); and *An Account of Col. Crockett's Tour to the North and Down East* (1835), which Bartlett used as a source for his dictionary. Several issues of *Davy Crockett's Almanack* appeared in the years after Crockett's death. His autobiography, *A Narrative of the Life of David Crockett*, appeared in 1834. He authored it with substantial help from his friend Thomas Chilton, a congressional representative from Kentucky.
27. *"the land is so rich"*: *Davy Crockett's Almanack of Wild Sports in the West, Life in the Backwoods, & Sketches of Texas, 1837* (Nashville: Heirs of Col. Crockett, 1837), 2, 8.
28. *"I was so wrothy"*: *Crockett's Almanack*, 2, 17, 20.
29. *"Some people are going to try"*: Crockett, *Tour to the North*, 205.
30. *"Not knowing whether he intended"*: Crockett, *Tour to the North*, 16.
31. *"On my way"*: J. K. Paulding, *The Lion of the West* [1830] (Stanford: Stanford University Press, 1954), 21, 27, 54. An 1833 revision of the play includes a character named Mrs. Wollope, a traveling Englishwoman who is aghast at Wildfire's crudeness, even as she contemplates how to use him in her book. That would have made the play even more amusing for American audiences. The play's performance history is discussed in the introduction to the Stanford edition by James N. Tidwell.

Chapter 5: Slang-Whanging in Congress

1. *"He was a powerful advocate"*: Thomas Jefferson to Dr. Benjamin Rush, Jan. 16, 1811, quoted in Thornton, *American Glossary*, 1:335.
2. *"the introduction of legislative balances"*: Alexander Hamilton, Federalist paper no. 9, in *The Federalist, on the New Constitution, Written in 1788* (Hallowell, ME: Masters, Smith and Co., 1852), 39.
3. *"the rich and well-born"*: United States Constitutional Convention (1787), *Secret Proceedings and Debates of the Convention Assembled at Philadelphia, in the Year 1787* (Albany, NY: Websters and Skinners, 1821), 135.
4. *"That will do for a salamander"*: Different versions of this story appear in a number of nineteenth-century publications. The drawing is often wrongly attributed to Gilbert Stuart. Elmer C. Griffith, *The Rise and Development of the Gerrymander* (Chicago: Scott Foresman, 1907), 17, cites the *Boston Gazette* of Mar. 26, 1812, as the first appearance of Tisdale's drawing, which accompanied an editorial. Both the *Oxford English Dictionary* and *A Dictionary of American English on Historical Principles* give a quotation from the May 23, 1812, *Columbian Centinel*—"this 'Gerry-mander'"—as their earliest example of the term.
5. *"It is called a bittered sling"*: A sling is a nineteenth-century American drink composed of rum, brandy, or other liquor, plus water, sugar, and a flavoring like mint. Presumably, a bittered sling included bitters.
6. *"electioneering activity"*: Thomas Jefferson to Levi Lincoln, Oct. 25, 1802, in Jefferson, *Writings*, 4:451.
7. *"You may say fellow citizens"*: John Witherspoon, *Pennsylvania Journal and Weekly Advertiser* 5, May 9, 1781, quoted in Mathews, *Beginnings of American English*, 18.
8. *"Loss upon loss"*: Quoted in Albert Matthews, "Uncle Sam," *Proceedings of the American Antiquarian Society* 19 (1908): 33. Other newspaper examples of *Uncle Sam* and the nicknames for President Madison in the following paragraph are also taken from this source.

   A widespread story claims that *Uncle Sam* is based on the initials of a Troy, New York, meat-packer named Samuel Wilson, who provided supplies during the war. He stamped his shipping crates with the initials of the contractor, Elbert Anderson, and the abbreviation for *United States* (E. A.—U. S.). The story goes that when one of the contractor's employees asked what the initials stood for, a coworker jokingly replied, "Elbert Anderson and Uncle Sam." However, Matthews shows that the story is almost certainly wrong for a number of reasons, including the fact that *U. S.* was a well-known abbreviation by that time. Also, the story did not begin circulating until the 1840s. No mention is made of it in either Wilson's or Anderson's obituaries.
9. *"It often happened"* and *"No matter where"*: Royall, *Sketches of History*, 165.
10. *"a famous squire"*: Quoted in Matthews, "Uncle Sam," 43.

11. *"is used by the Democratic party"*: Hamilton, *Men and Manners*, 18–19. Hamilton mentions the Federalists as opponents to the Democrats, but the Federalist Party was defunct by 1824. John Quincy Adams ran as a National Republican.
12. *"even though he know'd"*: David Crockett, *Sketches and Eccentricities of Col. David Crockett* (London: O. Rich, 1834), 167, 164.
13. *"They will go the whole hog"*: *Philadelphia Spirit of the Times*, May 21, 1842.
14. *"A Democrat of the Jeffersonian school"*: Rep. Gordon of New York, *Congressional Globe*, Jan. 5, 1843, 124.
15. *"When [politicians] are contending for victory"*: *Register of Debates in Congress*, vol. 8, col. 1325, Jan. 25, 1832.
16. *"Uneducated people invent words"*: Bartlett, *Dictionary of Americanisms* [1848], xviii.
17. *"a noisy talker"*: Pickering, *Vocabulary*, 173.
18. *he was speaking to Buncombe*: Versions of this story abound in historical dictionaries and other reference sources, including Bartlett. Many claim that the representative in question was Felix Walker, but it's unclear whether he was in fact the originator of the term. Its first appearances in print don't come until several years after Walker's purported speech.
19. *"not for the purpose of bringing light"*: Quotations are from the *Congressional Globe* for Feb. 20, 1841, 340; Jan. 30, 1844, 193; and June 18, 1838, 436.
20. *"A practice exists in the State capitals"*: J. S. Buckingham, *America: Historical, Statistic, and Descriptive*, vol. 3 (London: Fisher, 1841), 421.
21. *"shillings sterling per diem"*: Benjamin Franklin, *Works*, vol. 3 (New York: G. P. Putnam's Sons, 1904), 15.
22. *"Have we not heard it proclaimed"*: Rep. Wick, *Congressional Globe*, July 21, 1840, 545; Rep. Duncan, *Congressional Globe* App., July 7, 1838, 474.
23. *"one of the most reckless"*: Rep. Kennedy of Indiana, *Congressional Globe*, Aug. 2, 1841, 276; Sen. Sevier of Arkansas, *Congressional Globe* App., Feb. 20, 1840, 186; Sen. Benton of Missouri, *Congressional Globe*, Mar. 3, 1845, 393.
24. *"I have no highland fling"*: Sen. Roane of Virginia, *Congressional Globe* App., Feb. 15, 1839, 185; Rep. Giddings of Ohio, *Congressional Globe*, Aug. 12, 1850, 1563.
25. *"Give him a barrel of Hard Cider"*: Quoted in John Bach McMaster, *A History of the People of the United States from the Revolution to the Civil War*, vol. 6 (New York: Appleton, 1906), 562.
26. *campaign songs*: Harrison fans who wanted to learn all the campaign songs could find them in *Log Cabin and Hard Cider Melodies*, *The Tippecanoe Songbook*, and similar collections.
27. *"as splendid as that of the Caesars"*: Quotations are taken from Robert Gray Gunderson, "Ogle's Omnibus of Lies," *Pennsylvania Magazine of History and Biography* 80 (Oct. 1956): 443–51.

28. *"omnibus of lies"*: Rep. Duncan, *Congressional Globe* App., Jan. 25, 1841, 153.
29. *the expression* keep the ball rolling: Games that involve pushing a small ball over a frozen pond or, in modern times, an ice rink, go by several names, including shinny, shinty, bandy, and pond hockey. Although few modern-day Americans have heard of these games, they are still popular in Europe and Canada.

Chapter 6: American Words in the News

1. *"The proceedings were entered"*: *Boston Morning Post*, June 26, 1838. All examples are taken from two articles by Allen Walker Read—"The First Stage in the History of 'O.K.,'" *American Speech* 38 (Feb. 1963): 5–27, and "The Second Stage in the History of 'O.K.,'" *American Speech* 38 (May 1963): 83–102. Read was the first to discover and document the newspaper origin of *okay*. Before his articles appeared, various origin theories were put forward. One widespread myth claimed that the word comes from Choctaw. Another, spread by Andrew Jackson's enemies, is that Jackson, a self-admitted poor speller, used *o.k.* to sign off on papers that he'd read and considered "oll korrect." The evolution of *okay* is also recounted in Allan Metcalf, *OK: The Improbable Story of America's Greatest Word*.
2. *"This is a species of spoken short-hand"*: "Initial Language," *New York Evening Tattler*, July 27, 1839, quoted in Read, "First Stage," 15. The term *gentlemen of the fancy* usually refers to boxers but could also mean amateurs of a hobby or sport, such as pigeon fancying.
3. *"curious short-hand phraseology"*: *Philadelphia Gazette,* November 12, 1839, quoted in Read, "First Stage," 17.
4. *"Why is the city of Boston"*: The riddle is from the *Boston Morning Post*, Dec. 14, 1838, quoted in Read, "First Stage," 23.
5. *the 1960s* A-OK: Alan Shepard is often credited with coining *A-OK*, but the real inventor was Col. John "Shorty" Powers, public relations officer for the Project Mercury spaceflight program, as explained in Mark Straus, "Ten Enduring Myths About the U.S. Space Program," Smithsonian .com, Apr. 14, 2011, www.smithsonianmag.com/science-nature/ten-enduring-myths-about-the-us-space-program-1969206.
6. *"'All right' has already virtually disappeared"*: *London Observer*, July 25, 1954. For a short discussion of the use of *okay* outside the United States, see Metcalf, *OK*, chapter 14, "The World—and England."
7. *around 260 newspapers*: The number of newspapers in circulation in the 1790s comes from Foner, *Give Me Liberty!*, 276.
8. *about twelve hundred papers*: Numbers of newspapers in circulation during the nineteenth century comes from William E. Huntzicker, *The Popular Press, 1833–1865* (Westport, CT: Greenwood, 1999), 170.
9. *"candidly express our opinion"*: *New York Herald*, Aug. 31, 1835.

10. *"every week-day morning"*: *New-York Tribune*, 1847, quoted in Bartlett, *Dictionary of Americanisms* [1848], 53.
11. *"In this debate"*: Quoted in Bartlett, *Dictionary of Americanisms* [1848], 66.
12. *The newspapers looked to current slang*: Examples in this paragraph come from the *New-York Tribune*, May 12, 1877; *Tribune*, Dec. 10, 1845; *New York Herald*, June 21, 1848.
13. *"These men are incendiaries"*: Quoted in Gustavus Myers, *The History of Tammany Hall* (New York: Boni & Liveright, 1917), 140. The speaker was apparently referring to a story well known in New York, of a Dutch farmer who took this radical step to get rid of rats.
14. *"I knew these men would give way"*: Quoted in the *New Brunswick (NJ) Times*, Apr. 13, 1820.
15. *"a tumultuous and confused scene ensued"*: The quote and the story of the name's origin come from Jabez D. Hammond, *The History of Political Parties in the State of New York*, vol. 2 (Syracuse, NY: Hall, Mills, 1852), 490–91. It's unclear which newspaper "the *Times*" refers to. The *New York Times* didn't start publication until 1851.
16. *"there seems no other way"*: Bartlett, *Dictionary of Americanisms* [1848], vi.
17. *"Those who do the most mischief"*: Edward S. Gould, *Good English* (New York: Middleton, 1867), 7; White, *Words and Their Uses*, 29.
18. *"We never eat"*: Henry Alford, *A Plea for the Queen's English* [1864] (New York: George Routledge, 1878), 248–49.
19. *"a policemen went"*: Quoted in White, *Words and Their Uses*, 31.
20. *"Illumined by the lyric muse"*: Bartlett, *Dictionary of Americanisms*, 2nd ed., xxix.

Chapter 7: American English Takes Its Station

1. *"It is like the course of the Mississippi"*: Basil Hall, *Travels in North America*, vol. 2 (Edinburgh: Cadell, 1829), 203–4. Both Hall and Webster may have been less rigid in their outlook than they sound. Webster later offered the mitigating comment that he didn't suppose there could be more than fifty words in use in the United States and not in England, which Hall seemed to find reassuring. He notes in his memoir that the dictionary maker gave him "some new views" to ponder.
2. *seventy thousand words*: The number of new words and definitions is taken from Webster, *Notes on the Life*, 2:309. The grammar book included in the dictionary is Webster's *Philosophical and Practical Grammar of the English Language* (New Haven, CT: Oliver Steele, 1807).
3. *"It is not only important"*: Quotations in the chapter that describe Webster's goals for the dictionary are taken from the preface to Webster, *American Dictionary*, 1:vi–viii.

4. *a number of legal terms*: Webster explained how he redefined legal terms in a three-page summary of the dictionary's contents. It is not included in the original edition of the dictionary but appears as an "Advertisement" at the front of the 1832 edition that was printed in England.
5. *The final word*: The date when Webster finished the dictionary comes from a memorandum that he wrote, quoted in Webster, *Notes on the Life*, 2:293.
6. *The first print run*: The numbers of copies in the first American and English print runs also come from Webster, *Notes on the Life*, 2:304, 2:305.
7. *The reception of the* American Dictionary: American reviews of the dictionary come from *Religious Intelligencer*, Jan. 16, 1830, 544; *New-York Evening Post*, June 16, 1829; *Western Recorder*, Jan. 20, 1829, 12; *North American Review*, Apr. 1829, 433–82.
8. *some reviewers*: British reviews of the dictionary come from *Westminster Review*, Jan. 1831, 56–92; *Dublin Literary Gazette*, Apr. 17, 1830, 251; *Edinburgh New Philosophical Journal*, Apr. 1830, reprinted in *Museum of Foreign Literature, Science, and Art*, July 1830, 71; *Edinburgh Literary Journal*, Mar. 13, 1830, 161.
9. *first installment of* The Sketch Book: As mentioned in chapter 3, *The Sketch Book* was published simultaneously in England and the United States, in a series of seven paperback installments. The collected stories and essays were first published as a single hardback volume in 1824. The two best-known stories of the collection today are "Rip Van Winkle" and "The Legend of Sleepy Hollow." Two essays about the English that received attention at the time were "English Writers on America" and "John Bull."
10. *"most formidable enemy"*: Irving, *History of New York*, 359.
11. *The origins of the word* cocktail: Several fanciful origin stories have historically circulated, although there is no evidence for any of them. One widely held theory derives the word from the French *coquetier*, meaning *egg cup*. In this story, it was the practice of New Orleans apothecary Antoine Peychaud, inventor of Peychaud bitters, to serve customers strong liquors in these tiny cups "for medicinal purposes." Another suggestion is that the word is derived from *cock-tailings*, a term for the dregs of liquor barrels, which were combined and sold cheaply. (The barrel's spigot was called a cock.)
12. *"The almighty dollar"*: "The Creole Village" in *Chronicles of Wolfert's Roost and Other Papers* [1855] (New York: G. P. Putnam, 1861), 40, 47.
13. *"balls of sweetened dough"*: Irving, *History of New York*, 151.
14. *"the remnants of those great Indian Tribes"*: Washington Irving to Peter Irving, Dec. 18, 1832, quoted in *Athenaeum*, Mar. 2, 1833, 137.
15. *"a grand prairie"*: Irving, *Tour on the Prairies*, 106.
16. *"One of those deep, funnel-shaped pits"*: Irving, 124.
17. *"We still had to traverse"*: Irving, 159.

18. *"Their hunters and 'braves'"*: Irving, 10.
19. *"We found it impossible to lay down the volume"*: Reviews quoted appear in *Dublin University Magazine* 5, May 1835, 554–72; *Quarterly Review*, Sep. 1835, 392–418; *Harvardiana*, July 1, 1835, 335–41; *Knickerbocker*, May 1835, 458–59; *North American Review*, July 1835, 1–27.

Chapter 8: A Collection of Words "Peculiar to the United States"

1. *"a late work"*: Bartlett talks about writing the *Dictionary of Americanisms* in his *Autobiography*, 32–33.
2. *He whizzed through a series*: Bartlett gives details of his word collecting in the introduction to *Dictionary of Americanisms* [1848], iii–ix.
3. *"all those words usually called provincial"*: Bartlett, *Dictionary of Americanisms,* iv.
4. *"Geography, Archaeology, Philology"*: Bartlett, *Autobiography*, 25. Today the American Ethnological Society has evolved into a branch of the American Anthropological Association, with over one thousand members. The New-York Historical Society is a thriving institution that includes a library and the oldest museum in New York.
5. *"with much labor"*: Bartlett, *Autobiography*, 46. The scrapbooks are now housed in the Special Collections of the Providence Public Library. The title page of each volume of the scrapbook says, "History of the Great Conspiracy and Rebellion in the United States Gleaned from the Newspapers of the Day, Embracing a Daily record of Events, Narratives, Letters, Military and Naval Orders, Official Reports and Documents, Speeches, Lectures, Statistics, Editorial Comments, etc., Commencing in September 1860." Details of Bartlett's Civil War scrapbooks, and other scrapbooks that he compiled over the years, can be found in his *Autobiography*, 196n52.
6. *"purely technical," "obscene and blasphemous,"* and *"low, or vulgar"*: Bartlett, *Dictionary of Americanisms* [1848], viii, viii, iv.
7. *His entry on* hasty pudding: The second verse of "Yankee Doodle" goes as follows: "Father and I went down to camp, / Along with Captain Gooding, / And there we saw the men and boys / As thick as hasty pudding." For some background on the song, see Sonneck, *Report*, 134–35.
8. *"I have . . . attempted to illustrate"*: Bartlett, *Dictionary of Americanisms* [1848], v.
9. *"In the arternoon"*: Seba Smith, *The Life and Writings of Major Jack Downing of Downingville* (Boston: Lilly, Wait, Colman and Holden, 1834), 159.
10. *"We trust to* 'soft sawder'": Thomas Chandler Haliburton, *The Clockmaker*, vol. 1 [1836] (London: Richard Bentley, 1843), 15.

11. *"the Jack Downing and David Crockett taste"*: "Philological," *Family Magazine*, May 1836, 196. Other reviews mentioned are from *North American Review*, Jan. 1844, 211–27; *Literary Cabinet and Western Olive Branch*, Jan. 18, 1834, 191; *Western Literary Journal and Monthly Review*, Jan. 1845, 178–81.
12. *"These books show"*: "Yankeeana," *London and Westminster Review*, reprinted in *Museum of Foreign Literature, Science, and Art*, Jan. 1839, 75–76.
13. *"Among some of the Western people"*: Bartlett, *Dictionary of Americanisms*, 2nd ed., xxvi.
14. *the annual per capita consumption*: Rorabaugh, *Alcoholic Republic*, 15.
15. *"The Drinker's Dictionary"*: A reprint of the *Gazette* article is included in Franklin's memoirs in the section titled "Bagatelles," *Memoirs of Benjamin Franklin*, vol. 2 (New York: Derby & Jackson, 1859), 496.
16. *The end product*: For the first occurrence of *bourbon*, see Gerald Carson, "How Old Is 'Bourbon'?" *American Speech* 38 (May 1963): 157–58. Carson believes the word first appeared in print in the Dec. 19, 1846, New York *Spirit of the Times*, which mentions "a jug of old Bourbon."
17. acknowledge the corn: For more on this expression see Jeffrey Alan Hirschberg, "Going Whole Hog to Acknowledge the Corn," *American Speech* 51 (Spring–Summer 1976): 102–8. At some point, long "shaggy dog" stories grew up around this phrase to explain its origins, even though the connection with being corned is fairly obvious from early instances of its use in the newspapers. One popular explanation, which Bartlett quotes from in his entry, first appeared in the *Pittsburgh Commercial Advertiser* sometime during the 1840s. It concerns a gullible young man from the Louisiana countryside who arrives in New Orleans with a flatboat each of corn and potatoes to sell and promptly gambles them away. The flatboat carrying the corn later inexplicably sinks to the bottom of the river. When the winner of the betting game arrives the next day to take possession of the flatboats, their owner says, "I acknowledge the corn, but the potatoes you can't have, by thunder!" Rather than an origin story, this tale is more likely to be a joke, playing off the already understood meaning of *acknowledge the corn*.
18. *"I have signed"*: Quoted in Bartlett, *Dictionary of Americanisms* [1848], under *tee-total*.
19. *"meetin' houses"*: Thomas Chandler Haliburton, *The Attaché; or Sam Slick in England*, vol. 1 (London: Bentley, 1843), 218.
20. *Bartlett recognized the importance*: Bartlett's historical information about the religions comes mainly from a book that he refers to as *Evans's History of Religions*, American edition. It's unclear which book he's referring to. The only book I've found with that title and author, *A History of Religions* by Elizabeth Edson Gibson Evans, wasn't published until 1892 (New York: Truth Seeker Co.).

The information "American edition" suggests that the book Bartlett used was originally published in England.

21. *"a known coin"*: Thomas Jefferson, *Memoirs, Correspondence, and Private Papers of Thomas Jefferson*, vol. 1, ed. Thomas Jefferson Randolph (London: Henry Colburn and Richard Bentley, 1829), 136.
22. *"On the Pacific coast"*: John Norcross, "'Dollars,' 'Bits,' 'Picayune,'" *Notes & Queries* 10 S. VIII (July 27, 1907): 64.
23. *Van Buren won 14 percent of the northern vote*: Foner, *Give Me Liberty!*, 453.
24. *"our best and strongest title"*: Rep. Winthrop, *Congressional Globe*, Jan. 3, 1846, 134.
25. *"Buildings of every description"*: Teresa Vielé, *Following the Drum* [1858] (Lincoln: University of Nebraska Press, 1964), 104. The origin of *Manifest Destiny* is detailed in Julius W. Pratt, "The Origin of 'Manifest Destiny,'" *American Historical Review* 32 (July 1927): 795–98.
26. *"We are a great people"*: The quoted reviews come from the *Southern Literary Messenger*, Oct. 1848, 623–29; *Christian Register*, Sep. 23, 1848, 154; *Littell's Living Age*, July 13, 1849, 79–80; *North American Review*, July 1849, 94–110.
27. *the first print run*: Bartlett published the first edition of *Dictionary of Americanisms* through his own bookselling business, Bartlett and Welford. The Boston publisher Little, Brown brought out the subsequent editions. Although the 1861 book is called the third edition, it is identical to the 1859 version.

Chapter 9: The Words Keep Coming

1. *"Since the last edition"*: Bartlett, *Dictionary of Americanisms*, 4th ed., iii. The third edition, published in 1861, was identical to the second.
2. *"after a struggle"*: Bartlett, iv.
3. *Two companies built it*: The miles of track laid comes from the *Encyclopedia of the American West*, vol. 4 (New York: Macmillan Reference, 1996), 1611.
4. *one of the first word historians to collect college slang*: Probably the earliest such collection was produced by the "other" John Bartlett, better known as the publisher of *Familiar Quotations*. The book was *A Collection of College Words and Customs* by Benjamin Homer Hall (Cambridge, MA: John Bartlett, 1851).
5. *According to most estimates*: Foner, *Give Me Liberty!*, 404.
6. *a railroad that "went underground"*: Eber M. Pettit, *Sketches in the History of the Underground Railroad* (Fredonia, NY: W. McKinstry & Son, 1879), 35–36.
7. *"Our escort who put on"*: John Russell Bartlett, *Personal Narrative*, vol. 2 (New York: Appleton, 1854), 500.
8. *"all neat stock found running at large"*: *Laws Passed at the Fifth Session of the General Assembly of the State of Colorado* (Denver: Collier and Cleveland, State Printers, 1885), 348.

9. *"In the mining districts"*: Bartlett, *Dictionary of Americanisms*, 4th ed., vi–vii.
10. *"the richest and most infinitely varied"*: Mark Twain, *Roughing It* (Hartford, CT: American Publishing, 1872), 330.
11. *"I'll have to pass"*: The conversation between Buck and the preacher takes place in *Roughing It*, chapter 47, 330–37.
12. *"a faithful mirror"*: Schele de Vere, *Americanisms*, 5.
13. *"Mr. Bartlett's admirable"*: Schele de Vere, 4.
14. *"investigation of the English dialects"*: Louise Pound, "The American Dialect Society: A Historical Sketch," *Publication of the American Dialect Society*, no. 17 (Apr. 1952): 5, 6. The American Dialect Society is still thriving. Their work with word lists eventually led to the six-volume *Dictionary of American Regional English*, completed in 2013. They also publish the journal *American Speech*.
15. *"Of course a complete investigation"*: *Dialect Notes* 1 (1896): 4.
16. *"have long been a bugbear"*: Farmer, *Americanisms*, vi.
17. *"daily gaining ground"* and *"indicative of the vitality and creative vigor"*: Farmer, vii, viii.

Select Bibliography

Abbott, O. L. "The Preterit and Past Participle of Strong Verbs in Seventeenth-Century American English." *American Speech* 32 (Feb. 1957): 31–42.

———. "Verbal Endings in Seventeenth-Century American English." *American Speech* 33 (Oct. 1958): 185–194.

Alexander, Henry. "Early American Pronunciation and Syntax." *American Speech* 1 (Dec. 1925): 141–148.

Barth, Gunther, ed. *The Lewis and Clark Expedition: Selections from the Journals Arranged by Topic*. Boston: Bedford/St. Martin's, 1998.

Bartlett, John Russell. *The Autobiography of John Russell Bartlett*. Edited by Jerry E. Mueller. Providence, RI: John Carter Brown Library, 2006.

———. *Dictionary of Americanisms: A Glossary of Words and Phrases Usually Regarded as Peculiar to the United States*. New York: Bartlett and Welford, 1848. Reprinted with foreword by Richard Lederer. Hoboken, NJ: John Wiley, 2003.

———. *Dictionary of Americanisms*. 2nd ed. Boston: Little, Brown, 1859.

———. *Dictionary of Americanisms*. 4th ed. Boston: Little Brown, 1877.

Boller, Paul. *Presidential Campaigns from George Washington to George W. Bush*. Oxford: Oxford University Press, 2004.

Boorstin, Daniel J. *The Americans: The National Experience*. London: Phoenix, 1965.

Bradford, William. *Bradford's History of Plymouth Plantation: 1606–1646*. Edited by William T. Davis. New York: Charles Scribner's Sons, 1908.

Burstein, Andrew. *The Original Knickerbocker: The Life of Washington Irving*. New York: Basic Books, 2007.

Cairns, William B. *British Criticisms of American Writings, 1815–1833*. Madison: University of Wisconsin, 1922.

Carver, Craig M. *American Regional Dialects: A Word Geography*. Ann Arbor: University of Michigan Press, 1987.

Clemens, J. R. "George Washington's Pronunciation." *American Speech* 7 (Aug. 1932): 438–441.

Cresswell, Nicholas. *The Journal of Nicholas Cresswell, 1774–1777*. New York: Dial Press, 1924.

Criswell, Elijah Harry. *Lewis and Clark: Linguistic Pioneers*. Columbia: University of Missouri, 1940.

Crockett, David. *An Account of Col. Crockett's Tour to the North and Down East.* Philadelphia: Carey and Hart, 1835.

———. *A Narrative of the Life of David Crockett, of the State of Tennessee*. Philadelphia: Carey & Hart, 1834.

Cross, Whitney R. *The Burned-Over District: The Social and Intellectual History of Enthusiastic Religion in Western New York, 1800–1850.* Ithaca, NY: Cornell University Press, 1950.

Crowell, Russell G. "John Russell Bartlett's Dictionary of Americanisms." *American Quarterly* 24 (May 1972): 228–242.

Crozier, Alan. "The Scotch-Irish Influence on American English." *American Speech* 59 (Winter 1984): 310–331.

Cutler, Charles L. *O Brave New Words! Native American Loanwords in Current English.* Norman: University of Oklahoma Press, 1994.

Dakin, Robert F. "South Midland Speech in the Old Northwest." *Journal of English Linguistics* 5 (Mar. 1971): 31–48.

Davis, Harold. "On the Origin of Yankee Doodle." *American Speech* 13 (Apr. 1938): 93–96.

Douglas, George H. *The Golden Age of the Newspaper*. Westport, CT: Greenwood, 1999.

Farmer, John S. *Americanisms, Old and New: A Dictionary of Words, Phrases and Colloquialisms Peculiar to the United States, British America, the West Indies, &c, &c*. London: Thomas Poulter, 1889.

Fischer, David Hackett. *Albion's Seed: Four British Folkways in America.* Oxford: Oxford University Press, 1989.

Foner, Eric. *Give Me Liberty! An American History*. 2nd ed. New York: W. W. Norton, 2009.

Grandgent, C. H. "From Franklin to Lowell: A Century of New England Pronunciation." *PMLA* 14 (1899): 207–239.

Griffith, Elmer C. *The Rise and Development of the Gerrymander*. Chicago: Scott, Foresman, 1907.

Grimes, William. *Straight Up or on the Rocks: A Cultural History of American Drink.* New York: Simon & Schuster, 1993.

Hamilton, Thomas. *Men and Manners in America.* Vol. 1. Edinburgh: William Blackwood, 1833.

Hogg, Richard M., ed. *The Cambridge History of the English Language*. Vol. 6, *English in North America*, edited by John Algeo. Cambridge: Cambridge University Press, 2001.

Irving, Washington [Diedrich Knickerbocker, pseud.]. *A History of New York, from the Beginning of the World to the End of the Dutch Dynasty* [1809]. Philadelphia: David McKay, 1848.

———. *The Sketch Book of Geoffrey Crayon, Gent.* [1820]. New York: Longman's, 1905.

———. *A Tour on the Prairies* [1835]. Edited with an introductory essay by John Francis McDermott. Norman: University of Oklahoma Press, 1956.

Jefferson, Thomas. *The Writings of Thomas Jefferson*. 9 vols. Edited by H. A. Washington. Washington, DC: Taylor & Maury, 1854.

Kime, Wayne R. "Washington Irving and Frontier Speech." *American Speech* 42 (Feb. 1967): 5–18.

Krapp, George Philip. *The English Language in America*. 2 vols. New York: Frederick Ungar, 1925.

Lamar, Howard R., ed. *The Reader's Encyclopedia of the American West*. New York: Thomas Y. Crowell, 1977.

Lamont, Edward M. *The Forty Years That Created America: The Story of the Explorers, Promoters, Investors, and Settlers Who Founded the First English Colonies*. Lanham, MD: Rowman & Littlefield, 2014.

Lewis, Meriwether, William Clark, et al. *The Journals of the Lewis and Clark Expedition*. Edited by Gary E. Moulton. Lincoln: University of Nebraska Press, 1983–2001.

———. *Original Journals of the Lewis and Clark Expedition, 1804–1806*. 8 vols. Edited, with introduction, notes, and index, by Reuben Gold Thwaites. New York: Dodd Mead, 1904.

Mathews, Mitford McLeod. "Mrs. Anne Royall as an Observer of Dialect." *American Speech* 2 (Jan. 1927): 204–207.

———, ed. *The Beginnings of American English*. Chicago: University of Chicago Press, 1931.

Mencken, H. L. *The American Language*. 4th ed. New York: Knopf, 1936.

Metcalf, Allan. *OK: The Improbable Story of America's Greatest Word*. Oxford: Oxford University Press, 2011.

Metcalf, Allan, and David K. Barnhart. *America in So Many Words: Words That Have Shaped America*. Boston: Houghton Mifflin, 1997.

Norcross, John. "'Dollars,' 'Bits,' 'Picayune.'" *Notes & Queries* 10th series, vol. 8 (July 27, 1907): 63–64.

Parton, James. *Life of Andrew Jackson*. 3 vols. New York: Mason Bros., 1861.

Pickering, John. *A Vocabulary, or Collection of Words and Phrases Which Have Been Supposed to Be Peculiar to the United States of America*. Boston: Cummings and Hilliard, 1816.

Poplack, Shana, ed. *The English History of African American English*. Malden, MA: Blackwell, 2000.

Read, Allen Walker. "American Projects for an Academy to Regulate Speech." *PMLA* 51 (Dec. 1936): 1141–79.

———. "The Assimilation of the Speech of British Immigrants in Colonial America." *Journal of English and Germanic Philology* 37 (Jan. 1938): 70–79.

———. "Bilingualism in the Middle Colonies, 1725–1775." *American Speech* 12 (Apr. 1937): 93–99.

———. "British Recognition of American Speech in the Eighteenth Century." *Dialect Notes* 6 (1933): 313–334.

———. "The Collections for Pickering's 'Vocabulary.'" *American Speech* 22 (Dec. 1947): 271–286.

———. "The First Stage in the History of 'O.K.'" *American Speech* 38 (Feb. 1963): 5–27.

———. "The Philological Society of New York, 1788." *American Speech* 9 (Apr. 1934): 131–136.

———. "The Second Stage in the History of 'O.K.'" *American Speech* 38 (May 1963): 83–102.

———. "The Speech of Negroes in Colonial America." *Journal of Negro History* 24 (July 1939): 247–258.

Rorabaugh, W. J. *The Alcoholic Republic, an American Tradition*. Oxford: Oxford University Press, 1979.

Royall, Anne Newport. *Sketches of History, Life, and Manners in the United States*. New Haven, CT: Printed for the author, 1826.

Schele de Vere, Maximilian. *Americanisms: The English of the New World*. New York: Charles Scribner, 1872.

Shackford, James Atkins, and John B. Shackford. *David Crockett: The Man and the Legend*. Chapel Hill: University of North Carolina Press, 1986.

Smith, John. *Works: 1608–1631*. Edited by Edward Arber. Birmingham, UK: English Scholar's Library, 1884.

Sonneck, Oscar George Theodore. *Report on "The Star-Spangled Banner," "Hail, Columbia," "America," "Yankee Doodle."* Washington, DC: Government Printing Office, 1909.

Sturtevant, William C., ed. *Handbook of North American Indians*. Vol. 15, *Northeast*, edited by Bruce G. Trigger. Washington, DC: Smithsonian Institution, 1978.

Thornton, Richard H. *An American Glossary*. 2 vols. Philadelphia: Lippincott, 1912.

Travers, Leonard. "Reconstructing an Early-Seventeenth-Century 'American' Dialect." In *American Speech: 1600 to the Present*, edited by Peter Benes, 120–131. Boston: Boston University Press, 1985.

Trollope, Fanny. *Domestic Manners of the Americans* [1832]. Edited with an introduction and notes by Pamela Neville-Sington. London: Penguin Books, 1997.

Webster, Noah. *An American Dictionary of the English Language*. 2 vols. New York: S. Converse, 1828.

———. *A Compendious Dictionary of the English Language*. Hartford, CT: Hudson & Goodwin, 1806.

———. *Dissertations on the English Language*. Boston: Isaiah Thomas, 1789.

———. *Notes on the Life of Noah Webster*. Compiled by Emily Ellsworth Fowler Ford. Edited by Emily Ellsworth Ford Skeel. 2 vols. New York: Privately printed, 1912.

White, Richard Grant. *Words and Their Uses*. Boston: Houghton Mifflin, 1870.

Index

Note: Page numbers in *italic* refer to images.